BEST
Weekend
PROJECTS

Quick-and-simple ideas to improve your home and yard

Reader's Digest

The Reader's Digest Association, Inc.
Pleasantville, New York/Montreal

FOR THE FAMILY HANDYMAN

Editor in Chief	KEN COLLIER
Executive Editor	SPIKE CARLSEN
Special Projects Editor	MARY FLANAGAN
Design Director	SARA KOEHLER
Administrative Manager	ALICE GARRETT
Graphic Designer	TERESA MARRONE
Production Manager	JUDY RODRIGUEZ

Editorial and Production Team: Donna Bierbach, Tom Caspar, Steven Charbonneau, Jean Cook, Roxie Filipkowski, Joe Gohman, Jeff Gorton, Shannon Hooge, Shelly Jacobsen, Duane Johnson, Randy Johnson, Tim Johnson, Vern Johnson, Travis Larson, Dave Munkittrick, Lisa Pahl, Peggy McDermott, Becky Pfluger, David Radtke, Judy Rodriguez, Bob Ungar, Gary Wentz, Marcia Wright Roepke.

Photography and Illustrations: Mike Krivit, Don Mannes, Ramon Moreno, Frank Rohrbach, Eugene Thompson, Bill Zuehlke

FOR READER'S DIGEST

Chairman	ERIC SCHRIER
President, U.S. Magazines	BONNIE BACHAR
Group Director, Home & Garden Group	KERRY BIANCHI
Publisher	RICK STRAFACE
Newsstand Sales	DAVID ALGIRE
Associate Art Director	GEORGE MCKEON
Executive Editor, Trade Publishing	DOLORES YORK
Manufacturing Manager	JOHN L. CASSIDY
Director of Production	MICHAEL BRAUNSCHWEIGER
Associate Publisher	ROSANNE MCMANUS
President and Publisher, Trade Publishing	HAROLD CLARKE

ISBN 13: 978-0-7621-0881-7
ISBN 10: 0-7621-0881-9

Previously published as *Best Weekend Projects* 2006.

Text, photography and illustrations for *Best Weekend Projects* are based on articles previously run in **The Family Handyman** magazine (2915 Commers Dr., Suite 700, Eagan, MN 55121, www.familyhandyman.com) and **Backyard Living** magazine (5400 S. 60th St., Greendale, WI 53129, www.backyardliving.com).

For more Reader's Digest products and information, visit our website: www.rd.com (in the United States)

Printed in China

1 3 5 7 9 10 8 6 4 2

A NOTE TO OUR READERS: All do-it-yourself activities involve a degree of risk. Skills, materials, tools and site conditions vary widely. Although the editors have made every effort to ensure accuracy, the reader remains responsible for the selection and use of tools, materials and methods. Always obey local codes and laws, follow manufacturer instructions and observe safety precautions.

Contents

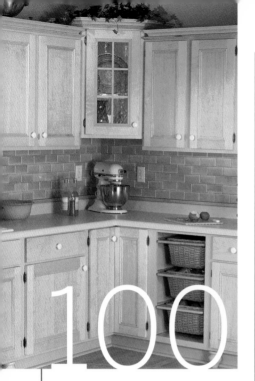

100

138

184

130

Practical products for weekend improvements

Amazing folding ladder

Everyone who sees this ladder is impressed. Open, it's a solid and stable stepladder. Folded, it's tiny enough to tuck away in a corner of the hall closet.

The Super Fold 3-Step from Cosco (model 11-670 AGO1) is an engineering marvel with a 250-lb. load rating. Unfolding the ladder is simple. A gentle tug on the handles opens the frame. A light pull on the frame and the Super Fold starts to look like a ladder. Downward pressure on the rungs snaps supports into place, and you're ready to climb to new heights. The top rung gets you 29-1/2 in. off the floor.

Folding the ladder is just as easy. Tug on the release straps to collapse the rungs and supports. Squeeze the frame closed. Wrap and hook the binding strap, and tuck it away for another day.

The Super Fold costs $70. It's available at Costco and Meijers stores, through QVC and at amazon.com.

Cosco Home and Office Products, (888) 818-5110.

Wrap-anything repair roll

Drainpipe drippin'? Radiator hose wrecked? Garden hose gushin'? X-Treme Tape, $6, may be the solution for wrapping up your problems. It's a silicone-based repair tape that stretches like crazy, conforms to almost any shape and fuses to itself. It remains flexible down to -60 degrees F, and doesn't melt until it hits 500 degrees F. Use it to fix anything from drainpipes to mufflers.

X-Treme Tape (item No. 96825) begins to bond as soon as it's wrapped over itself. It fuses permanently after 24 hours. This is a great product to keep in your toolbox for those emergency repairs that sneak up on you when you least expect it. It's available from Duluth Trading Co.

Duluth Trading Co., (877) 382-2345. www.duluthtrading.com

A tool basket for your ladder

When you're about to climb a stepladder, do you usually stuff your pockets with the tools du jour? A paintbrush in this pocket, a rag in that one, a scraper in that one. Unfortunately, the can of paint and the caulk gun won't fit in a pocket, so you have to struggle up the ladder with them in hand. Once on the ladder, you're constantly patting down your pockets to find the tool of the moment. Argh!

If this is a painful reminder of the last time you worked on a stepladder, consider getting a LadderMaxx caddy ($30). This handy little basket is a great way to organize your stuff, get it to the worksite and keep it organized while you're working on the ladder

The basket is 10 x 16 in. Fill it with whatever you'll need on the job and off you go. Once you're on the stepladder, you can loop either basket handle over the top of the ladder, giving you a handy spot to store materials and tools. The LadderMaxx even has a built-in cord retainer. If you're working with a power tool, the extension cord can be looped through the retainer so that the LadderMaxx carries the weight of the dangling cord.

Find a retailer near you by contacting the company.

Bee Safety Wise: (800) 230-5364. www.laddermaxx.com

Two ways to fix squeaky floors

1. From-down-under fix

If you can get at the squeaky floor from underneath (usually an unfinished basement or crawlspace), the Squeak-Relief kit is one way to go. Have someone spring up and down to activate the squeak while you prowl around downstairs ready to home in on the rascal. It'll most likely be a nail rubbing on a subfloor that wasn't glued down to the joist. The gap is what allows the subfloor to move independently of the framing. Using the special nail that's included in the kit, tack the bracket to the side of the joist with the top against the bottom of the subfloor. Then run the long screw into the joist and the short screw into the subfloor. Simple, elegant, effective and fast. Order a package of four (item No. 105064) for about $15.

**Improvements Mail Order Catalog, (800) 642-2112.
www.improvementscatalog.com**

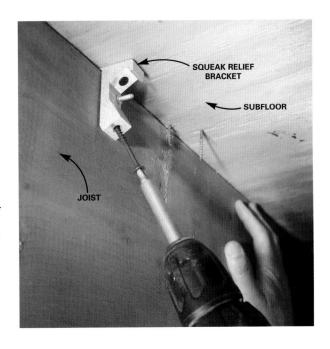

SQUEAK RELIEF BRACKET

SUBFLOOR

JOIST

2. From-the-top fix

If you can't get at a floor squeak from underneath, another good solution is the Squeeeeek No More kit (item No. 110189) designed to send a snap-off screw right through the carpet—without unraveling the fibers. The kit comes with a screw designed to help you find the joist under the squeak. Then you run a specially scored screw through the middle of the depth-control jig, which stops the screw at the right distance from the floor. Use a recess on one of the wings on the jig to snap off the screw just below the floor surface. For $30, you get the jig, the joist-finding screw and 50 of the scored screws, enough to fix all the floors in a haunted mansion.

**Improvements Mail Order Catalog, (800) 642-2112.
www.improvementscatalog.com**

SCREW DRIVE

DEPTH CONTROL JIG

Screw Gripper

Made in USA (800) 459-8428 Pat. pend.

SCREW SNAP RECESS

The indispensable dozen

True do-it-yourselfers know you can never have too many tools, but if you were stranded on the proverbial deserted island (with an electrical outlet and a house that needs remodeling!) and had to pick your best 12, here's a mix that would be tough to beat. Opinions vary, but these tools rank as must-have items in even a modest toolbox, and they'll allow you to tackle a wide array of projects. If we had to add a 13th, it would surely be the basic pliers.

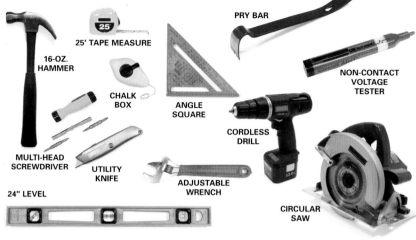

PRY BAR

25' TAPE MEASURE

16-OZ. HAMMER

CHALK BOX

ANGLE SQUARE

NON-CONTACT VOLTAGE TESTER

CORDLESS DRILL

MULTI-HEAD SCREWDRIVER

UTILITY KNIFE

24" LEVEL

ADJUSTABLE WRENCH

CIRCULAR SAW

16-oz. hammer. Nimble enough to drive a small finish nail and stout enough for a 16-penny sinker, these midsize hammers have a curved claw for nail pulling or rip/straight claw for prying.

Pry bar. Great for dismantling framing, pulling nails, removing trim and moldings, and for demolition work.

Multi-head screwdriver. This self-contained kit typically features #1 and #2 Phillips tips, plus small and midsize standard slotted or square-drive tips.

Non-contact voltage tester. Guesswork is not recommended when working on electrical repairs or improvements. A non-contact voltage tester detects live current in a wire or cable.

25-ft. tape measure. A 25-ft. tape measure is light and compact for small-scale work and still stretches enough to handle bigger chores, such as framing.

Cordless drill. A middleweight 12-volt model will handle most drilling and screwdriving tasks. Get a kit with two battery packs and a one-hour charger; add a good set of drill and driver bits.

Angle square. Use this versatile tool for layout or cutline marking, to check corners for square or to find and mark angles from zero to 90°. It's great for rafter layout.

Circular saw. Get a model with 7-1/4-in.-blade diameter with a ball-bearing motor rated at 12 amps minimum. Substituting specialty blades allows you to cut plastics, a variety of metals and concrete.

Adjustable wrench. A 10-in. (25-cm) model is a good all-around size; buy a smaller one as a spare and because you often use them in pairs.

24-in. level. This midsize level is compact enough for aligning pictures, yet big enough to plumb a fence post or level a hefty deck beam.

Utility knife. Use to cut vinyl flooring, roofing shingles, builder's felt and other building materials.

Chalk line. Use a chalk line to snap straight guidelines for cutting plywood, installing shingles or establishing tile layout on a floor. Locking versions double as plumb bobs.

Safety & safety equipment

Whatever tools you might assemble for a project, the list should start with items that help keep you safe and healthy. Item one? Your brain. Trust its intuition when a task seems inherently dangerous or too difficult to tackle alone. Don't work in adverse conditions that can make a routine job dangerous, and never work with tools if your judgment or motor skills are impaired by medication, alcohol or other substances.

Equally important, don't think only in terms of acute injuries or accidents. Cumulative health risks often pose greater hazards to your sight, hearing and respiratory functions, so take preventive measures to protect yourself.

Hearing protection. Irreversible hearing loss from exposure to loud noise is deceptively gradual, often going undetected until it's too late. You can

FOAM EARPLUGS

prevent this by taking simple precautions in the form of disposable foam earplugs, reusable rubber earplugs (tethered pairs stay intact longer) or earmuffs.

Eye protection. A ricocheting nail or a splash of harsh solvent can permanently damage an eye before you have time to react. Safety glasses or goggles help protect you from these and other needless injuries. The best have impact-resistant polycarbonate lenses and wraparound side shields to prevent indirect impact.

Respiratory protection. Fine sawdust, drywall dust, insulation fibers and vapors from solvents or adhesives all pose respiratory risks. To avoid breathing these and other airborne contaminants, wear a dust mask or a respirator, depending on the task at hand. Moldable form-fitting masks are better than the single-layer disposables. Use a respirator with cartridge filters for fumes.

Folding peg board cabinet

Organize your tools and workshop with this clever cabinet.

Peg board is a great way to organize tools. It displays them in clear view so they're easy to grab and, just as important, easy to put away. This cabinet has the hanging space of almost an entire 4 x 8 ft. sheet of peg board, yet packs it into a compact 24 x 32 in. package. Two overlapping doors open, utilizing the front and back of each for tools. About 4 in. of space separate each panel, leaving a 2-in. depth for tools placed directly across from each other. If you place fat tools across from skinny ones, you can utilize the space even better.

project at a glance

skill level
intermediate

special tools
clamps
drill
circular saw

approximate cost
$110

figure a
cabinet details

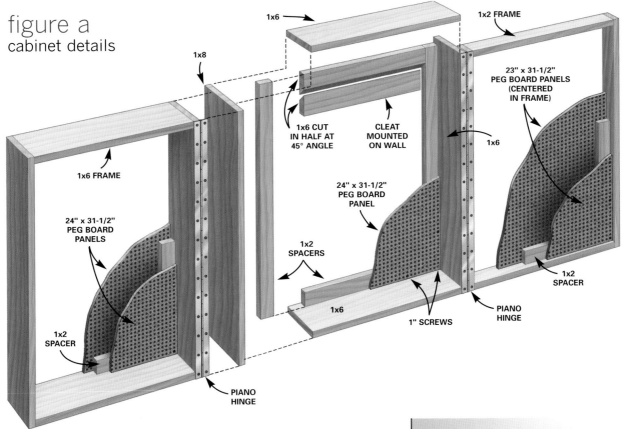

1x6

1x2 FRAME

1x8

**23" x 31-1/2"
PEG BOARD PANELS
(CENTERED
IN FRAME)**

1x6 FRAME

**1x6 CUT
IN HALF AT
45° ANGLE**

**CLEAT
MOUNTED
ON WALL**

1x6

**24" x 31-1/2"
PEG BOARD
PANELS**

**24" x 31-1/2"
PEG BOARD
PANEL**

**1x2
SPACERS**

**1x2
SPACER**

**1x2
SPACER**

1x6

1" SCREWS

**PIANO
HINGE**

**PIANO
HINGE**

Materials, cost and tools

This cabinet costs $110 to build. The knot-free poplar boards drive up the price, but the straight, stable wood allows the doors to fit well, minimizes twisting, and keeps the cabinet square. In addition to the materials listed at right, we purchased four eye screws and 2 ft. of small chain to hold the doors open. All the supplies are available at a home center or lumberyard.

You don't need any special tools to build this cabinet, but a pair of 1-ft. clamps are helpful when you're attaching the hinges.

Cut accurately for tight-fitting doors

Cut the 4 x 8-ft. peg board sheet lengthwise into two pieces, one 24 in. wide and the other 23 in. wide. Then cut the two pieces into 31-1/2-in. lengths. You must cut the peg board panels accurately for the doors to fit evenly. Carefully measure and use a straightedge to guide your circular saw cuts. Some lumberyards will cut the sheets to size for you. Ask them to be precise.

Then assemble the peg board panels (Photo 1), following the pattern shown in Figure A. You don't have to make fancy joints. Cut and screw on the 1x2 side spacers first, then measure and cut the 1x2 ends to fit between them. You'll have one 23 in. peg board panel left over to hang on the wall for items that won't fit in the cabinet.

Substitute one half of the cleat for the top 1x2 on the back panel (Photo 3 and Figure A). Watch the angle. Orient it so it hooks onto the other half you screw to the wall (Photo 5).

materials list

One 4'x8' sheet of 1/4" peg board

Five 10' lengths of 1x2 poplar

Two 10' lengths of 1x6 poplar

One 3' length of 1x8 poplar

One 6' piano hinge

One lockable hasp

1 lb. of 2" finish nails

1 lb. of 1" screws

Eight 3" screws

cutting list

1/4" peg board panels
   three 24" x 31-1/2"
   two 23" x 31-1/2"

1x2 spacers, 1x6 cleat, and 1x6, 1x8 and 1x2 frames—measure and cut to fit around panels.

tip

Punch a starter hole with a nail for the piano hinge screws to keep them centered.

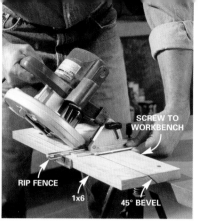

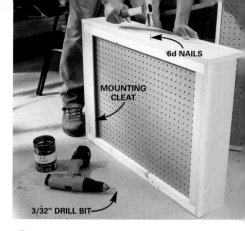

1 Cut the peg board to the sizes shown on Figure A with a circular saw guided by a straightedge. Cut the 1x2s to length and fasten the peg board to them with 1-in. screws spaced every 8 in.

PEG BOARD
1x2

2 Cut the 1x6 mounting cleat in half at a 45-degree angle. For safety before cutting, screw it to a firm work surface with one edge overhanging 3 in. Use one half of the mounting cleat in place of the top 1x2 on the back peg board panel.

SCREW TO WORKBENCH
RIP FENCE
1x6
45° BEVEL

3 Measure and cut the 1x6 frame boards to fit around each panel. Glue and nail the top and bottom first, then the sides, to the 1x2 spacers with 2-in. (6d) finish nails spaced every 8 in. Fasten the frame board corners with two nails and glue. Predrill all holes with a 3/32-in. drill bit to avoid splitting the wood.

6d NAILS
MOUNTING CLEAT
3/32" DRILL BIT

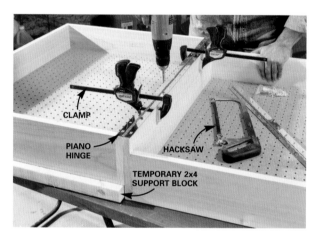

4 Cut the piano hinge to length with a hacksaw and screw it on with the screws in the hinge package. Support and clamp the hinge sides in position to simplify hinge attachment. Close the doors and attach the hasp.

CLAMP
PIANO HINGE
HACKSAW
TEMPORARY 2x4 SUPPORT BLOCK

5 Position the other half of the mounting cleat about 40 in. above the work surface and fasten it to the wall studs with four 3-in. screws. Hang the cabinet and drive two 3-in. screws through the bottom 1x2 into the wall studs for extra strength.

MOUNTING CLEAT

Wrap the panels to form the cabinet and doors

The frames for the three panels are all slightly different. The back panel frame consists of three 1x6s and a 1x8; the middle panel has four 1x2s; and the front has four 1x6s (Figure A). These differences allow them to hinge together.

Measure the lengths and nail on the frames. Make sure to run a bead of carpenter's glue along the panel edges and at the corner joints to make them stronger.

Clamp the piano hinge to a firm surface, and cut it to length with a hacksaw (about 32-5/8 in.). Set the top, bottom, and middle screws to align the hinge, then fill in the remaining holes (Photo 4).

A hasp will hold the doors closed. We used a chest-style one that pulls the doors tight together and has a slot for a lock.

Hang it on the wall

The mounting cleat is an easy way to hang this heavy cabinet. If you're mounting it over a workbench, hang it at least 16 in. above the work surface so you can open the doors without disturbing the project you're working on.

To hold the doors open when working, we installed eye hooks on the bottom of each door and on the wall. A short chain with small S-hooks holds the doors open.

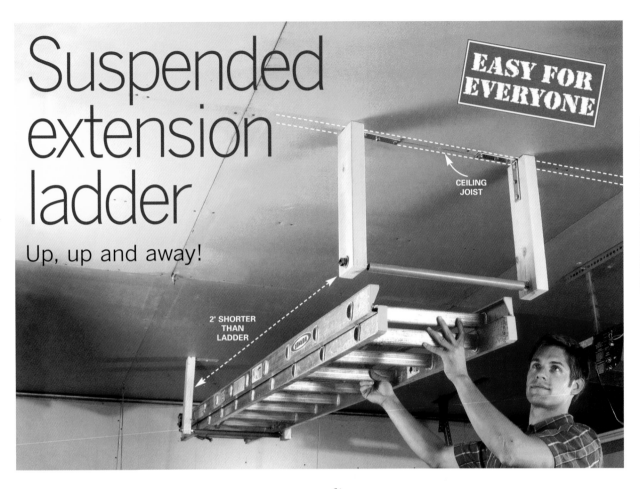

Suspended extension ladder

Up, up and away!

EASY FOR EVERYONE

CEILING JOIST

2' SHORTER THAN LADDER

It's always most convenient to hang an extension ladder on brackets on a wall. But unfortunately that wipes out all other storage potential for that wall. To save that valuable wall space, we designed a pair of 2x4 suspended brackets so a ladder can be stored flat along the ceiling.

Simply slide one end of the ladder into one bracket, then lift and slide the other end into the other bracket. Most people will need to stand on something solid to reach the second bracket. The 2x4 bracket sides are 16 in. long with 5-in. corner braces lag-screwed into the top for attachment to the ceiling joist (Figure A).

The bracket base is a 1/2-in. x 24-in. threaded steel rod ($2.75) that extends through 5/8-in. drilled holes on the bracket sides. It's held in place with flat/lock washers and a nut on each side of both 2x4 uprights. A 3/4-in. x 18-in.-long piece of PVC conduit pipe surrounds the rod for smooth rolling action when you slide the ladder in and out.

project at a glance

skill level
beginner

special tools
drill
drill bits

approximate cost
$10–$15

figure a ladder support detail

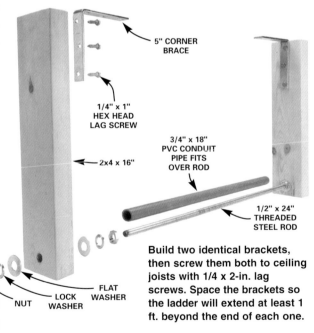

5" CORNER BRACE

1/4" x 1" HEX HEAD LAG SCREW

2x4 x 16"

3/4" x 18" PVC CONDUIT PIPE FITS OVER ROD

1/2" x 24" THREADED STEEL ROD

NUT

LOCK WASHER

FLAT WASHER

Build two identical brackets, then screw them both to ceiling joists with 1/4 x 2-in. lag screws. Space the brackets so the ladder will extend at least 1 ft. beyond the end of each one.

tip For extra security, wrap a bungee cord around the ladder and one bracket.

Hang-it-all storage wall

Organize your garage with a handsome, easy-to-build storage system that'll hold all that garage clutter.

The wall space in your garage is way too valuable just to hang rakes, bikes and garden hoses at random on nails, hooks or shelves. To make every square inch of that wall space work for you, we designed this wall storage system.

Our system is made entirely from plywood and standard hardware. It's easy to build and easy to customize to suit your needs. You can install it to fill any size wall or cover only part of a wall. You can hang shelves, bins or hooks and arrange them to make efficient use of wall space. With special store-bought hangers, you can hang

hard-to-hold items like bikes or wheelbarrows. Best of all, everything hangs from sturdy rails, so you can rearrange the wall in minutes without any tools. Some store-bought systems provide the same versatility, but they can cost two or even three times as much as this homemade system.

The only power tools you'll need are a circular saw and a drill. Other tools—a table saw, router, miter saw and brad nailer—will save you time, but aren't neces-

project at a glance

skill level
intermediate

special tools
circular saw
drill
router (optional)

approximate cost
$400 for
8 x 20-ft. wall
system

sary. All the materials you'll need are available at home centers. The total materials bill for our 8 x 20-ft. wall system and accessories was about $400. If you don't expect to hang anything from the lower half of the wall, you can cut time and expenses by covering only the upper half. If you completely cover a large wall as we did, expect to spend a weekend building the system and another finishing it and assembling shelves and hooks.

Cover the wall with plywood

You could nail and glue the rails directly to bare studs or drywall, but we chose to cover our wall with 1/4-in. plywood, for three reasons: First, the birch plywood matches the rails and gives the whole system a rich, finished appearance. Second, plywood won't scratch, gouge or dent as easily as drywall, and third, you can quickly clean it with a damp cloth.

The sheets of plywood should meet at studs, so start by locating studs with a stud finder. Chances are,

you'll have to cut the first sheet lengthwise so the edge aligns with a stud's center. Then you can use full sheets until you reach the end of the wall and cut the final sheet to

Hooks and shelves slip onto plywood rails, so you can move them anywhere instantly.

fit. Your cuts don't have to be perfect and the sheets don't have to fit tightly into corners because you'll cover the edges with trim later (see Photo 2).

If you're installing the plywood over drywall as we did, run a bead of construction adhesive around the edges of each sheet and cover the middle with a zigzag

materials list

All the tools and materials for this project are available at home centers. Here's what it took to build our 8 x 20-ft. wall system, including 12 shelves and 16 mounting plates. The various brackets and hooks aren't included—choose those to suit your needs.

ITEM	QTY.
4' x 8' 1/4" plywood (wall covering, rails)	7
4' x 8' 3/4" plywood (rails, shelves, mounting plates)	4
Tubes of construction adhesive (fastening 1/4" plywood and rails)	6
Wood glue (assembling rails, mounting plates)	12 ozs.
3/4" aluminum angle, 1/8" thick (shelf cleats)	8'
2" aluminum flat stock, 1/8" thick (mounting plate cleats)	8'
1-5/8" paneling nails (fastening 1/4" plywood)	1 lb.
3/4" brad nails (assembling rails)	4 ozs.
16d finish nails (fastening rails to studs)	1 lb.
No. 8 x 3/4" taper-head screws (fastening cleats to shelves)	100
1-1/4" drywall screws (fastening cleats to mounting plates)	1 lb.
No. 8 x 3/4" pan-head screws (fastening shelf brackets)	100
Water-based polyurethane (coating wall, rails, shelves and mounting plates)	1 gal.

1 Cover the wall with 1/4-in. plywood. Spread construction adhesive on each sheet, then nail them to studs. Mark stud locations with masking tape.

2 Frame the wall with 1-1/2 in. wide strips of 3/4-in. plywood. At corners, nail the strips flat against adjoining walls. Then run strips across the top and bottom.

pattern (Photo 1). Use at least half a tube of adhesive per sheet. If you're fastening plywood to bare studs, apply a heavy bead of adhesive to each stud. Nail the sheet to studs with 1-5/8 in. paneling nails to secure the plywood until the adhesive dries.

Frame the plywood-covered wall with strips of 3/4-in. plywood (Photo 2). Make the strips using the same techniques used to make the rails (see Photos 3 and 4). Rip 3/4-in. plywood into 1-1/2 in.-wide strips, chamfer one edge with a router and nail them into place with 16d finish nails.

Combine thick and thin plywood to make rails

Begin rail construction by cutting strips of 1/4-in. and 3/4-in. plywood. If you don't have a table saw, make a simple ripping guide to ensure straight cuts. Cut a 3-5/8 in. spacer block to position the ripping guide (Photo 3). If you make the guide from 1/2-in. plywood, you can rip two sheets of 3/4-in. plywood at once. Cut a 2-5/8 in. block to position the guide when cutting the 1/4-in. plywood strips. You'll get

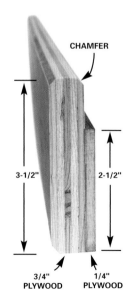

CHAMFER

3-1/2"   2-1/2"

3/4"   1/4"
PLYWOOD   PLYWOOD

13 rails from a sheet of 3/4-in. plywood; 18 strips from a sheet of 1/4-in. plywood. We made twenty-three 8-ft. long rails for our 8 x 20-ft. wall.

The chamfers on the rails are optional (Photo 4). The two on the face of the rail are purely decorative. The one on the back lets the aluminum cleats slip over the rail more easily. Instead of chamfering the edge, you can simply round it slightly with sandpaper. For appearance, we also chamfered our shelves and hook mounting plates. A carbide chamfer bit costs $20.

Fasten 1/4-in. strips to each rail (Photo 5). To save time, finish the rails before you install them. We used water-based polyurethane. But don't coat the back side; construction adhesive will grip bare wood better than sealed wood.

Use glue and nails for rock-solid rails

Attach rails with two beads of construction adhesive and a 16d finish nail driven at each stud (Photo 6). Cut rails so that the ends meet at stud centers. For better appearance and strength, avoid putting rail joints at plywood seams.

Use a level to make sure the lowest course of rails is straight and level. Then use a pair of spacer blocks to position the rest of the rails. You can space the rails however you like. The closer you position them, the more flexibility you'll have when hanging shelves or hooks. We began with a 10-in. space between the bottom strip of trim and the lowest rail, then spaced the rest of the rails 6 in. apart. When all the rails are in place, finish the entire wall with a coat of polyurethane.

3 Position your ripping guide using a spacer block and clamp it into place. Then cut the 3-1/2 in. wide plywood rails. Cut two sheets at once to speed up the job.

4 Cut three 45-degree chamfers 1/8 in. deep on each rail using a router and chamfer bit.

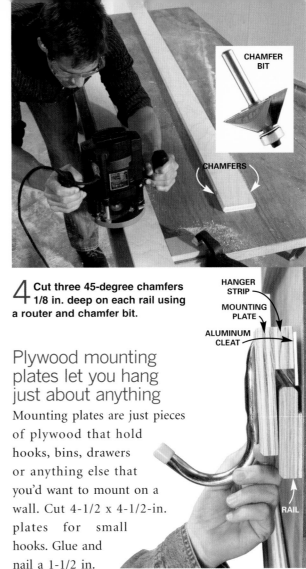

Mass-produce hanger cleats from aluminum stock

The cleats that hook onto the rails are made from 1/8-in. thick aluminum stock that's available in 2- to 8-ft. lengths. Use 3/4-in. x 3/4-in. angle for shelves and 2-in. wide flat stock for mounting plates (see Photos 9 and 11). Cutting and drilling aluminum is fast and easy. Cut the aluminum with a metal-cutting blade ($10; Photo 7). We cut all our cleats 4 in. long, but you can vary the length to suit your needs. Drill 3/16-in. screw holes and 3/8-in. recesses with standard drill bits (Photo 8). Wear eye protection when cutting and drilling aluminum.

Plywood mounting plates let you hang just about anything

Mounting plates are just pieces of plywood that hold hooks, bins, drawers or anything else that you'd want to mount on a wall. Cut 4-1/2 x 4-1/2-in. plates for small hooks. Glue and nail a 1-1/2 in.

Hanging options

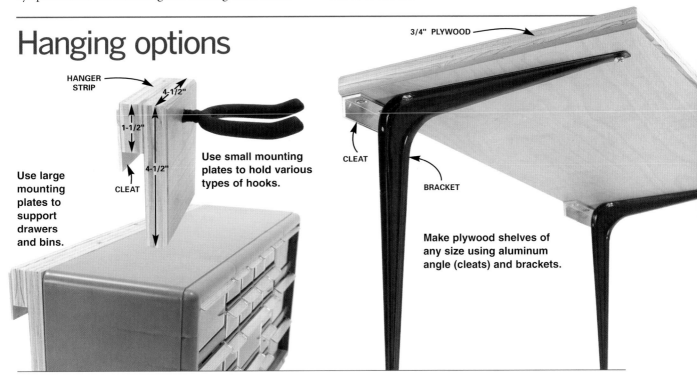

Use large mounting plates to support drawers and bins.

Use small mounting plates to hold various types of hooks.

Make plywood shelves of any size using aluminum angle (cleats) and brackets.

5 Glue 2-1/2 in. wide strips of 1/4-in. plywood to the back of each rail, even with the non-chamfered edge. Tack the strip into place with a pair of 3/4-in. brads every 12 in.

3/4" BRADS

NON-CHAMFERED EDGE

6 Spread two beads of adhesive on each rail and nail them to studs with 16d finish nails. Start at the bottom and work up.

6" POSITIONING BLOCK

6"

6"

10"

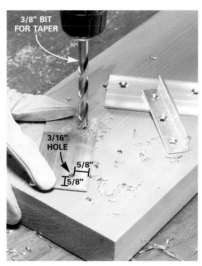

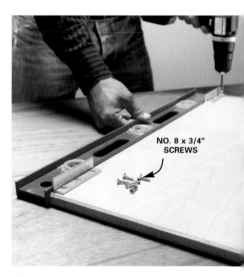

METAL-CUTTING BLADE

3/8" BIT FOR TAPER

3/16" HOLE

5/8"

5/8"

NO. 8 x 3/4" SCREWS

7 Cut aluminum angle and flat stock into 4-in. long sections. Round off the razor-sharp edges of each cut with a file or sandpaper.

8 Drill three 3/16-in. screw holes in angled cleats and two in flat cleats. Then drill a shallow screw-head recess with a 3/8-in. bit.

9 Screw cleats to the shelf about 1/4 in. from the ends. Use a straightedge to position the cleats flush and parallel with the back edge of the shelf.

wide plywood hanger strip across the back of each plate. Coat the plates with polyurethane. When the finish is dry, position the aluminum cleats about 1/4 in. from the upper edge of the hanger strip and fasten it with 1-1/4 in. drywall screws (Photo 11). Finally, screw hooks to the plates (Photo 12). We also made larger mounting plates for bins, drawer units and a bicycle holder.

Don't hang plates or shelves on the rails until the polyurethane has dried for at least 24 hours. Otherwise, the fresh polyurethane can "glue" parts together.

Make a dozen sturdy shelves in an hour

The shelves are made from aluminum angle cleats, 3/4-in. plywood and brackets that are available in a range of sizes ($1 to $2 each). We made shelves 6, 12 and 15 in. deep and 24 in. long. You could make yours longer than that, but remember that long shelves are less versatile than short ones. To keep shelves from sagging, place brackets no more than 30 in. apart. We chamfered three sides of each shelf with a router and coated them with water-based polyurethane before adding cleats and brackets (Photos 9 and 10).

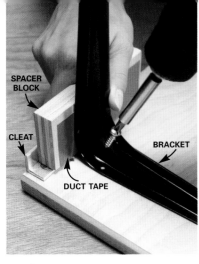

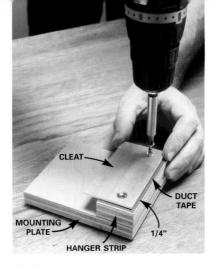

10 Position shelf brackets with a 3/4-in. plywood spacer block. Add a strip of duct tape to slightly widen the space so the cleat slips easily onto rails.

11 Glue a hanger strip to the mounting plate. Then add a strip of duct tape and screw on the cleat 1/4 in. from the top edge.

12 Predrill and screw hooks near the top of the plate where they can penetrate two layers of plywood.

tip We put our deepest shelves near the ceiling where they would be out of the way. That out-of-reach space is the best place for stuff you don't use often and a good spot for child hazards like lawn chemicals.

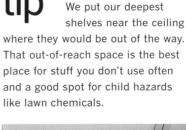

13 Slip the cleats over the rails and push down to anchor the shelves and mounting plates.

14 Use plywood scraps and your imagination to build custom racks for hard-to-store items.

Custom racks, too few hooks and a missed opportunity

One of the things we like most about this storage system is its adaptability. With a little ingenuity, you can make special holders for all those oddball items that don't fit conveniently on shelves or store-bought hooks (Photo 14). But before you make a custom holder, visit a home center. We spent a couple of hours building a bike rack only to find a better one at a hardware store for $7.

We also wasted time on the storage system project because we made too few mounting plates for hooks. Assembling five or six extras would have taken just a few minutes. Instead, we had to drag out our tools and run through the whole process a second time.

But here's our biggest mistake: Like most garages, this one has too few electrical outlets. We could have hacked holes in the drywall to easily run new electrical lines. No need to patch up the wall, since it was about to be covered with plywood anyway. Unfortunately, this occurred to us just as we nailed the last rail into place.

Super-simple utility cabinets

You can knock any of these cabinets together in a couple of hours and have that garage clutter tucked away by dinnertime!

Build 'em and fill 'em. We designed these sturdy cabinets for simple assembly. You just glue and screw plywood together to make the basic box, then add a premade door, actually an inexpensive bifold door panel. Since bifolds are readily available in several styles, including louvered and paneled, you can make a wide range of practical yet handsome cabinets, without the time and hassle of making the doors.

We built a set of five cabinets in different sizes to show you how versatile this design is. You can make them big and deep to store clothing and sports gear; shallow and tall for shovels, rakes, skis or fishing rods; or shallow and short to mount on walls for tools, paint cans and other small items. You can even mount them on wheels and roll your tools right to the job. The only limitation is the size of standard bifold doors.

In this article, we'll demonstrate how to build one of the smaller hanging wall cabinets. You can build the others using the same techniques and the Cutting Lists on p. 22.

You don't need advanced skills or special tools to build this entire set of cabinets. However, you do have to cut a lot of plywood accurately. A table saw helps here, but a circular saw with a guide works fine too. Add a drill

or two, a couple of clamps and some careful advance planning, and you're set.

Buying the bifolds and plywood

When planning your cabinets, begin by choosing the bifold door and build the rest of the cabinet to match its dimensions. Standard bifolds are 79 in. high and available in 24-in., 30-in., 32-in. and 36-in. widths. Keep in mind that you get two doors for each of these widths, each approximately 12, 15, 16 or 18 in. wide. Your cabinet can be any of the single-door widths or any of the double-door widths. You can also cut the doors down to make shorter cabinets, as we demonstrate here. Make them any depth you choose.

Bifolds come in several styles and wood species. We chose louvered pine doors ($56 for 30-in. wide) and birch plywood ($40 per sheet) for a handsome, natural look. All the materials for our cabinet, including hardware, cost about $70. The five cabinets cost $320. You can cut that cost considerably by using less expensive plywood, bifolds and hinges.

You can also save by using plywood efficiently. Once you decide on the door sizes, lay out all the cabinet pieces on a scale drawing of a 4 x 8-ft. sheet of plywood (graph paper helps). You can even adjust the cabinet depths a bit to achieve best use. We built the five cabinets shown from four sheets of 3/4-in. plywood and two sheets of 1/4-in. plywood for the backs.

project at a glance

skill level
intermediate

special tools
circular saw
drill
clamps
table saw
 (optional)

approximate cost
$75–$100 per cabinet

GARDEN FAVORITE

BLUE LAKE 274
GARDEN BEAN

$1.00

GARDEN FAVORITE

BEAN

gardening

a commonsense guide

GARDENING

penelope ody

1 Mark the door length and clamp a straightedge to the door to guide your saw. Cut the other cabinet pieces using the straightedge as well.

2 Predrill screw holes through the sides 3/8 in. from the ends. Drive 1-5/8 in. screws with finish washers through the sides into the top and bottom. Stack extra shelves in the corners to keep the box square.

The "partial wrap-around" hinges we used may not be available at home centers or hardware stores. However, woodworking stores carry them; see p. 25. If you don't mind exposed hinges, simply use bifold hinges, which cost less than $1 each at home centers.

Cut out all the parts

Begin by cutting the bifold doors to size (Photo 1). This will determine the exact cabinet height. Be sure to use a guide and a sharp blade for a straight, crisp cut. Center the cut on the dividing rail. Be prepared for the saw to bump up and down slightly as it crosses each stile (Photo 1). Then trim each newly created door so that the top and bottom rails are the same width.

Some bifold door manufacturers use only a single dowel to attach each rail to the stile. If this is the case with your doors, you may find that one of your rails (after being cut in half) is no longer attached to the door. Don't panic. Dab a little glue on each rail and stile and clamp them back together. After 20 minutes or so, you'll be back in business.

Then cut the plywood to size using a guide to keep all the cuts straight and square. If the plywood splinters a bit, score the cutting line first with a utility knife.

tip* Most lumberyards and home centers have a large saw (called a panel saw) for cutting sheets of plywood. For a nominal fee, you can have them rip all of your plywood to proper widths. (You'll cut the pieces to length later.) You have to plan your cabinet depths in advance, but it's quicker than ripping the plywood yourself and makes hauling it home a lot easier.

cutting lists
for cabinet styles shown on p. 23

Storage locker
Door: One 11-3/4" x 79" (half of a 24" bifold)*

Sides: Two 3/4" x 11-1/4" x 79"

Top, bottom, shelf: Three 3/4" x 11-1/4" x 10-1/4"

Cleats: Two 3/4" x 3" x 10-1/4"

Front cleat: 3/4" x 3" x 10-1/4"

Back: One 1/4" x 11-3/4" x 79"

Closet on wheels
Doors: Two 15-3/4" x 79" (32" bifold)*

Sides: Two 3/4" x 22-1/2" x 79"

Top, bottom, shelf: Three 3/4" x 22-1/2" x 30-1/8"

Cleats: Three 3/4" x 3" x 30-1/8"

Back: One 1/4" x 31-5/8" x 79"

Casters: Four 3"

Paneled wall cabinet
Doors: Two 14-3/4" x 32-1/4" (30" bifold)*

Sides: Two 3/4" x 11-1/4" x 32-1/4"

Top, bottom, shelves: Four 3/4" x 11-1/4" x 28-1/8"

Cleats: Two 3/4" x 3" x 28-1/8"

Back: One 1/4" x 29-5/8" x 32-1/4"

Narrow floor cabinet
Door: One 11-3/4" x 79" (half of a 24" bifold)*

Sides: Two 3/4" x 11-1/4" x 79"

Top, bottom, shelves: Nine 3/4" x 11-1/4" x 10-1/4"

Cleats: Two 3/4" x 3" x 10-1/4"

Back: One 1/4" x 11-3/4" x 79"

*Exact door sizes vary. Measure your doors before deciding cabinet dimensions.

Ventilated wall cabinet

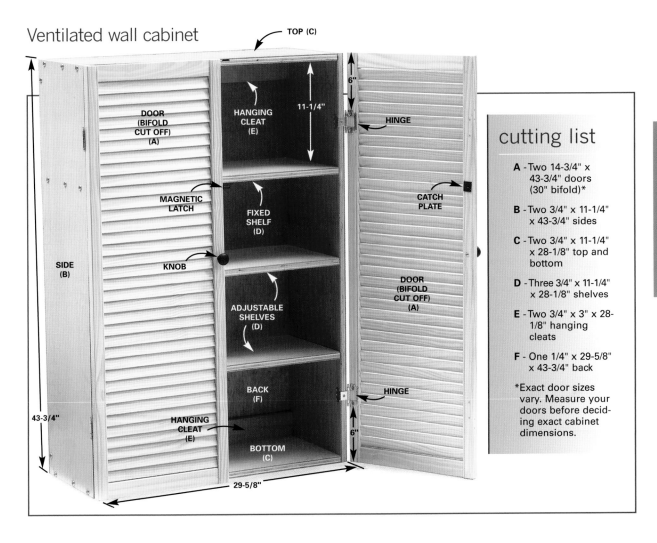

TOP (C)

DOOR (BIFOLD CUT OFF) (A)

HANGING CLEAT (E)

11-1/4"

6"

HINGE

MAGNETIC LATCH

FIXED SHELF (D)

CATCH PLATE

KNOB

SIDE (B)

ADJUSTABLE SHELVES (D)

DOOR (BIFOLD CUT OFF) (A)

43-3/4"

BACK (F)

HINGE

HANGING CLEAT (E)

BOTTOM (C)

6"

29-5/8"

cutting list

A - Two 14-3/4" x 43-3/4" doors (30" bifold)*

B - Two 3/4" x 11-1/4" x 43-3/4" sides

C - Two 3/4" x 11-1/4" x 28-1/8" top and bottom

D - Three 3/4" x 11-1/4" x 28-1/8" shelves

E - Two 3/4" x 3" x 28-1/8" hanging cleats

F - One 1/4" x 29-5/8" x 43-3/4" back

*Exact door sizes vary. Measure your doors before deciding exact cabinet dimensions.

Other cabinet options (Cutting Lists and dimensions on p. 22)

Storage locker
Compact storage for long items like skis, fishing rods, long-handled tools; either on floor or wall-hung; 12-in. wide door and one fixed shelf.

Closet on wheels
Large storage capacity (about 32 in. wide and 22-1/2 in. deep); fixed shelf; closet rod; 3-in. swivel casters ($6 each).

Paneled wall cabinet
Shorter version of cabinet above; made from the paneled portion of partial louvered doors; one adjustable shelf.

Narrow floor or wall cabinet
Shelf version of storage locker (left); top and bottom shelves fixed; intermediate shelves mounted on adjustable shelf standards ($2 each).

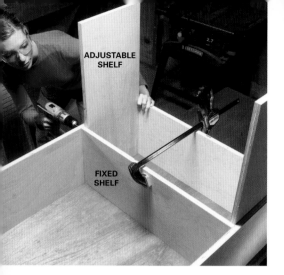

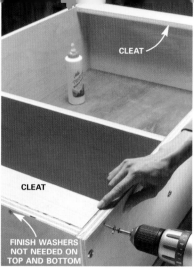

3 Predrill, clamp and screw the fixed shelf to the sides. Use adjustable shelves as a guide to space it and keep it square.

4 Glue and clamp hanging cleats to the top and bottom. Predrill and drive screws through the top, bottom and sides into the cleats.

5 Spread a bead of glue on all back edges. Then align the plywood back with the top and nail with 1-in. brads. Align the other sides and nail in the order shown.

Assemble the box

Assemble the box face down on a flat surface. The garage floor works well for this step.

Mark and predrill screw holes through the sides for the top and bottom pieces (Photo 2). If you've got two drills, this is the time for them both. Use one for drilling holes and the other for driving screws.

We added finish washers (8¢ each; available at full-service hardware stores) for a more decorative look.

Attach the fixed shelf next to stiffen and strengthen the box (Photo 3). Use the extra shelves as guides to help position and square the shelf. Predrill and drive three screws through each side into the fixed shelf.

Attach cleats at the top and bottom of the cabinet to use for screwing the cabinet to a wall (Photo 4). Use three or four screws across the top and bottom. Clamp the cleat into place until you drive the screws. Because the screws won't be visible on the top and bottom, you can skip the finish washers. Use your finger to make sure the cleat sits flush with the side (Photo 4).

The 1/4-in. plywood back stiffens the frame and keeps it square, which is essential for the doors to fit accurately. Spread glue along the cabinet edges, including the fixed shelf and the hanging cleats (Photo 5). Carefully set the back onto the cabinet, keeping the top flush with the cabinet top. Nail in the order and direction shown in Photo 5. Align the edges carefully before nailing each side to keep the cabinet perfectly square. (You cut the plywood back perfectly square, right?)

Shelves, hinges and other hardware

Use a scrap of peg board to help lay out the holes evenly for the adjustable shelf support pins. Mark each hole clearly (red circles, Photo 6) on the front and back of the peg board. Mark each hole position on one side of the cabinet, then slide the peg board across to the other side for marking. Don't flip the peg board over; it can throw the pattern off and the shelves will rock rather than lie flat.

Most shelf support pins require a 1/4-in. hole, but check the pins you buy to be sure. In addition, measure how far the pins are supposed to go into the cabinet sides. Wrap a piece of masking tape around your drill bit at this depth (photo at right). This ensures that you won't drill completely through the side of your cabinet. Check the bit after every few holes to make sure the tape hasn't slipped.

Install your door hinges 6 in. from the top and bottom of the doors (add a third hinge on taller doors). The best type is a "partial wrap-around" hinge (Photo 7). Its hinge leaves are hidden when the door is closed, and the design allows you to avoid driving screws into the weak plywood edge grain.

Begin by installing the hinges on the door (Photo 7). Keep them perfectly square to the door edge and predrill screw holes as precisely as possible. An extra set of hands will be helpful when attaching the doors to the cabinet.

STILE

6 Mark shelf pin locations on both front and back sides of a peg board template. Mark one side of the cabinet, then slide (not flip) the peg board to the opposite side and mark matching holes. Drill the 1/4-in. pin holes.

7 Screw the hinges to the cabinet doors. Align the door edges with the cabinet top and bottom. Then predrill and screw the hinges to the cabinet sides.

8 Attach cabinet knobs to the doors and install a pair of magnetic latches to hold the doors closed. For full-length doors, install latches at both the top and the bottom.

Have your partner align the door exactly with the top or bottom of the cabinet while you mark, predrill and screw the hinges to the cabinet side. Repeat for the other door. Ideally the doors will meet evenly in the center with about a 1/8-in. gap between. You may have to "tweak" the hinge positions slightly with paper shims, or plane the doors a bit to make them perfect.

Choose any type of knob and magnetic latch you like. However, bifold door stiles (the vertical edges) are narrow, so make sure the neighboring door will clear the knob when opened (Photo 8). If you have a rail (the horizontal door frame member), mount the knobs there.

Another problem: Bifold stiles are usually 1 to 1-1/8 in. thick and most knobs are designed for 3/4-in. doors. So you may have to look for longer knob screws at your local hardware store. Or try this trick: With a 3/8-in. bit, drill a 1/4-in. deep hole on the backside of the stile to recess the screwhead.

To mount a magnetic latch, first mount the magnet to the underside of the fixed shelf (Photo 8). Stick the catch plate to the magnet with the "mounting points" facing out (photo below). Close the door and press it tightly against the latch. The points on the catch plate will indent the door slightly and indicate where to mount the plate.

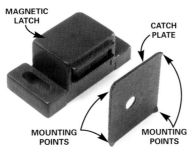

MAGNETIC LATCH

CATCH PLATE

MOUNTING POINTS

MOUNTING POINTS

Finishing

That's about it. Now that you've built one cabinet and know the ropes, you can probably build the second cabinet in half the time. We finished our cabinets inside and out with two coats of clear water-based satin polyurethane. It dries quickly (half hour), has little or no odor, and cleans up with soap and water. The first coat raises the wood grain a bit, so you have to sand it lightly with fine sandpaper (150 grit or finer). Whether you use a clear finish, paint or stain, it's generally faster if you remove the doors and hardware first.

Partial wrap-around hinges

The hinges shown are available at woodworking stores such as Rockler Woodworking and Hardware (800) 279-4441; www.rockler.com; No. 31456; $5.99 per pair). Less expensive styles are also available.

Heavy-bicycle lift

More space with less hassle.

WALL CLEAT

Hanging bikes by one or both wheels on bicycle storage hooks is the quickest and cheapest way to get them off the floor and out of the way. But the hooks won't always work if your bike is too heavy to lift easily. Then the best solution is a convenient pulley system that allows you to quickly and easily raise the bike out of the way.

We couldn't design a system much cheaper or better than a purchased system like the Hoist Monster from ProStor (about $40 through Ace, TrueValue, or www.racorinc.com). It can lift up to 100 lbs. with its quality mechanical system of pulleys and hooks, and its dual safety design (locking mechanism and rope tie-down cleat) keeps the bike secure.

Attach the pulley brackets to a ceiling joist with wood screws. Position the hooks the same distance apart as the distance from the handlebar to the seat rear. Choose a location that's convenient yet doesn't interfere with vehicles or people, since the bike will hang down about 4 ft. from the ceiling. If the joists aren't spaced just right, lag-screw 2x4s to them and then screw the brackets to the 2x4s.

project at a glance

skill level
beginner

special tools
drill

approximate cost
$40

1 Attach the lift assembly hardware to the center of the ceiling joists with the screws provided. Mount the safety rope cleat to a garage wall stud, out of a child's reach. Wrap the cord around the cleat to secure the bike (photo at top of page).

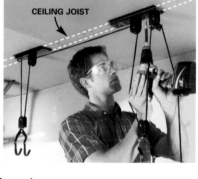

CEILING JOIST

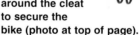

INSTALL SO THIS DISTANCE EQUALS MEASUREMENT FROM HANDLEBAR TO REAR OF SEAT

7 low-cost storage projects

Ideas for every room in the house.

Shoe-bag storage

Expand the limited storage space in your garage by hanging clear plastic shoe bags on the wall. They take up very little room and are great for holding garden sprays, spray paints, lubricants and other bottles and cans. And, since the items are in plain sight instead of buried at the back of a shelf, you always know what you've got and where it is.

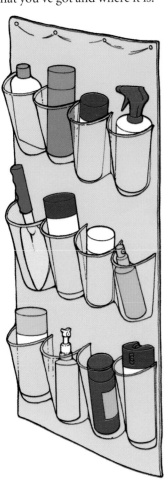

project at a glance

skill level
beginner

special tools
circular saw, jigsaw, drill

approximate cost
$10–$25 each

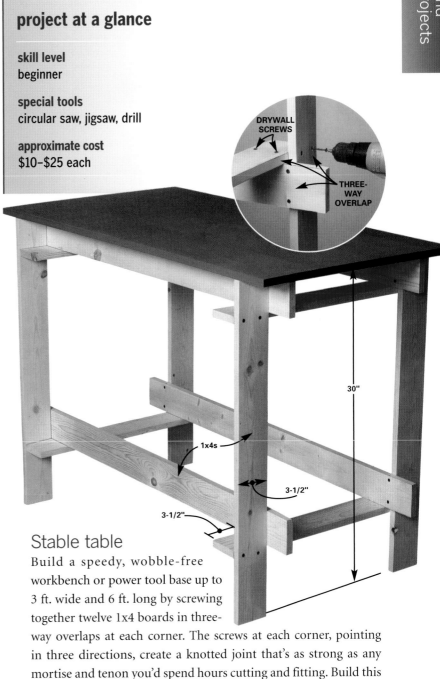

DRYWALL SCREWS

THREE-WAY OVERLAP

30"

1x4s

3-1/2"

3-1/2"

Stable table

Build a speedy, wobble-free workbench or power tool base up to 3 ft. wide and 6 ft. long by screwing together twelve 1x4 boards in three-way overlaps at each corner. The screws at each corner, pointing in three directions, create a knotted joint that's as strong as any mortise and tenon you'd spend hours cutting and fitting. Build this base in a half hour and spend the rest of Saturday using it!

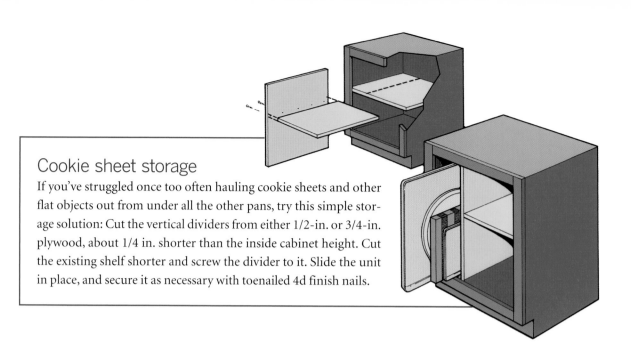

Cookie sheet storage

If you've struggled once too often hauling cookie sheets and other flat objects out from under all the other pans, try this simple storage solution: Cut the vertical dividers from either 1/2-in. or 3/4-in. plywood, about 1/4 in. shorter than the inside cabinet height. Cut the existing shelf shorter and screw the divider to it. Slide the unit in place, and secure it as necessary with toenailed 4d finish nails.

Mobile stacking totes

Make these stacking totes from 1/2-in. birch veneer plywood. The dimensions we give allow each tote to interlock snugly with the one above and below it. You can cut four totes from one full sheet of plywood—five from about a sheet and a third. Cut all the plywood parts to size, cut out the hand grips, and sand all edges smooth. Then glue and assemble the totes with 4d finishing nails. Leave them unfinished or apply paint or stain. Mount 2-in. casters on the bottom tote to make the stack mobile.

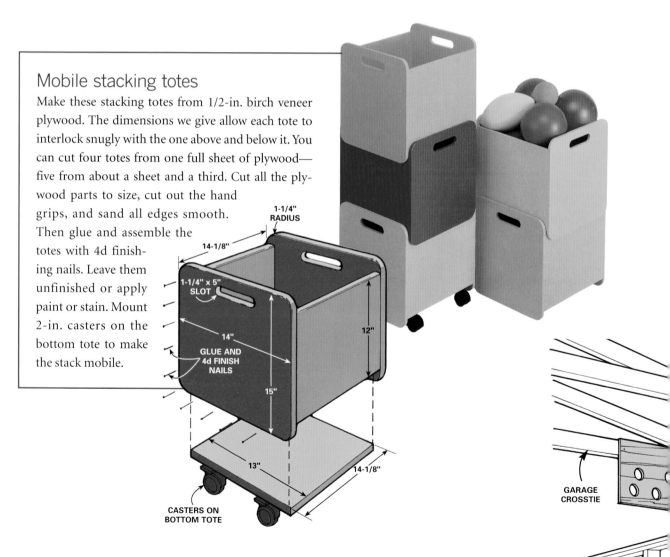

1-1/4" RADIUS

14-1/8"

1-1/4" x 5" SLOT

14"

GLUE AND 4d FINISH NAILS

12"

15"

13"

14-1/8"

CASTERS ON BOTTOM TOTE

GARAGE CROSSTIE

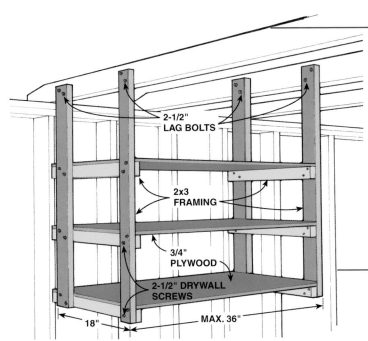

2-1/2"
LAG BOLTS

2x3
FRAMING

3/4"
PLYWOOD

2-1/2" DRYWALL
SCREWS

18" **MAX. 36"**

Hanging garage rack

This hold-anything rack mounts over the hood of your car and takes up no valuable garage floor space. Build the two 2x3 end support frames first, determining shelf width and spacing to suit your needs. Hang the frames from overhead beams with 2-1/2 in. lag bolts. If you build the rack in a corner, you can mount the shelf supports for one side directly to the side wall of the garage.

Utility shelves

This sturdy, freestanding shelf unit is made from any inexpensive 1-by lumber (3/4 in. thick) for the legs, and plywood or particleboard for the shelves. Glue and nail the four L-shaped legs together with 6d finish nails. Clamp the shelves in place, getting them evenly spaced and level, then secure each shelf with eight 2-in. screws through the legs.

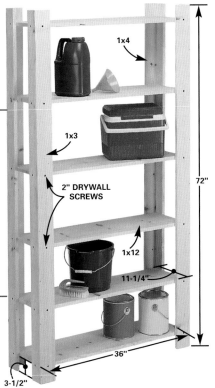

1x4

1x3

2" DRYWALL
SCREWS

1x12

72"

11-1/4"

36"

3-1/2"

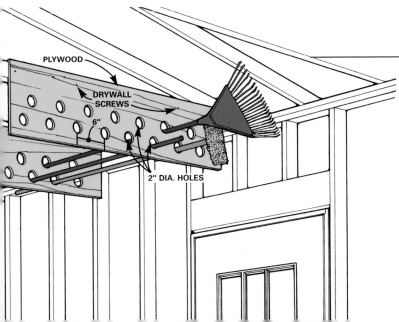

PLYWOOD

DRYWALL
SCREWS

6"

2" DIA. HOLES

Overhead storage for garden tools

Rakes, shovels, brooms and other long-handled tools seem to be in the way no matter how they're stored in the garage. Here's a rack that works: Cut two pieces of plywood about 12 in. x 48 in. and drill matching 2-in. holes in each, spaced about 6 in. apart. Mount the racks on crossties below your garage roof rafters.

Maximize your closet!

Double your closet capacity with smart and efficient built-ins, shelving and rod space.

I s your closet too small and overstuffed? Do your cluttered shelves, packed and sagging clothes rods, and jumbled shoes all cry out for more space? Of course, the coolest solution would be to expand the existing closet, but that's usually impossible. Instead, you can organize your existing closet to make every cubic inch count and get more dresser space to boot.

It's surprisingly easy and economical to squeeze more storage out of limited space. In this story, we'll show you how to remodel a standard 8-ft. long, 30-in. deep closet, a size that's found in millions of homes. Here's what we've done to maximize storage.

● **Cabinet module:** The 2-ft. wide, 23-in. deep, 78-in. tall cabinet module is designed to provide extra drawer and shelving space. The unit is mounted 6 in. above the floor for easy cleaning. The mounting height also makes installation easier because you don't have to fool with removing and reinstalling carpeting or baseboards.

● **Clothes rods:** Rod capacity is maximized because the rods are double-stacked at one end of the closet for shorter clothes like shirts and skirts. The single rod at the other end of the closet is for slacks and dresses.

● **Shoe shelves:** To tame shoe scatter, we've designed a two-tier shoe shelf. Including the space under the shelves, you'll have 9 luxurious ft. of shoe storage—enough for even those beat-up, knockabout shoes you can't bear to part with.

project at a glance

skill level
intermediate

special tools
circular saw
drill
clamps
brad nailer

approximate cost
$300–$350

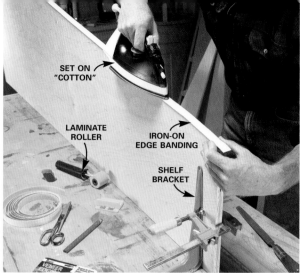

1 Cut the sides to length and width using a ripping jig (p. 35). Rip the drawer dividers to width only. Cut the angles on the front edge of each cabinet side.

2 Clean off any sawdust on the edges and then iron the edge banding onto the outside edges of the sides and the two lengths of drawer divider stock.

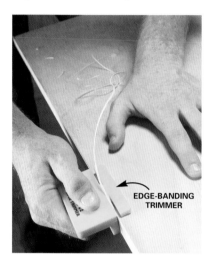

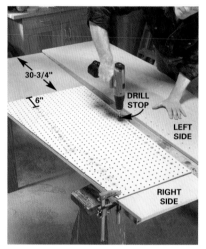

3 Trim the overhanging edges of the edge banding with a trimming tool, then file and sand the edges smooth and flush with the edge.

4 Mark the shelf bracket hole locations on peg board and use it as a drilling template. Flip the peg board to drill the other side.

materials list

ITEM	QTY.
3/4" plywood	3 sheets
1/2" plywood (buy a 4x4 sheet if it's available)	1 sheet
1/4" plywood	1 sheet
Iron-on edge banding	3 rolls
Construction adhesive	1 tube
Woodworking glue	
8' chrome closet rods	1
6' chrome closet rods	1
Closet rod end brackets	3 sets
No. 8 finish washers	50
No. 8 2" oval head screws	40
No. 8 3" oval head screws	12
22" "Liberty" bottom-mount drawer slides	4 sets
Drawer pulls	4 (or 8)
Shelf brackets	12

Custom-build your own closet system

It's easy to upgrade the typical single rod and shelf found in standard closets for more efficient "closetry." Home centers offer several lines of mix-and-match closet cabinets and organizers so you can design and install a custom closet system. Those systems look inexpensive—until you start adding up all the parts! A similar-size Melamine cabinet module alone will cost about $300. We offer a more handsome, lower-cost alternative—custom-building your own. For that same $300, you'll have a closet full of cabinetry that's so doggone good-looking that you'll want to leave the closet doors open.

This project doesn't call for any fancy woodworking joints. All the parts are end-cut and simply screwed together. While that makes for easy construction, it means you'll have to use plywood-core, veneered plywood (any type) because it'll hold screws and has a smooth, even surface ready for finishing. If you want to use particleboard-core sheets, plan on joining parts with biscuits, dowels or any other fastening system you're familiar with. We chose birch plywood to match the bedroom's existing woodwork. All of the materials shown are found at any well-stocked home center. See the list above.

As for tools, you don't need much aside from a good circular saw, a screw gun, a carpenter's square and two 30-in. bar clamps. You'll also have to blow the dust off

figure a closet assembly

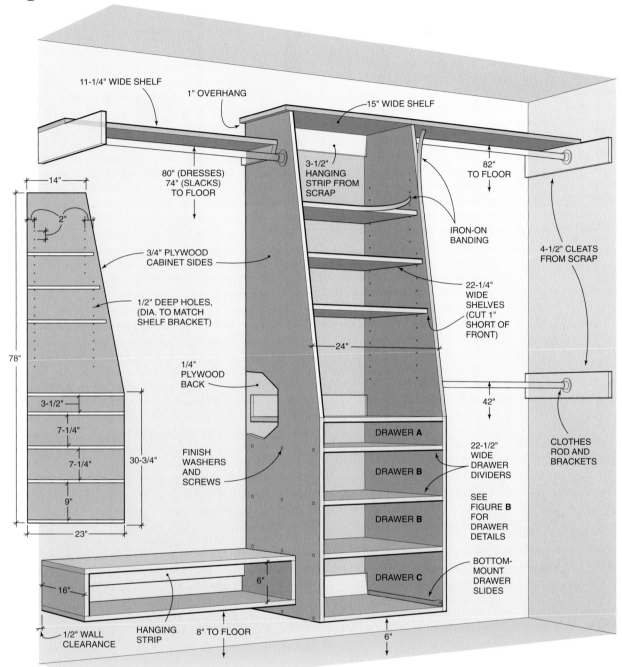

11-1/4" WIDE SHELF

1" OVERHANG

15" WIDE SHELF

3-1/2" HANGING STRIP FROM SCRAP

80" (DRESSES) 74" (SLACKS) TO FLOOR

82" TO FLOOR

14"

2"

3/4" PLYWOOD CABINET SIDES

1/2" DEEP HOLES, (DIA. TO MATCH SHELF BRACKET)

IRON-ON BANDING

4-1/2" CLEATS FROM SCRAP

22-1/4" WIDE SHELVES (CUT 1" SHORT OF FRONT)

78"

1/4" PLYWOOD BACK

24"

3-1/2"

7-1/4"

7-1/4"

9"

30-3/4"

FINISH WASHERS AND SCREWS

42"

DRAWER A

DRAWER B

22-1/2" WIDE DRAWER DIVIDERS

SEE FIGURE B FOR DRAWER DETAILS

CLOTHES ROD AND BRACKETS

DRAWER B

23"

DRAWER C

BOTTOM-MOUNT DRAWER SLIDES

16"

6"

1/2" WALL CLEARANCE

HANGING STRIP

8" TO FLOOR

6"

figure b
drawer assembly

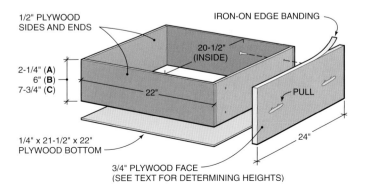

1/2" PLYWOOD SIDES AND ENDS

IRON-ON EDGE BANDING

20-1/2" (INSIDE)

2-1/4" (A)
6" (B)
7-3/4" (C)

22"

PULL

1/4" x 21-1/2" x 22" PLYWOOD BOTTOM

24"

3/4" PLYWOOD FACE (SEE TEXT FOR DETERMINING HEIGHTS)

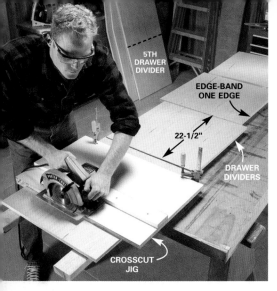

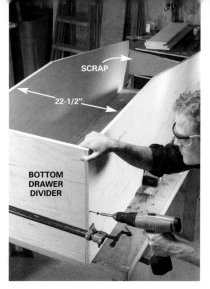

5 Cut the five edge-banded drawer dividers to length with the crosscutting jig, four from one length and one from the other.

6 Screw a scrap to the top of the cabinet, spacing the sides 22-1/2 in. apart, then clamp the bottom drawer divider between the sides. Predrill and fasten.

7 Stand the cabinet upright and rip spacer blocks from scrap to space and support the other drawer dividers as you screw them into place.

the clothes iron and use it to apply the edge banding (Photo 2). But there are a few other optional tools you'll find useful. While it is possible to hand-nail the parts together, a brad nailer (Photo 9) will speed up construction. (Since you can now buy a brad nailer for under $100, this project is a good excuse to add it to the tool collection.) Also pick up an edge-banding trimmer for quick, accurate edge trimming (less than $10; Photo 3).

Building the cabinet box

Start the project by cutting the cabinet box sides (Photo 1) and two 23-in. wide lengths for the drawer dividers; see Photos 1 and 5. Consult Figure A on p. 33 for all of the cutting dimensions. Before you cut the drawer dividers to length, edge-band one edge. That way the exposed edges will be finished before they're cut to length (Photo 5).

Before you assemble the cabinet, drill the holes for the adjustable shelving. We show the old trick of using a peg board jig for consistent hole spacing (Photo 4). Because the sides taper, you'll have to shift over a row or two of holes to keep the narrower top shelf brackets within a few inches of the front. Try to keep the front and rear holes about 2 in. from the edge. Buy a drill bit that matches the shaft on the shelving brackets that you chose. It's best to use a "brad point" drill bit to keep from splintering the veneer. Either use a depth stop or mark the drill bit with a piece of tape to keep from drilling through the plywood.

Begin assembling the cabinet on its back by attaching a spacer strip at the top and then screwing the bottom drawer divider into place (Photo 6). Predrill using a 1/8-in. bit and drive 2-in. long No. 8 oval head screws with finish washers (below). Then stand the cabinet and, using spacer blocks ripped from scraps, position and hold the drawer dividers in place while you screw them to the sides. Keeping the dividers tight to the spacers as you screw them into place is important for the drawers to work properly.

Edge-banding basics

If you've never used iron-on edge banding, it'll only take you a couple of attempts to achieve proficiency. Don't worry if you make a mistake; run the iron over it again and the heat-sensitive glue will release so you can adjust the piece and iron it back on again. Cut each strip of banding about 1 in. extra long with a sharp scissors. Leave about 1/2 in. or more of banding overhanging the starting corner because it tends to creep when you iron it. Move the iron along (set on "cotton") at about 1 in. per second all the way to the other end, guiding it with your other hand as you go. As you guide it, make sure the banding edges hang over each side of the plywood. Before it cools, push a block or roller over it to embed the banding. Then let the banding cool for 30 seconds or so and check for voids. Re-iron and embed any loose spots.

NO. 8 FINISH WASHER

2" NO. 8 OVAL HEAD SCREW

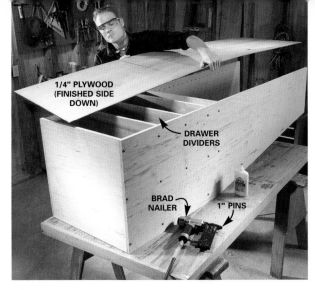

1/4" PLYWOOD (FINISHED SIDE DOWN)

DRAWER DIVIDERS

BRAD NAILER

1" PINS

1/4" PLYWOOD

SIDE

FRONT OR BACK

1-1/4" SHORT OF OPENING

1/2" PLYWOOD

8 Glue and pin the cabinet back to the sides and dividers to square the cabinet. Then glue and pin the hanging strips to the back and sides.

9 Glue and pin the drawer sides together with 1-in. brads. Before the glue sets, square each drawer by gluing and pinning the bottom in place.

Cutting plywood with simple jigs and a circular saw

If you have a full-size table saw, great—you'll be able to use it for most of the plywood cuts. If you have a portable table saw, use it for the smaller ripping jobs like making the shelving and drawer parts. But you can also do a fine job with only a circular saw fitted with a plywood blade and a couple of simple, screw-together jigs made from cheap Melamine closet shelving stock.

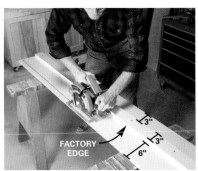

FACTORY EDGE

3"

3"

6"

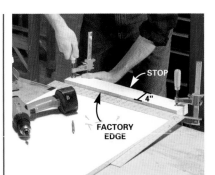

STOP

4"

FACTORY EDGE

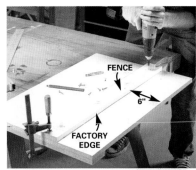

FENCE

6"

FACTORY EDGE

RIPPING JIG: Use an 8-ft. length of 16-in. wide shelving to build the ripping jig. Draw a line 3 in. from the edge and cut along it with the circular saw. Screw this piece to the larger piece about 3 in. away from one edge with the factory edge facing the widest section of shelving, as shown. Then use that edge as a guide to cut off the Melamine. Now it's just a matter of lining up that edge with marks on plywood stock and clamping it to make perfect cuts up to 8 ft. long on any piece of plywood (Photo 1).

CROSSCUTTING JIG: You can use the ripping jig for crosscutting, too, but this crosscutting jig has the advantage of a stop on the bottom. Push the stop against the plywood, align it with the cutting mark and clamp for quick, accurate crosscuts. Make it from a 4-ft. length of 24-in. wide Melamine shelving (or plywood if wide shelving isn't available). Cut a 4-in. wide strip for the stop from one end and another 4-in. wide strip from one edge for the fence. Align the factory edge of the short piece with the factory edge at the other end of the shelving to make the stop. Then clamp and screw the two pieces together while checking alignment with a carpenter's square. Flip the jig over and measure from the long factory edge 6 in. to position and screw the long saw guide, as shown. The key with both jigs is to use the straight factory edges for guiding the saw.

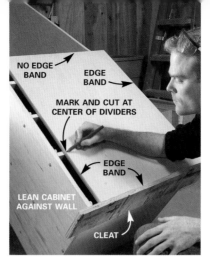

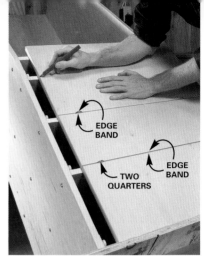

10 Screw the drawer slides into the cabinet and bottom edges of the drawer boxes. Slide each drawer into place to check the fit.

11 Set drawer front panel (edge-banded on three sides) on a temporary cleat screwed to cabinet bottom. Mark and cut lowest drawer front. Edge-band the raw edges.

12 Space each panel two quarter thicknesses apart, then measure and cut the next. Edge-band the two raw edges that meet, then repeat the procedure for the next panel.

13 Place crumpled newspaper behind each drawer and replace the drawers. They should stick out about 1/2 in. beyond the cabinet front.

14 Apply four beads of construction adhesive to the drawer boxes and restack the drawer fronts, spacing them with double quarters.

15 Lay a board across each edge of the fronts and clamp overnight. Then drive four 1-in. screws through each box into the fronts.

Cut the ends as close to the plywood as possible with the scissors and then run the edge-band trimmer down both sides to trim off the overhang. You'll have to make multiple passes to get all of the spots flush. The trimmer works best if you trim with the grain. Sometimes that means reversing direction in the middle of trimming. Use a file held at a 45-degree angle to remove oozed-out glue and banding that's still a little proud, then sand all the joints smooth with a sanding block and 100-grit paper.

You'll save a lot of time simply by edge-banding all the parts after ripping them to width and before cutting them to length. Then you won't have so many individual parts to edge-band,

IRON-ON EDGE BANDING

or those pesky short drawer front ends to deal with. Pay attention to the simple little clamping tip shown in Photo 2: Screw a shelf bracket down and clamp the wood to it. That'll hold the pieces steady for edge banding.

Drawer construction

The prospect of building drawers makes most beginner woodworkers' knees rattle, but don't worry—it's not all that hard. The key is to build the cabinet and the drawer boxes square. If you're using drawer slides other than the ones we call for, be sure to read the directions before building the drawers. They'll tell you the necessary height and side-to-side clearances.

Building a square drawer is easy if you pin together the sides and then square them up with the plywood bot-

16 Set cabinet on blocks and center it in closet. Plumb it, shimming as needed, and drill 1/8-in. pilot holes through the cleats into studs or drywall.

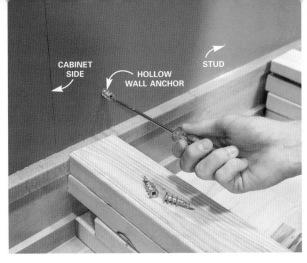

17 Remove the cabinet and screw drywall anchors into the holes without stud backing. Reposition the cabinet and screw it to the wall.

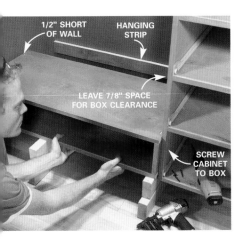

18 Build the shoebox about 1/2 in. short of the wall. Screw a cleat to the wall, then screw the box to the cabinet and nail it to the cleat.

19 Screw the closet rod brackets to the cleats and the cabinet, then install the clothes rods. Cut the top shelves and fasten them to cleats (Figure A).

20 Add the drawer pulls and adjustable shelves, then fill it up. Still not enough space? Donate whatever doesn't fit!

tom before the glue dries (Photo 9). Accurate side-to-side dimensions are crucial. You can always shim out the drawer slides if the drawers are a little narrow, but if they're too wide, you'll have to rebuild them.

Now is a good time to finish ripping and edge-banding your adjustable and fixed shelves. Don't cut them to final width until the cabinet is mounted so you can measure and cut exact widths to fit their selected positions. Stain and finish everything at the same time prior to installation. We used an oil-based honey maple stain and top-coated it with two coats of satin polyurethane.

Making it fit in your closet

The cabinet unit is 78 in. tall, so it will fit in any closet with 8-ft. walls, even with the 6-in. gap at the floor. Alter the height if you have a lower ceiling.

You'll have to set the cabinet aside before mounting it to install drywall anchors unless you're lucky enough to have the cabinet fall in front of two studs. Position the cabinet in the closet, then plumb and mark the wall (Photo 17) so the pilot holes line up with the anchors after you reset it. Then measure to the wall to determine the final length for the top shelf—don't forget to add 1 in. for the left-side overhang. Place cleats and shelves anywhere you wish. Build the cabinet taller, wider or with more drawers. Drawer sizes can be easily altered too—make deeper ones for sweaters or shallower ones for socks. The project how-to techniques shown will work for any configuration that best suits your needs.

Simple shelves
Strong, quick to build and no visible supports.

Made from only two parts:

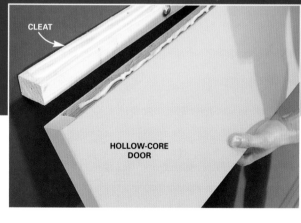

CLEAT

HOLLOW-CORE DOOR

These "floating" shelves are perfect for displaying your collectibles, photos, travel mementos or just about anything. Without the brackets and clunky hardware you'd find with store-bought shelves or kits, they seem to be suspended in midair.

These shelves are strong, too. While they're not designed to hold your old set of Encyclopaedia Britannicas, they're certainly capable of it. No one would believe that they're made from plain, old lightweight and inexpensive hollow-core doors.

In this article, we'll show you how to install these shelves (and shorter ones) securely with basic tools. Even if you think you have no DIY skills, you can tackle this project.

Surprise—a low-cost project that requires only basic tools

Each shelf is made from half of an 18-in. hollow-core door, which costs $18. That's only about $9 a shelf, plus the minimal cost of the lag screws (Photo 4) and cleat

that hold the shelf to the wall. You can buy new hollow-core interior doors at a home center or lumberyard (just be sure the door doesn't have predrilled holes for locksets). You may find only 24-in. wide doors, but the door can be any width; just try to minimize the waste. And you might be able to get doors free from yard sales or other sources.

As far as tools go, you can get by with just a circular saw and edge guide (Photo 2) to cut the door. Use a table saw to cut the cleat because a clean, straight cut is important for

a good-looking shelf. (If you don't own a table saw, use a friend's or have the cleat cut at a full-service lumberyard.) You'll also need a stud finder, a chisel, a hammer, a wrench, 1-in. brads, 3-1/2 in. lag screws, carpenter's glue and a level. Simply follow photos 1–9 for information on building these simple shelves.

Want a different look?

We chose to paint our shelves, but if you want the beauty of real wood, you can buy the

project at a glance

skill level
beginner

special tools
circular saw
drill
level
edge guide

approximate cost
$10–$20
per shelf

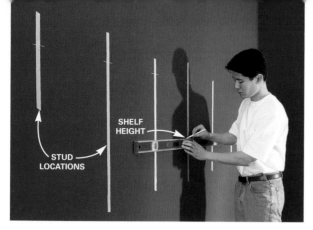

1 Trace the horizontal location for each shelf using a 4-ft. level as your guide. Use a stud finder to mark the locations of the studs and lightly press masking tape over each one. If you don't have a string line, use a long straightedge and mark the wall with a pencil. Check your marks with the 4-ft. level.

STUD LOCATIONS

SHELF HEIGHT

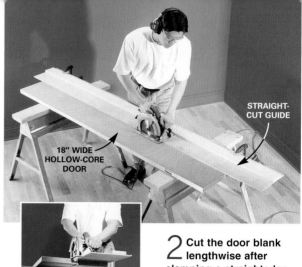

STRAIGHT-CUT GUIDE

18" WIDE HOLLOW-CORE DOOR

2 Cut the door blank lengthwise after clamping a straightedge guide to the door. Be sure to use a 40-tooth carbide blade for a smooth cut.

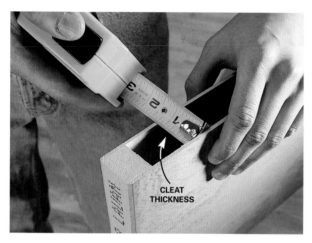

CLEAT THICKNESS

3 Measure the space between the outer veneers of the door and cut cleats from a 2x4 to this thickness. Our measurement was 1-3/32 in. Use straight, dry lumber for the cleats.

ALIGN CLEAT TO MARK

1-3/32" THICK, 1-1/2" DEEP

4 Predrill 1/4-in. dia. holes at the stud locations after you cut the cleats to length (the measurement between the end blocks of the door half). Hold the cleat to your line on the wall and drill into the stud with a 1/8-in. bit. Using a wrench, install one lag screw into each stud until it's tight. Use 1/4-in. x 3-1/2 in. lag screws. Each cleat must be straight as an arrow.

tip If you intend to paint the room, do so before you install the shelves because it's a drag to cut around each shelf with a paintbrush.

door in wood veneers like oak or maple (ours was lauan). If you decide on a natural wood finish, you'll need to cover the exposed edges with a matching wood trim. If you go this route, first shave off 1/8 in. from the front and side edges with a table saw to eliminate the slight bevel on each edge, then apply the matching trim. You can also cover the entire shelf with plastic laminate if you want a tough, hard-surfaced shelf.

You may want to change the depth of your shelves as well. Don't exceed 9 in. or you'll start to weaken the cantilever strength of the shelf. Feel free to make narrower or shorter shelves, as shown in Photo 9.

Create a rock-hard finish with a low-gloss enamel paint

The whole job will go a lot smoother if you paint the shelves before you install them. Just be sure to sand your wood door with 150-grit sandpaper before you paint. If the surface is still rough and porous after sanding, fill the pores by applying a paste wood filler (like

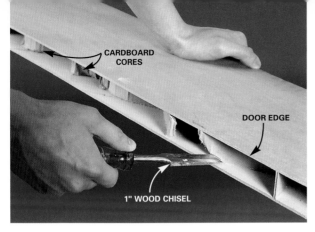

5 Cut away the corrugated cardboard cores at least 1-1/2 in. from the cut edge. Scrape away the glue carefully without gouging the wood surface.

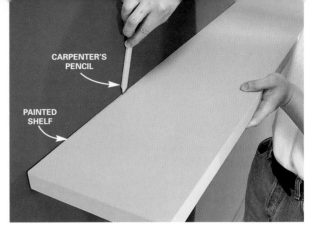

6 Dry-fit the shelf to make sure the blank fits over the cleat. Check the back side of the shelf and scribe it to the wall if necessary. Use a block plane or sander to remove material from the back edge for a tight fit.

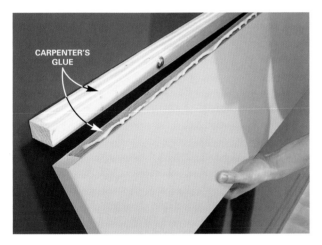

7 Apply glue to the top of the cleat and the inside bottom edge of the door blank. Slide the shelf over the wood cleat.

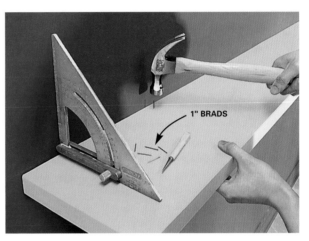

8 Nail the shelf to the cleat using a square as your guide. Start at the middle and work your way to each end. Use 1-in. brad nails spaced 8 in. apart.

Elmer's wood filler) with a 3-in. drywall knife. Let it dry and sand the surface again.

These shelves are permanent— they're tough to remove!

The glue not only makes the shelves strong but also impossible to remove without ruining them. You'll have to cut them in place 2 in. away from the wall with a circular saw to expose the lag screws and then remove the cleats with a wrench. That's unfortunate, but you can always make another set cheaply and easily.

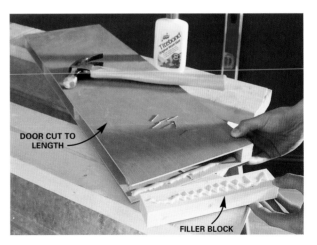

9 Build shorter shelves by cutting the shelf to length. Glue a filler block flush with the end and nail each side with small brad nails.

EASY FOR EVERYONE

Under-sink shelf

Make every square inch count.

project at a glance

skill level
beginner

special tools
aviation snips
drill
circular saw

approximate cost
$5

Tired of moving all that stuff under the sink every time you mop the floor? Just buy a Melamine closet shelf ($5) from a home center and a length of suspended-ceiling wall angle (sorry, it only comes in 10-ft. lengths, but it's cheap and you can have it cut for transport). Also pick up four 1/2-in. No. 8-24 bolts, washers and nuts. Follow Photos 1 – 3.

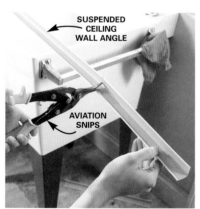

1 Using an aviation snips, cut two lengths of suspended ceiling channel to support the undersink shelf.

2 Clamp pieces of ceiling angle or aluminum angle to your sink legs (about 11 in. from the floor) and drill through with a 3/16-in. bit. Insert 1/2-in. long No. 8-24 bolts from the inside and thread on acorn nuts to cover sharp bolt edges.

3 Cut a shelf from 3/4-in. Melamine board and drop it onto the angle braces. You may need to notch your shelf if the sink trap is in your way. Paint the raw edges of the board to protect them from moisture.

2 section

weekend yard & garden projects

Micro irrigation

Reduce the time you spend watering to practically zero.

Whether you're growing roses to win prizes or just trying to keep a few flowerbeds looking good, you know what a chore watering is, lugging hoses around the yard and moving them every half hour or so. Micro irrigation—a network of plastic tubing and low-volume drippers and sprinklers that reach every part of the garden you want to water—takes the hassle out of watering.

The materials are inexpensive (you can get started for less than $100) and easy to install using nothing more than a pruning shears and a special hole punch tool. Once you lay out the tubing and connect the drippers, sprinklers or sprayers, you'll be able to water your plants by simply turning on the water and letting it run for an hour or two. Add a battery-operated controller for about $40 more and you won't even have to remember to turn on the water. It'll turn the water on and off automatically at the times you select.

Micro irrigation saves more than time and energy; it saves water by distributing it more efficiently. Because you use dozens of watering devices to replace one regular sprinkler, you have much greater control over where the water goes and how much is supplied to each plant. Instead of flooding the ground all at once, micro irrigation lets you apply a small amount over longer periods, allowing it to soak into the plants' root zone for maximum benefit. And since runoff and evaporation are kept to a minimum, micro irrigation uses less water.

In this article, we'll introduce you to the basics of micro irrigation, including planning tips and step-by-step installation instructions. For more details, especially in the planning phase, we recommend that you also read through one of the manufacturers' free planning guides or browse the Internet sites we've listed (see Buyer's Guide on p. 47).

project at a glance

skill level
beginner

special tools
pruning shears
hole punch tool

approximate cost
$100 for a
small garden

1 Mount a "Y" with shutoff valves to your faucet. Then attach the optional timer, backflow preventer, filter, pressure regulator and adapter.

2 Connect the 1/2-in. poly tubing to the faucet end. Then lay the tubing through the garden according to your plan. Stake it down about every 5 or 6 ft.

Make a sketch and plan the system

The basic planning strategy is to pick the best watering device to serve each type of plant. Then determine a flow rate that supplies adequate water to every plant in the watering zone. Set up the system to run between one and two hours at a time, two or three times a week.

Start by measuring your garden and making a simple sketch. Choose the type and flow rate of the watering devices based on your soil and the plants' water needs. Mark these on the plan and draw in the tubing route to connect them. This will involve a little guesswork. See "Drippers, Bubblers, Sprinklers and Sprayers" on p. 47 for information that will help you choose the right watering device. Try to cover all the root zones of your plants. Don't worry about getting everything perfect at first. Add a few extra of each type of watering device and buy the watering devices, tubing and the basic parts shown in Figure B for the faucet hookup. Once you see how the system works, you'll find it's easy to relocate or add emitters to get a more balanced water flow or better coverage.

tip If this is your first venture into micro irrigation, start small and experiment to get a feel for how the system works. Choose one or two flowerbeds or a garden and install a simple one-zone system.

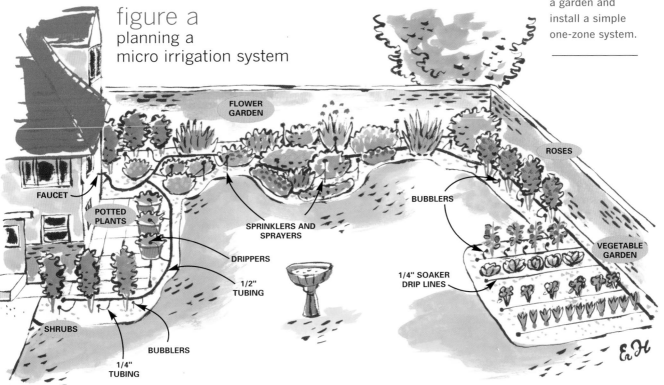

figure a
planning a
micro irrigation system

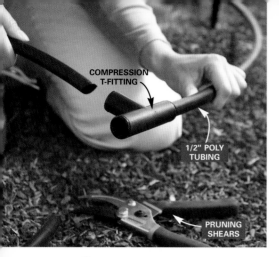

3 Cut the tubing with a pruning shears and install T- and 90-degree fittings where they're needed. Twist and press the tubing firmly into the fitting.

4 Punch holes in the tubing wherever you want to install a watering device. Push and twist until the tip of the punch creates a clean hole.

5 Press a barbed connector into the hole in the 1/2-in. tubing. If the 1/4-in. tubing isn't already attached, add a length of 1/4-in. tubing to reach your dripper, sprayer or sprinkler location.

Planning rules of thumb:

- Use 1/2-gph (gallons per hour) drippers in clay soil, 1-gph drippers in loam and 2-gph drippers in sandy soil.
- Add the gph rate of all drippers, bubblers, sprayers and sprinklers you plan to use. If you're using 1/2-in. tubing for the main line, limit the total to between 150 and 220 gallons per hour (check with the manufacturer).
- Limit the length of 1/2-in. tubing on one zone to a maximum of about 200 ft.
- Limit the total gph on a length of 1/4-in. tubing to 25 to 30.

As you add to the system, it's best to divide your yard into groups of plants that have similar watering requirements. With this strategy, you add a separate system (zone), starting at the water source, for each group of plants or area of the yard.

For help with planning a large, more complicated system (and for the best prices), work with a retailer that specializes in selling micro irrigation products (see Buyer's Guide on p. 47).

figure b
starting from the faucet

A. Battery-operated controller turns the water on and off at specified times. This is optional but should be the first component, if used.

B. Backflow preventer protects your household water from accidental contamination.

C. Filter screens out particles that could clog the holes in the drip parts.

D. Pressure regulator reduces the high house pressure to the lower pressure required by drip systems.

E. Adapter connects the 1/2-in. plastic (polyethylene) tubing to the hose threads on the pressure regulator.

Begin at the outside faucet

Figure B and Photo 1 show the parts you'll need and the order in which to install them. The Y-splitter with shut-offs allows you to keep the drip system on all the time (and operated by a controller) and still use your regular garden hose (Photo 1). You don't have to use a controller, but you must use a backflow preventer. Some of these components are available with hose thread or pipe thread, so make sure to match the thread type when you buy parts. Joining hose thread to pipe thread will result in leaks.

Lay the 1/2-in. tubing

Next, run the 1/2-in. tubing to the garden bed (Photo 2) and position it according to your plan. The tubing will be more flexible and easier to work with if you let it sit in the sun for a while to warm up. Remember, you can

Drippers, bubblers, sprinklers and sprayers

One of the first things you'll notice when you're browsing the brochures or Web sites is a wide variety of watering devices. Here are the basic types and a few things you need to know about each one. While the ones shown here are the most common, there are many other, more specialized emitters. See the micro irrigation catalogs for the other types and their uses.

weekend yard & garden projects

Sprinklers (45¢ to $2 each)
These are miniature versions of sprinklers you might use in the yard. Most have flow rates between 14 and 40 gph and cover a radius of 3 to 30 ft. Since most sprinklers have a relatively high flow rate, you can't use more than about 15 or 20 in one zone of 1/2-in. tubing.

Drippers (20¢ to 70¢ each)
Use these to water individual plants, or buy "inline" drippers and use them in a series with a 1/4-in. tube. Drippers work great for container plants too. They're color-coded for different flow rates between 1/2 gph (gallons per hour) and 4 gph. In general, use lower flow rates for less porous soil, like clay, to allow more time for the water to soak in. Buy pressure-compensating (PC) drippers to maintain a steady flow despite the water pressure.

Bubblers (45¢ to 70¢ each)
A cross between drippers and sprayers, many bubblers are adjustable for flows up to 35 gph and diameters to 18 in. Since they put out more water than drippers, they're good for larger plants like roses, tomatoes and shrubs.

Soaker drip line (20¢ to 35¢ per linear foot)
Also called emitter tubing, drip line consists of 1/2-in. or 1/4-in. tubing with built-in drippers. It's available with emitters spaced different distances apart for different flow rates. Drip line is great for vegetable gardens or rows of plants. You can use it to encircle shrubs and large plants, or lay it out in a grid pattern as a substitute for sprinklers in a densely planted flowerbed. Use 1/4-in. drip line for maximum flexibility.

Sprayers (45¢ to $1.70 each)
These are like sprinklers without moving parts. You can choose a spray pattern from a quarter circle up to a full circle, or buy sprayers with adjustable spray patterns. They spray from 4 to 34 gph and up to a radius of about 12 ft. Use sprayers to water ground cover or densely planted flowerbeds.

Buyer's Guide

- DIG Irrigation Products: (800) 322-9146. www.digcorp.com. Free planning guide available where DIG products are sold. Products available at retail and online stores.

- DripWorks: (800) 522-3747. www.dripworks.com. Free design service. Catalog and mail order sales. Excellent Web site and online sales.

- The Drip Store: (866) 682-1580. www.dripirrigation.com. Step-by-step online tutorial, forum and shopping for all your micro irrigation needs.

- Raindrip: (877) 237-3747. www.raindrip.com. "Micro-Watering Handbook" is free where RAINDRIP products are sold. Free phone advice. Call and ask for Dr. Drip to answer your micro irrigation questions.

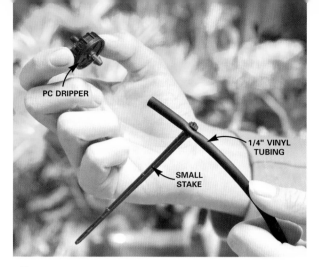

6 Press pressure-compensating (PC) drippers, sprinklers or sprayers onto the end of the 1/4-in. tubing. Use a stake to support the dripper and anchor it in the root zone of the plant.

7 Flush the system by running water through it. Then use end cap fittings to close the open ends of the 1/2-in. tubing.

cover the tubing with decorative mulch later to hide it. Cut the tubing with a pruning shears. Use T-fittings to create branches and elbows to make 90-degree bends (Photo 3). Be aware that there are a few different sizes of what's called "1/2-in." tubing, depending on which brand you use. Buy fittings to match the brand of tubing you're using. If you need to join two different brands of tubing or you're not sure which you have, you can buy universal fittings that will work on all diameters of tubing. Use special plastic tubing clamps to nail the tubing to the house or deck.

You can bury 1/2-in. poly tubing in a shallow trench to conceal it as it crosses a path or small section of lawn, but for longer lengths, especially in high-traffic areas, we recommend substituting 1/2-in. PVC pipe instead. Buy adapters to connect the 1/2-in. poly tubing to the ends of the PVC pipe. Check with your local plumbing inspector before burying any pipe to see whether special backflow prevention is required.

Connect the emitters

Now add the various types of emitters for the particular plants—drippers, sprayers, sprinklers or drip line. The technique is simple. Use a hole punch tool to poke a hole in the tubing wherever you want to add a watering device (Photo 4). You can insert a dripper directly into the hole in the 1/2-in. tubing or use a barbed connector and connect a length of 1/4-in. vinyl tubing. Then connect a watering device to the end of the 1/4-in. tube (Photo 6).

You can buy sprinklers and sprayers as assemblies that include a barbed connector, a short length

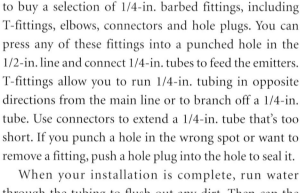

of 1/4-in. tubing and a plastic stake (Photo 6), or buy the parts separately and assemble them yourself. Remember to buy a selection of 1/4-in. barbed fittings, including T-fittings, elbows, connectors and hole plugs. You can press any of these fittings into a punched hole in the 1/2-in. line and connect 1/4-in. tubes to feed the emitters. T-fittings allow you to run 1/4-in. tubing in opposite directions from the main line or to branch off a 1/4-in. tube. Use connectors to extend a 1/4-in. tube that's too short. If you punch a hole in the wrong spot or want to remove a fitting, push a hole plug into the hole to seal it.

When your installation is complete, run water through the tubing to flush out any dirt. Then cap the ends (Photo 7). Now you're ready to turn on the water and see how your new micro irrigation system works. Let the water run for an hour. Then check around your plants to make sure the root zone has been thoroughly wetted. Fine-tune the system by adjusting the length of time you water or by adding or relocating watering devices.

Maintain your system

- Clean the filter once a month (more often if you have well water with a lot of sediment).
- Inspect the drippers occasionally to make sure they're working.
- In cold climates, prepare for winter by removing the shutoff Y-splitter, backflow preventer, controller, filter and pressure regulator and bringing them inside. Remove end plugs and drain or blow the water out of the system. Replace the caps and plug the faucet end of the tubing as well.

Simple walkway ideas

TOP OF 5-GALLON BUCKET

Steppingstone form

Don't discard that partial bag of concrete mix! Build your own steppingstone form from a 5-gallon bucket. Cut around a 5-gallon bucket just above the handle. Set the cutout ring on a sheet of plywood and fill it with concrete. When the concrete has set, remove the form—you now have your first homemade steppingstone.

project at a glance

skill level
beginner

special tools
5-gallon bucket
trowel

approximate cost
$1 per
steppingstone

Edge a concrete walk

Dress up a plain concrete walk with a border of bricks placed in a line or a basketweave pattern. Bluestone or flagstone pieces, cut at the quarry in pieces 6 in. to 1 ft. wide and at least 1 ft. long, also look handsome along the edges of a walk or a cement patio. Large Belgian pavers like those shown in the photo work well too: Their extra width keeps weeds away from the walk; their weight holds them firmly in place; and their warm, golden color and rough texture make a nice contrast with plain concrete.

No matter which type you choose, set the pavers in about 2 in. of pea gravel. It'll keep the pavers from settling or heaving and lets you easily adjust their height during installation.

project at a glance

skill level
beginner

special tools
shovel

approximate cost
$1 per paver

PAVERS

PEA GRAVEL

7 simple steps to a lush, green lawn

A healthy lawn takes a bit of extra effort in the first two years but saves work and money later.

Having the best lawn possible doesn't mean you have to sweat and fret all summer long. Establishing and maintaining a nice yard are mostly just a matter of quenching your lawn's thirst with long drinks of water, feeding it three or four times a year and mowing it at the right height. If your lawn's been neglected, it may take up to two years of extra work to rejuvenate it. But once you get it going, a healthy, lush lawn largely takes care of itself. Weeds can't get a foothold, the soil retains moisture better, and insects and disease have a harder time getting established.

In this article, we'll tell you the seven simple steps for a healthy, low-maintenance lawn. None of these are difficult, expensive or particularly time-consuming. But several require timing (fertilizing) and a watchful eye (when to mow and water). And several may ask you to follow through on simple tasks you've never done (pH test, soil moisture check). The results will be worth it.

Following our recommendations won't necessarily guarantee you the best lawn in the neighborhood. There are simply too many variables in soil quality, sun exposure and grass types to say that. But we can promise this: If you follow our general advice, soon your lawn will be in the best shape ever and it'll stay that way with very little effort.

project at a glance

skill level
beginner

special tools
broadcast
  spreader
aerator

approximate cost
varies

STEP 1 Identify your grass and its growing cycle

You need to know what type of grass you have to determine the best care regimen for your lawn. Different grasses have different cutting heights and watering and fertilizer needs, and all can be harmed by certain herbicides.

There are dozens of varieties of grasses, but they break down into two broad categories: warm and cool climate grasses. **Warm climate grasses** are found mainly in the Southern United States where hot (and sometimes humid) conditions predominate during the summer and the winter is mild. They grow most rapidly before and after the hottest summer period. **Cool climate grasses** are found nearly everywhere else with the exception of the desert regions. They thrive just before and after the hot summer months and go

dormant in the dead of winter. In the transitional zone, both types can be found.

It's easy to identify your grass type. Simply pull a plug of the most dominant variety (or varieties; most lawns have a combination of species) and show it to experts at a local garden center. They will be a wellspring of regional advice and be able to recommend the timing and application of the lawn care products that work best with your grass and in your local climate and soil conditions. They'll also know how to deal with local garden pests, weeds and soil conditions.

Can't find professional help? Become your own lawn expert. It's easier than you think. In "For More Information," p. 57, we list a few of our favorite resources for advice on identifying and treating pests and weeds. You can also figure out what type of grass you have and find mowing and special care information.

Cool climate grasses
Transitional zone
Warm climate grasses

Growth calendar for warm climate grasses

Warm climate grasses grow slower during the summer months when the temperatures are above 95 degrees F. When the weather cools down (below 80 degrees), the growing rate speeds up. It slows down again when temperatures fall below 55 degrees.

Growth calendar for cool climate grasses

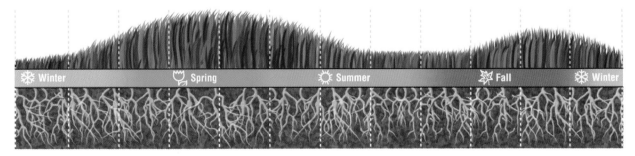

Cool climate grasses have two distinct growing periods, the main one being in the spring and a shorter one in the fall. During the hot, stressful summer months, growth slows.

STEP 2 Feed your lawn four times a year

If you were fed only sporadically, you probably wouldn't feel or look too healthy. The same goes for grass. It hungers for four "meals" during specific periods throughout the growing season. Feeding (fertilizing) means supplying your grass with three basic nutrients: nitrogen (N), phosphorus (P) and potassium (K). In general, the many other trace nutrients your grass may need occur naturally in the soil. All fertilizers have a label detailing the proportions of N-P-K they contain. Most lawns are content with a 4-1-2 mixture. Some grasses need more nitrogen and some soils need more of one or more ingredients (or trace nutrients) at least until they become balanced. A soil test (p. 55) will let you know of any deficiencies. Advice from the garden center will help you tailor a mixture for your soil and grass type.

Four lawn feedings each season are needed for healthy grass:

First feeding:
Fertilize your lawn in the spring after it's up, green, growing and has been mowed at least twice. This feeding picks up where the last feeding in the fall leaves off. And the grass is vigorous enough to absorb the nutrients. If you fertilize before the grass is able to use it, you're just wasting time and money.

Second feeding:
Just before the hot weather starts, fertilize the grass to keep it nourished during the stressful summer months. In most parts of the country, that's early June, but in the Sunbelt states, it can even be early May.

Third feeding:
Apply this treatment later in the fall when dew starts forming on the grass in the morning. That's after the hot weather subsides and the temperature generally stays below 80 degrees F. This feeding replenishes the nutrients used up during the summer and helps the root structure begin regenerating.

Fourth feeding:
Apply the fourth feeding (sometimes called a "winterizer") about three weeks before the last expected mowing. *This is the most important treatment of the year* because the roots are multiplying and storing food for the winter. Then, when the grass comes out of dormancy in the spring, it'll have a bellyful of food for that initial growth spurt.

tips on fertilizing

- Select fertilizers that are a combination of "slow" and "fast" release. They give the grass both immediate and longer-term nutrients.
- Never fertilize wet or damp grass; wait until it's completely dry. Otherwise, the fertilizer will stick to the blades and could damage them. An exception to this rule is combination fertilizer/herbicides. They should be applied to damp grass, when no rain is forecast (and no watering) for 48 hours. Water after that.
- We prefer a "broadcast" spreader to distribute the fertilizer because it spews out the granules, distributing them faster and more evenly than a "drop" spreader.
- Fill the spreader on a hard surface like a driveway, patio or sidewalk—never on the grass. You'll be able to reclaim any spills and keep them from damaging the grass. Use a shop vacuum to pick up spills. You'll never be able to sweep up fine granules.
- Water thoroughly after fertilizing to dissolve and drive the fertilizer into the soil.
- If you aerate (see p. 57) in the fall, apply the fertilizer afterward so the fertilizer will drop into the aeration holes for better soil penetration.
- Never fertilize when the ground is frozen because it won't penetrate the soil. Instead the fertilizer will run off and find its way into streams and waterways.

STEP 3 Water thoroughly but only when it's needed

The key to a good watering regimen and a healthy lawn is to water not only when the grass needs it but also enough to penetrate the soil to a depth of 3 to 4 in. That encourages healthy, deep root growth and gives the soil moisture reserves, so it'll need less frequent watering. Moist soil also helps the roots absorb and metabolize nutrients and keeps the grass cooler in hot weather. But keep in mind that different parts of your yard need more or less water. Sunny and hilly areas will need more water than shady or low areas.

To develop a sound watering strategy, perform this experiment (after a dry spell) in any of these areas your lawn may have: flat, sunny, shady, on a slope, and a couple of feet from the street/driveway (or sidewalk) intersection. Shove a spade into the grass about 6 in. and pull the shovel back and forth until you can see a cross section of the soil. Look for a level of moister, darker soil at some point below the surface. It indicates how deep the soil moisture penetrates. Your lawn needs watering any time the top 3/4 to 1 in. of soil is dry. Water and keep track of the watering time until repeated tests indicate a moisture depth of about 3 to 4 in. at each location. That'll tell you how long to water specific areas each time.

Perform the shovel test once a week for three to four weeks, keeping track of watering duration. After that testing period, you'll have a good feel for the water retention of your soil and intuitively know how much to water and when without performing the digging test. Sounds like a lot of work, right? The results will save you big on water and you'll have a healthier lawn to boot.

Digging soil-moisture inspection slits

Shove a spade into the ground about 6 in. and wiggle it back and forth to create a slit. You'll be able to see or feel the soil to determine soil moisture depth.

tips on watering

- The morning hours are the optimal watering time because the grass blades will dry before nighttime. Lawns that stay moist at night encourage harmful mold and fungal growth. Quit watering one to two hours before sunset. You'll also lose more water to evaporation if you water during those hot afternoons.

- An impact (or impulse) sprinkler will lose 20 percent less of its water to evaporation than the types of sprinklers that send thin streams of water into the air. But oscillating sprinklers do work better on smaller, rectangular yards.

- Never give your yard just a "sip" of water, thinking that's better than nothing. That encourages shallow rather than healthier deep roots.

- Don't overwater, either. If water puddles or is streaming off the yard, you're simply wasting water.

- Attach a water timer ($20 to $40) to your hose, and set it each time you water. Once you know how long to water, a water timer will do the thinking for you. You won't have to worry about shutting off the water at the right time.

STEP 4 Mow your grass to its ideal height and don't wait too long between cuttings

Each type of grass has an ideal height range for cutting, where you leave enough blade length to sustain the health of the plant and keep the grass thick enough to crowd out weeds. Two mistakes are to cut the grass too low and to let it grow too long before cutting. The chart below shows the cutting range for each grass type. Pick a height within that range that's suitable for your terrain. Then set your mowing height by placing the mower on a flat, hard surface, measuring to the bottom of

the mowing deck and adjusting the wheels accordingly. Your grass needs mowing when it's 1-1/2 times the ideal cutting height. That means if the cutting height is 2 in., cut the grass when it's about 3 in. high.

Use a mulching blade instead of a standard blade in your lawn mower. It chops up the grass more finely so it can fall in between the grass blades and decompose easier. The clippings are a free source of nitrogen for your lawn and help retain soil moisture.

Ideal mowing height ranges

Cool climate grasses

Bent grass	1/4 to 3/4 in.
Chewing hard or red fescue	1-1/2 to 2-1/2 in.
Tall fescue	1-1/2 to 3 in.
Kentucky bluegrass	1-1/2 to 3 in.
Perennial ryegrass	1-1/2 to 3 in.

Warm climate grasses

Bahia grass	2 to 3 in.
Bermuda grass	1/2 to 1 in.
Blue grama grass	2 to 3 in.
Buffalo grass	2 to 3 in.
Carpetgrass	1 to 2 in.
Centipedegrass	1 to 2 in.
St. Augustinegrass	1 to 3 in.
Zoysia grass	1/2 to 1 in.

---

tips on mowing

- **Change mowing directions each time you mow to lessen soil compaction (from you with a walk-behind mower or the tires from a riding mower).**
- **Mow with a sharp cutting blade.** A dull blade rips off the blades rather than cutting them. That stresses the grass and leaves a brown shredded end on each blade, which detracts from a lush, healthy look. It's not a bad idea to have two blades on hand so you'll always have a sharp one when the other's at the sharpening shop.
- **Rake or catch clippings if it's necessary.** Long grass should be removed if it's so long that it clumps when it's discharged. Those clumps can smother or even kill underlying grass and encourage fungi and molds.
- **In climates that receive snow, reduce the first and last seasonal mowing to 1-1/2 to 1-3/4 in.** That will discourage snow mold and reduce shrew and vole damage during the winter, especially with fescues and bluegrass.
- **If you've neglected your lawn and the grass is long, just cut off the top one-third of it on the first mowing.** Let it recuperate from the stress for a few days before mowing again. This time, too, cut off no more than one-third until you reach the right height.

Soil pH is often overlooked but is one of the key ingredients to a healthy lawn. If you've watered, mowed and fertilized properly and still have a sickly lawn, overly acidic or alkaline soil could well be the problem. Grass is most content in a soil that's slightly acidic. If you've never checked your lawn's soil pH, it's a great idea to take soil samples and have them tested. Don't be intimidated; it's a simple process both to test and to correct any problems.

Check your soil pH by calling a garden center or a university or county extension service that tests soil samples (for $3 to $10). They'll tell you how to collect and submit samples. Different parts of the yard can vary significantly. The best way to collect samples is to follow the grid shown.

Once you know the pH, the garden center will help you determine the best treatment to achieve a more grass-friendly pH. It's inexpensive and just a matter of applying the specified amounts with a spreader.

tips
on pH

- Once you adjust your lawn's pH, test it again in four months to see if it has maintained the correct pH range. Treat it again if necessary. Once you've established a consistent level, retest and adjust it (if necessary) every three years.

- Inexpensive, do-it-yourself test kits for pH testing are available at garden centers but aren't very accurate. For reliable results, get a professional analysis.

- Don't mix the front and back yard samples. The whole idea is to tell which areas need treatment. Pay to have them tested separately.

- Pelletized limestone is the best way to raise pH levels. Iron sulphate or sulphur is generally used to lower pH. Applied incorrectly, however, this treatment is potentially damaging to your lawn, so be sure to follow the directions.

- Grasses in soils with high or low pH values won't make the best use of naturally occurring or added fertilizers.

Mix together samples from the center of the yard near the house and at spots at opposite sides of the yard. Use the same sampling pattern for the back yard and have the two mixed samples tested separately.

The best pH level for grass

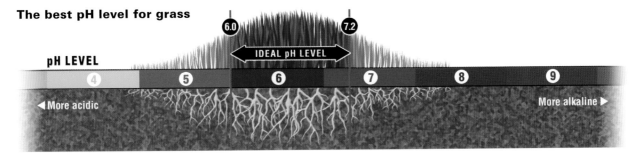

The acidity level is gauged on the pH scale. A pH of 7 is neutral. Below that is acidic and above it is alkaline. Soil that has a pH of between 6 and 7.2 is best for grass. Above or below that range can be highly detrimental to root development and leaves grass susceptible to heat stress and disease.

STEP 6 Identify the weed before choosing a weedkiller

The real key to a weed-free lawn is to nurture a healthy one. When the turf is dense, weed seeds have a hard time getting through to the soil. And once there, they can't get the sun they need to germinate and grow. But if you already have weeds, it's easy to eliminate them, provided you use the correct weedkiller at the proper time of year and within the temperature parameters called for in the directions.

Lawn weeds fall into three simple categories and require different treatment strategies. If you don't know the weed category, take a sample to a garden center for identification.

Broadleaf weeds

Dandelions, clover, creeping Charlie and plantain are all examples of broadleaf weeds. They not only survive the winter but also go to seed, propagating new generations the following spring. Kill broadleaf weeds with either liquid sprays or granular herbicides (weedkillers) distributed with a spreader while the weeds are growing heartily. That's usually when the lawn is growing well too.

Liquid herbicides should be applied to dry or slightly damp lawns, but only apply granular herbicides when the weeds are wet, either after you water or when they're still damp from dew or rain. When the leaves are wet, the chemical sticks to the leaves, where it will be absorbed and sent to the roots to kill the plant. It's usually best to apply herbicides when the temperature will remain below 80 degrees F (preferably even lower), and it's not expected to rain for at least 48 hours. Hot days cause liquid herbicides to vaporize before the weed can absorb it. And if it rains too soon, the granules will wash off the leaves and be ineffective.

Perennial weedy grasses

Perennial weedy grasses are ones that, like your lawn itself, survive the winter and reappear every spring. Quack grass and Dallis grass are common examples. Perennial weedy grasses have to be killed one by one with carefully applied general weedkillers like Roundup or Kills-All, either by spraying individual weeds or simply by wiping the concentrated herbicide (10 percent or higher) on the blades of grass. Be careful when spot-killing. General plant killers kill your yard grass just as easily as they kill weeds. Replace clumps of dead weeds by raking fresh seed through the dead grass into the soil below after the weeds turn brown. Then water daily until the grass is established.

Annual weedy grasses

Annual weedy grasses like crab grass or foxtail die at the end of every growing season after seeding the yard for the following spring. While they too can be spot-killed, the best remedy is to apply a pre-emergent herbicide in the early spring right after the first or second mowing. A pre-emergent works by preventing the weed seeds from sprouting. Talk to a local expert to help nail down the timing; it's the difference between success and failure.

Some types of weed grasses can be killed with specific herbicides without harming your grass. One example is a post-emergent crab grass spray, which will kill some other annual weedy grasses as well. For more details on these, bring a sample plant to the garden center for advice or check out the books or Web sites we recommend for help.

tips on weed-killing

- Don't waste your money or time applying herbicides (except preemergence treatments) when there aren't any weeds. No weeds? Just fertilize.
- Use a pump-up type sprayer to spot-treat weeds that are limited to specific areas. Only mix the amount of liquids you need that day. They have a very short shelf life once mixed with water.
- The soil should be moist and the grass growing before you apply any herbicides.
- Apply liquid herbicides only on calm, windless mornings. When the wind's blowing, you'll not only waste material but also possibly kill nearby shrubs and flowers.
- Water your lawn thoroughly before any weed treatment.
- Granular herbicides work poorly on viney broadleafs like clover or creeping Charlie. Use liquid herbicides on those. Some work better on hard-to-kill broadleaf weeds. Ask for advice at the garden center.
- Buy concentrated liquid herbicides; they're cheaper than premixed solutions.

STEP 7 Aerate to eliminate compacted soil under your lawn

Grass roots need "friable" (crumbly) rather than dense, compacted soil so they can spread and have access to the water, nutrients and oxygen they need to thrive. Soil can be compacted because it has too much clay or simply because of too much foot or mower traffic. To test for compaction, shove a large screwdriver into the soil after watering. If it doesn't easily penetrate a couple of inches, you should aerate.

An engine-driven machine called an aerator is the easiest way to aerate your yard. It pulls out thousands of plugs of soil and grass and drops them on the yard, where they eventually break down. Aerating loosens the soil and helps oxygen and water penetrate to augment deeper root development.

Aerate in the fall once dew begins forming regularly but stop at least three weeks before frost in the Snowbelt. Plan to aerate heavily compacted soils three years in a row and after that, whenever the screwdriver test calls for it. Aerating in the spring will encourage weedy grass seeds to sprout in the aeration holes. If you aerate in spring, apply a pre-emergent herbicide to reduce germination.

tips on aerating

- Aerate only during cool weather. The exposed roots surrounding holes will dry out on hot summer days.
- Wait two years before aerating newly seeded yards and one year before aerating newly sodded yards.
- Make two passes at 90-degree angles. In heavily compacted soils, make a third diagonal pass for thorough aeration or before seeding.
- Don't bother aerating lawns growing in sand unless there is a buildup of thatch.
- The soil should be moist 3 to 4 in. deep before aerating. Otherwise the tines won't penetrate and extract the necessary 1 to 1-1/2 in. plugs.

for more information

- "Lawns, Your Guide to a Beautiful Yard," The Scotts Co. Available at bookstores, garden centers and home centers.
- "All About Lawns," Ortho Co. Available at bookstores, garden centers and home centers.
- www.scotts.com
- http://turf.ufl.edu

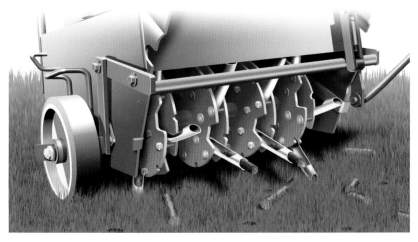

Rent an aerator at the rental shop or garden center for about $35 per half day. It's heavy, so you'll need a strong back to help you unload it.

Benefits of aeration

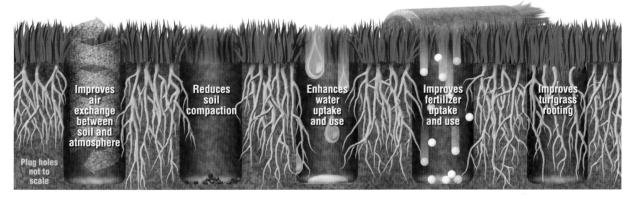

Improves air exchange between soil and atmosphere

Reduces soil compaction

Enhances water uptake and use

Improves fertilizer uptake and use

Improves turfgrass rooting

Plug holes not to scale

Small soothing fountain

Inexpensive, simple to build and a great place for the neighborhood birds to freshen up—now that's a fountain!

This quaint fountain is proof that good things come in small packages. You can build it in an afternoon for under $80. It's a "disappearing fountain" so there's no exposed standing water. This means there's less maintenance since there's less chance debris and critters will wind up in the water. Yet it provides the soothing sight and sound of running water people love. Another bonus—since birds love moving water, there's a chance you'll attract some of these outdoor friends.

You can personalize your fountain in a number of ways:

● Surround it with any type of rock. We used a natural wall stone, but you can use modular concrete retaining-wall blocks, boulders or flagstone.

● Top it off with any type of small stone. We used a decorative rock called "Western Sunset." You can use pebbles, lava stone or special rocks you've collected in your travels.

● Use any bowl, dish or plate you want for the water to splash into. We used three pieces so the water cascades from one piece into the next.

Let's Get Started

You can use a whiskey barrel liner from a local home center for the catch basin, but any large plastic container will do (see Photo 1 on p. 60). Some garden centers sell special pond liners just for this purpose.

Regardless of your soil conditions, nestle your catch basin or liner into a bed of sand. This helps protect the bottom of the tub from sharp rocks and makes it easier to level the tub and the first course of rock.

We constructed our fountain so we could gain access to the pump by removing a handful of rocks along with the hardware cloth trap door (Photo 5). This allows us to easily remove the pump for maintenance and for storing it indoors over the winter.

---

project at a glance

skill level
beginner

special tools
shovel
drill
ceramic tile bit

approximate cost
$75–$100

---

multiple spray patterns **All four of these interchangeable fountainheads, which provide different looks, came in one package. Use just one or switch them around from time to time for a new look and feel.**

1 Select a location where you'll enjoy your fountain, hollow out a 2-in.-deep area, then level in a bed of sand large enough to accommodate the plastic tub and the rock or block that will surround it.

2 Locate a sturdy plastic flower pot the same height as your plastic tub, cut a hole in the side near the bottom and feed the cord for the electric pump through it. Position this pot right side up in the center of your tub.

3 Cut a hole in the wire hardware cloth (available at home centers) large enough for the pump to fit through, then position the cloth over the tub and bend the edges over the tub lip.

Use a bag of sand as a workbench when drilling the holes in your bowls and dishes (Photo 6). It'll provide a cushion and help prevent breakage.

Many large garden centers and home centers sell water garden pumps and accessories. Or you can contact:

- Little Giant Pump Co., (888) 956-0000, www.littlegiant.com.

- MacArthur Water Gardens, (800) 695-4913, www.macarthurwatergardens.com.

Operating Tips

Keep your fountain liner full of water and check the level every day or so, especially in hot weather. You can use any thin stick as a dipstick to check the water level.

Plug your pump into a GFCI-protected outlet—ideally one located next to the fountain. If you use an extension cord, leave it exposed so you know where it is, and be careful with sharp garden tools and mowers.

As a precaution, unplug the fountain when you're not around to watch it (or put it on a timer). If the pump runs dry, it'll burn out.

Most pumps will accept a variety of fountainheads. Bear in mind that with some spray patterns, all the water may not drain back into the tub. You'll have to refill your tub much more often with this type of fountain.

figure a how it all goes together

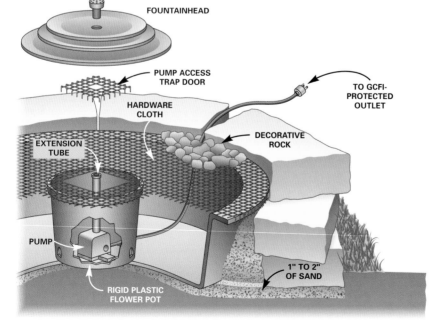

FOUNTAINHEAD

PUMP ACCESS TRAP DOOR

HARDWARE CLOTH

TO GCFI-PROTECTED OUTLET

EXTENSION TUBE

DECORATIVE ROCK

PUMP

RIGID PLASTIC FLOWER POT

1" TO 2" OF SAND

4 Surround the tub with flagstone or concrete retaining-wall blocks to match the rest of your landscape. The upper course should be about 2 in. higher than the top of the tub.

5 Cut a small piece of hardware cloth a few inches larger than the access hole to create a removable trap door, then cut a small opening for the pump stem. Cover the top of the hardware cloth with decorative stone.

SMALL OPENING
FOR PUMP STEM

REMOVABLE
TRAP DOOR

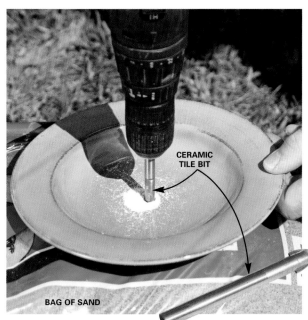

CERAMIC
TILE BIT

BAG OF SAND

OTHER
FOUNTAINHEADS

6 Drill a hole in your fountain dish by first scoring the glaze in the center of the bowl with a light tap of a nail (remember, light!), then boring a hole using a ceramic tile bit. If you need to enlarge the hole, use a larger bit or small file.

7 Install the fountainhead of your choice. Most pumps can accommodate a range of heads including mushroom-shaped, cup-shaped and fan-shaped patterns. Then fill the tub, plug in the pump and relax.

ti*p Have a little fun selecting your fountain dishes. It's the perfect opportunity to use those I-never-use-'em-but-I-can't-bear-to-throw-'em-out bowls, plates and even teapots.

Plant markers

Simple, fun and functional.

That favorite plant of yours deserves more recognition than a Popsicle stick with black ink spelling out its name. Try making these unique plant markers, which hold a label or a seed packet with bent copper wire set in a decorative base. They're easy to assemble, so let your creativity flow. Decorate them with rocks, glass beads or even seashells. They're also great gifts for friends and relatives, and at $2 apiece, you can make dozens of them.

You've probably got all the tools you'll need around the house to make these markers. A 2-gallon bucket and a wooden spoon are all you need for mixing the mortar. We used a 4- x 8- x 2-in. disposable plastic container as a form, but you could also try a cut-off milk carton or a bread pan. You should also round up a pair of pliers, wire cutters and a utility knife for working with the wire.

project at a glance

skill level
beginner

special tools
wire cutter
pliers
hand spade

approximate cost
$2 each

Perennial
125 mg
99¢

GARDEN
PLACE

Painted Daisy
Giant Mix

PLANT YOUR THOUGHTS IN THE GARDE

Full Sun | Excellent for Cutting

EASY FOR EVERYONE

1 Bend the copper wire. Hold a dowel 8 in. up from the end of a 5-ft. piece of wire folded in half. Wrap the wire around it as shown, forming a loop. Move the dowel over 3-1/2 in. (or the width needed to fit your seed packet) and wrap it again, making a second loop in the opposite direction. Cut the wire off even with the first leg, and bend a 1/2-in. 90-degree turn at the bottom of each leg to anchor it in the mortar.

2 Add the mortar. Mix up the mortar to the consistency of cookie dough, slowly adding water to the dry mix as needed. Mix the mortar thoroughly, let it sit for about 3 minutes, then remix, adding a dash more water if needed. Coat the plastic form with cooking spray. After filling the container, give it a few quick shakes to settle the mortar. Then form a mound using a spoon or small trowel so it resembles a loaf of baked banana bread.

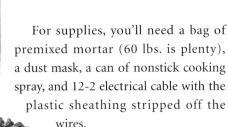

For supplies, you'll need a bag of premixed mortar (60 lbs. is plenty), a dust mask, a can of nonstick cooking spray, and 12-2 electrical cable with the plastic sheathing stripped off the wires.

For decoration, use rocks, glass beads or seashells—about 1/3 lb. of rocks per holder. Craft stores are loaded with materials. We added a latex bonding agent to the mortar. It's not absolutely necessary, but it'll make the mortar stick better to smooth rocks and glass. Buy it from a masonry supplier and follow the directions for mixing.

tip* When arranging the rocks, it's best to start at the edges and work toward the center.

3 Push the copper marker into the mortar so the 90-degree bends are about 1/2 in. up from the bottom and centered. If the mortar is too wet to support the wire, have a cup of coffee and let it stiffen up a little. Now arrange the rocks or beads to your liking. Embed the decorations at least halfway into the mortar so they're held tight. If you don't like how a rock looks, remove it, rinse it off and reposition. Once you're done with the arrangement, let the marker set for at least 24 hours before removing it from the form.

Stone path

Build this simple path with sand, stone and lots of muscle.

You don't have to be a skilled mason to lay a natural stone path like this one. If you have a strong back and an eye for fitting jigsaw puzzles, you can weave a casual garden path like this just about anywhere in your yard. There's no thick base to install or difficult cutting and fitting—you just lay natural stone over a simple sand bed.

You'll be moving a lot of dirt and stone, so a good shovel and wheelbarrow will pay off here. To simplify the grass removal, we rented a power sod cutter ($45 per half day, and you'll need a pickup truck to haul this brute). For smaller paths, a kick-type sod cutter would work fine ($20 per day to rent). Buy a heavy rubber mallet or deadblow hammer ($10 at hardware stores) to settle the stone into the sand bed. If your project requires a step or retaining wall like the one shown, you'll also need a level and a hand tamper (Photo 5). Buy a tamper for $28 or rent one for $8 per day. Finally, you'll need a garage broom to sweep the soil mixture into the cracks, and a good pair of heavy leather gloves to protect your hands.

project at a glance

skill level
beginner to intermediate

special tools
tamper
rubber mallet
wheelbarrow

approximate cost
$5–$10 per sq. ft. of path

1 Mark the path's edge with special upside-down spray marking paint. Spray along the path's edge outlined by the stakes.

2 Remove the sod in the area of the path with a sod cutter. Set the sod cutter to maximum depth to minimize additional digging. Dig out the path area to about 5 in. deep to allow for 3 in. of sand and 2-in. thick stone.

You'll order tons of stone

For our path, we chose a locally quarried limestone called Chilton. The 1-1/2 to 2-1/2 in. thick "stepper" stones cost about $300 per ton (a ton covers about 90 sq. ft.), but costs vary widely depending on what's locally available. Measure the length of your path and multiply this by its width to determine the square footage. Then add about 15 percent. Our 3-ft. wide by 70-ft. long path required about 3 tons of stone.

Check the Yellow Pages under "Stone, Natural" or call local landscaping suppliers to find stone in your area. Visit the stone yard to select the stone, since it varies in color, texture and cost. This is also a good time to discuss delivery options. Usually the stone will be stacked on pallets and dropped off near the street.

In addition to the steppers, we needed about a ton of 8-in. wide by 3- to 5-in. thick stone for the wall and a few 6-in. thick stones to build the step (Photos 4 and 6). Your stone dealer can help you figure the amount of stone you'll need for special projects like this.

Because this garden path is informal, we decided to set the stone on a 2- to 3-in. thick sand bed rather than the 6-in. deep compacted gravel base used under more heavily traveled walks and patios. Although you'll spend a lot less time digging and moving dirt with our method, you may have to reset a sunken or tipped stone every few years, because the base isn't as stable.

Landscape suppliers, sand and gravel companies, or your stone supplier will charge about $20 per cubic yard for the sand, plus delivery fees. Divide the square footage of your path by 108 to calculate how many cubic yards of sand you'll need for a 3-in. deep base.

Finally, you'll need some potting soil and mulch or compost to fill the spaces between stones. We mixed equal amounts of soil and sifted compost in a wheelbarrow and swept it into the cracks (Photo 10).

Use steps and low walls to manage sloping sites

You can lay a stone path like this almost anywhere that's not too steep for comfortable walking. If after laying out your path (Photo 1), you notice a section that seems too steep, plan on building in a step to break the path into sections that are more level (Photos 5 and 6). You'll have to buy a few stones about 6 in. thick and the right length to form the step. Then level them on a bed of packed gravel and fill behind them with sand before you continue laying path stones.

If your path runs along the edge of a slope like ours, level it by digging it into the slope and building a low retaining wall (Photos 3 and 4). We simply stacked wall stones on a compacted gravel bed for our retaining wall,

tip Don't worry about tight fits. The path will look more natural if you leave a few irregular spaces and an occasional stone jutting out into the yard.

HAND TAMPER

GRAVEL BASE FOR RETAINING WALL

STACKED WALL STONE

3 Pour and pack gravel into an 8-in. deep trench for the retaining wall footing only. Spread the gravel in 2-in. layers, packing each layer with a hand tamper before adding the next. Use a level and straightedge to level the final layer before you pack it down.

4 Stack the stone for the low retaining wall on the compacted gravel base. Stagger the joints in the stones and set each row back 1/2 in. behind the face of the stones below so the wall "leans into" the hill. Pack soil behind the stones as you build the wall.

HAND TAMPER

PACKED GRAVEL BASE FOR STEP

DEADBLOW HAMMER

STONES FOR STEP

3" SAND BED

5 Tamp gravel in 2-in. layers to form an 8-in. deep base under the step.

6 Set 6 x 8-in. wall stone into a 3-in. bed of sand to form the step. Settle and level the stones with a rubber mallet or a hammer and block of wood. Then fill behind the step stones with packed sand and set the path stones even with the top of the step.

but if it's more than a foot tall, consider stronger construction techniques.

A sand bed makes it easy to level the stones

Laying the stone is like assembling a big, heavy jigsaw puzzle (Photo 8). Spread the stones out on the ground so you can pick shapes and colors that fit. Use a wheelbarrow or a two-wheel dolly to move heavy stones, and always lift with your legs, not your back.

Start laying stones against walls, steps or other types of established borders. Then work out and along the path (Photo 8). Loosely assemble a half dozen stones and stand back to take a look at the arrangement. Reposition

7 Spread a 3-in. layer of sand. Use a rake to smooth the sand about 2 in. below the surface of the lawn. Tie a guide string to stakes about an inch above the finished height of the path. The string should follow the natural slope of the path; it doesn't have to be level.

8 Arrange the stone on the sand, mixing shapes and colors to create a natural-looking path. Leave about 2 in. between stones for plants to fill in.

9 Adjust the depth of the sand so the tops of the stones align under the string. Wiggle the stones into place and settle them down into the sand by pounding on the top with a rubber mallet.

10 Fill the cracks between stones with a 50/50 mix of potting soil and sifted compost or bark mulch. Spread the soil mix and sweep it into the cracks with a broom.

11 Plant creeping thyme or another durable spreading plant in the larger spaces. Dig down into the sand base to provide room for the roots. Loosen the roots and spread them out in the hole, then refill around the plant with potting mix and water the plant.

the stones if you like, and then set these stones before moving on.

The goal for placing the stones is to keep all the tops even. Adjust the height of each stone by scooping out or adding sand (Photo 9). As you gain experience, you'll be able to look at the thickness of the stone and judge how much sand to leave. We staked up string as a rough guide so that instead of waving up and down, our path dips gradually over its length to follow the natural terrain (Photo 9).

Complete the path by filling the joints between stones

with soil mix and planting a durable ground cover (Photo 11). We planted creeping thyme in the larger spaces. Eventually the thyme will spread and fill the cracks for a low-maintenance, fragrant path.

tip Check with your local nursery for advice on durable, spreading plants for your climate. If you'd rather not grow plants, fill the spaces with mulch or finely shredded bark.

Get your weekend workout and an attractive, hard-working wall with this DIY-friendly project.

project at a glance

skill level
intermediate

special tools
level
tamper
hand sledge
chisel

approximate cost
$8–$10 per sq. ft. of vertical wall

Concrete block retaining wall

Until concrete retaining wall systems muscled their way onto the scene 25 years ago, there were few do-it-yourself-friendly materials to choose from. Rock and stone were labor intensive to gather (or expensive to buy) and tricky to install. Treated timbers, despite claims to the contrary, often rotted within 15 years. Railroad ties looked like, well, railroad ties, and other options, like poured concrete or mortared brick, were best left to the pros. But concrete retaining wall systems—easy to install, widely available, reasonably priced, long-lasting and offered in a wide selection of colors and patterns—changed all that.

A retaining wall can solve many problems. It can convert steep or

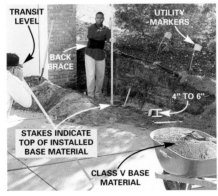

TRANSIT LEVEL
BACK BRACE
UTILITY MARKERS
4" TO 6"
STAKES INDICATE TOP OF INSTALLED BASE MATERIAL
CLASS V BASE MATERIAL

1 Excavate and level the area where you'll be installing the wall. Use a transit or a 4-ft. level taped to a straight 2x4 to establish a common stake height, indicating the top of your sand leveling bed (see Figure A). Create a flat area at least 4 to 6 in. deep and 24 to 28 in. wide for installing compactable base material. Provide a clear area of at least 12 in. behind the wall for installing the crushed rock as shown in Photo 7.

RENTED TAMPER
COMPACTED CLASS V (COMPACTIBLE BASE)

2 Install 4 to 6 in. of base material level to the tops of the stakes, then compact it until it's about 1 in. below the tops. Rent a hand tamper (about $5 a day) for small projects, or a gas-powered tamper (about $50 for a half day) for walls more than 30 ft. long.

3 Provide a flat-as-a-pancake sand base for installing the first course of blocks. With the tops of the stakes as guides, use a long, straight screed board to level the sand. A hand trowel is good for fine-tuning small dips and humps.

4 Install the first course of blocks, using a taut string line to establish a straight row. Use a 4-ft. level to level blocks lengthwise and a torpedo level to level them front to back. Pack native soil to grade level on both sides of this base course to anchor the wall in place. The brick tong makes positioning the 80-lb. blocks easier, faster and safer.

5 Drive in the pins to lock courses to one another and help establish the 3/4-in. backset for each row. Use an extra pin to set the installed pins below the surface of the blocks so they don't interfere with blocks on the next row. To maintain wall strength, offset the vertical joints of the row you're installing at least 4 in. from those of the row below.

hard-to-mow hills into terraced, usable planting beds. It can prevent erosion, help level a patio area, create tree borders, or simply add visual interest to a rolling yard.

figure a
anatomy of a retaining wall

- CAP BLOCK
- CONCRETE ADHESIVE
- REINFORCEMENT PIN
- 16" x 12" x 6" BLOCK
- 3/4" BACKSET
- RECOMPACTED NATIVE SOIL
- 4" TO 6" COMPACTED BASE MATERIAL
- RECOMPACTED NATIVE SOIL
- CRUSHED ROCK
- UNDISTURBED NATIVE SOIL
- 1" LEVELING SAND
- 12"
- 24" TO 28"

A retaining wall is only as straight and solid as the base it's built on. For a 4-ft. tall wall, excavate a trench deep enough to accommodate 4 to 6 in. of compacted base, 1 in. of leveling sand and half the height of the first course of blocks. Step succeeding courses back 3/4 in., overlap vertical joints at least 4 in. and secure one row to the next with pins. Backfill with crushed rock, except for the top, where you should install a 6-in. "cap" of native soil to help keep surface water from entering the rock-filled trench. Use concrete adhesive to secure the cap blocks.

The Versa-Lok brand retaining wall system shown here uses nylon pins to align and secure horizontal rows of 80-lb. blocks. (You can reach Versa-Lok at 800-770-4525 or www.versa-lok. com.) Other block systems use lips, gravity and filled cores to connect rows and increase strength. Your system may differ, but most of the preparation and installation steps remain the same. Here's how to install your wall.

Don't skimp on time, tools or materials

The wall shown here was a weekend-long project, and an exhausting one at that. It took a day to rip out the old, collapsing retaining wall, to dig farther into the hill to provide room for the backfill gravel and to help unload materials. It took another day to install the base, blocks and backfill.

Before launching into this project, contact your local building code official. Depending on the height and location of your wall, there may be structural, drainage and setback (the distance from wall to property line) considerations. A permit may be required.

tip For safety's sake, call your utility companies and have them mark the location of underground wires and pipes; the service is usually free. For more information, call the North American One-Call Referral System at (888) 258-0808.

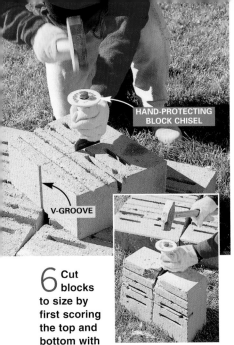

HAND-PROTECTING BLOCK CHISEL

V-GROOVE

CRUSHED ROCK

CONCRETE ADHESIVE

CAP BLOCKS

6 **Cut blocks** to size by first scoring the top and bottom with a block chisel, then turning the block on its side and finishing the task with a series of solid blows.

7 Backfill behind the retaining wall with crushed gravel. Crushed, rather than smooth, gravel locks together and helps direct backfill pressure downward (rather than out-ward). The backfill also provides a fast path for water drainage and acts as a tree root barrier.

8 Install the cap blocks using two 1/4-in. beads of concrete adhesive to secure them in place. Cap blocks can be positioned with a slight overhang or backset, or set flush with the wall face.

Unless you own a heavy-duty truck (and back!), have your blocks, compactable base, sand and backfill gravel delivered. Blocks may cost slightly more at specialty landscaping stores than at home centers, but landscaping stores are often better equipped to deliver the small batches of base, sand and gravel that you'll need for installing the blocks.

The Versa-Lok blocks and cap blocks we used cost about $4.50 each. Pins are about 75¢ each. Plan on spending $8 to $10 per square foot of retaining wall *face* (vertical surface) once you add in the base and backfill materials.

We used a transit level (Photo 1) to establish a flat base. But unless you own or rent one and know how to use it properly, just use a 4-ft. level taped to a long, straight 2x4, especially for short walls. The tamper, brick tongs and block chisel are available at rental yards.

Build straight and solid from start to finish

Every manufacturer and consultant we contacted stressed the absolute necessity of starting with a solid, level and well-compacted base. Failure to do this will result in a weak, wavy wall. Bear in mind:

● If your wall is higher than 4 ft., most concrete block manufacturers require extra engineering and installa-tion steps not shown here. These steps range from using

special reinforcement fabric to installing a series of ter-races rather than one tall wall. Most manufacturers pro-vide good printed installation guidelines. If you pur-chase your blocks from a specialty landscape center, there may be an on-site designer or engineer to help you.

● Before getting started, contact local utility companies to mark the location of underground wires and pipes. Telephone and cable TV wires are often buried just beneath the surface.

● In the Midwest, the compactable base material shown in Photo 2 is often referred to as "Class V" (as in the Roman numeral for five). In other regions, the rock may vary and the material may go by a different name. The important quality of the material is its different-sized rock and sand particles that interlock and compact to create a solid base. It's the same material used beneath road beds and paver patios. Make sure you use the right stuff. It's NOT the same as the crushed gravel you use for backfill.

● The 16-in. wide x 12-in. deep x 6-in. high blocks we installed weigh 80 lbs. each. A brick tong (Photo 4) doesn't make them lighter, but it does make them less clumsy to handle, easier to position and less likely to crush fingers.

● If your wall borders a sidewalk or deck, you may need a code-compliant rail. Contact your local building code department.

Path in a wheel-barrow

There's no heavy lifting, no fancy tools, and it's really, really cheap!

EASY FOR EVERYONE

This garden path is as easy to build as it is to look at and walk on. A bundle or two of cedar shakes, a roll of landscape fabric, a few bags of mulch and a couple of hours are all it takes to build it. You'll spend less than $5 per foot of 30-in.-wide path.

To create the path edging, we cut 18-in.-long cedar shakes in half, then pounded the 9-inch sections about halfway into the ground. Shakes are naturally rot-resistant and should last 5 to 10 years or more. And since they're tapered, they're easy to install. Bear in mind, shakes will split and break if you try to pound them into soil with lots of rocks, roots or heavy clay; this path works best in loose garden soil.

tip
Place a scrap 2x6 on top of each shake and pound on that if you find you're breaking shakes as you drive them in. The 2x6 will help distribute the blow more evenly across the top of the shake.

The landscape fabric helps prevent weeds from growing up into the path and creates a barrier so the dirt below remains separate from the path materials above. The path material itself can be wood chips, shredded bark, decorative stone—just about anything you can think of.

Here's how to do it in three easy steps:

project at a glance

skill level
beginner

special tools
hand sledge
utility knife
saw

approximate cost
$1–$2 per
sq. ft. of path

WEAR YOUR SAFETY GLASSES

CEDAR SHAKES

1 Pound the cedar shakes into the soil using a small mallet. Stagger every other shake, overlapping the previous shake by about 1/2 in.

2 Trim or fold the fabric so it follows the contour of the cedar shake edging. On sloped ground, use U-shaped sod staples to hold the fabric.

MULCH

3 Install a 2- to 3-in. layer of wood chips, shredded bark or stone over the landscape fabric.

section 3

weekend furniture & wood-working projects

Patio chair

The ultimate easy chair: easy to build, easy to tote, easy to set up and store.

Whether you're staking out a curbside spot for watching a parade, heading to the woods for a weekend or simply trying to catch a few rays, you'll love the portability and comfort of this chair. Interlocking legs and gravity keep the two sections together when in use. And when it's time to pull up stakes, the seat section tucks neatly inside the back. A handle cutout in the top slat makes for easy carrying and storing too.

What it takes

We made our chair from cedar because it's lightweight, but you could use cypress, fir, treated or other decay-resistant woods. We didn't want knots weakening the legs or seat, so we spent about $75 for knot-free "D-grade" cedar. You'll need basic tools: a jigsaw, drill, Phillips bit, file, combination square, carpenter's square and screwdriver, plus a table saw and belt sander. If you don't own these last two tools, borrow them (or use this project as an excuse to add a few more tools to your workshop).

Building one chair takes about eight hours. But once you're "jigged up" and have your patterns made, building additional ones only takes an hour or two more each.

Make the patterns (by connecting the dots or with a photocopier)

The backrest and seat support struts must be the exact length and shape for the chair to set up and "nest" for storage properly. You can ensure accuracy two ways: You can place the strut grid (below) on a photocopier, then enlarge it until the squares are exactly 1 in. On our office machine, that meant first enlarging the grid 2x, taking that copy and enlarging it 2x, then taking that copy and enlarging it 1.30x. We taped two pieces of 8-1/2 x 11 paper together lengthwise to create the 18-in. long pattern. Every machine is slightly different, *so make sure the final grid is 18 in., and 18 squares, long.* Then cut it out to create your pattern or use carbon paper to transfer the shape to your wood.

A second way is to use the transfer grid method (Photos 1 – 4). The shapes in Figure A below are drawn on a scaled-down grid. Draw a full-size grid of 1-in. squares on hardboard (Photo 1) and transfer the shapes to it; you'll have a template you can use over and over.

shopping list

- 2 pieces of 2x6 x 8' D and better-grade cedar
- 2 pieces of 1x6 x 8' D and better-grade cedar
- 1 piece of 1/8" x 24" x 48" hardboard (for templates)
- Eighty 2" galvanized deck screws
- 1 pint of Thompson's Water Seal finish
- Glue

cutting list

KEY	PCS.	SIZE & DESCRIPTION
A	2	1-1/2" x 5-1/2" x 36" cedar (backrest struts)
B	2	1-1/2" x 4-15/16" x 34" cedar (seat struts)
C	1	3/4" x 4" x 20" cedar (top slat)
D	2	3/4" x 2-1/2" x 20" cedar (seat supports)
E	11	3/4" x 2" x 20" cedar (slats)

figure a
patio chair details

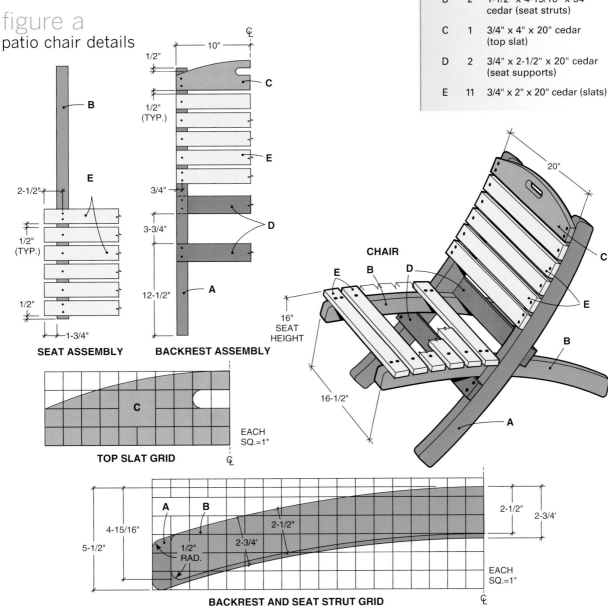

SEAT ASSEMBLY

BACKREST ASSEMBLY

CHAIR

TOP SLAT GRID

EACH SQ.=1"

BACKREST AND SEAT STRUT GRID

EACH SQ.=1"

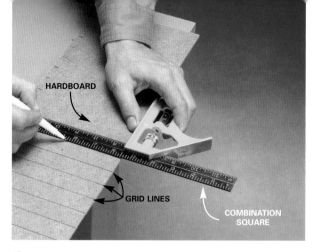

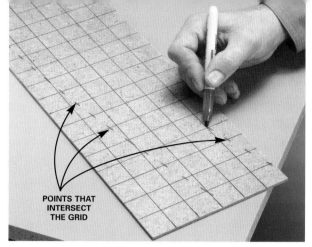

1 Measure and mark 1-in. increments on both ends and one side of the hardboard. Then draw grid lines using a combination square, straightedge and fine-point permanent marker. Or, if you like, you can use the photocopy method explained on p. 75.

2 To develop the pattern, transfer the points to your hardboard grid where the shape intersects the grid lines in the drawing.

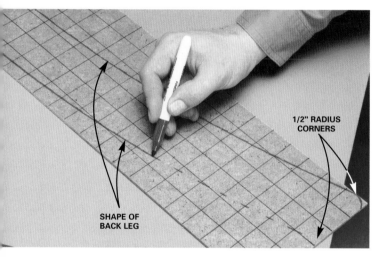

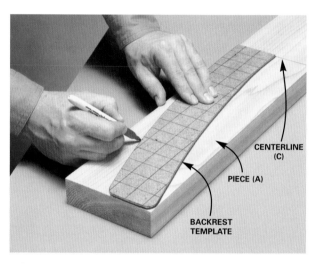

3 Draw lines connecting the points made on the grid. Use a smooth, arcing arm movement to draw the gradual curve. Use a quarter to trace the 1/2-in. radiuses at the bottom of the leg. Use a jigsaw to cut out the pattern.

4 Align the backrest strut template to the centerline and bottom edge of the cedar piece and trace the shape. Flip the template along the centerline to draw the other half. Cut out the pieces with a jigsaw.

We've drawn only half of the backrest and seat struts on our grids because the halves are symmetrical. Make one template for half of the shape, then flip it to draw the other half. Since the shapes of the seat and backrest struts are so similar, you can make only the backrest strut template, then use it to draw the seat strut pieces, making them 1/4 in. narrower and 1 in. shorter (2 in. shorter overall).

To use the template, align it to centerlines drawn on the boards (Photo 4), trace around it, then flip it over the centerline and trace the rest of the shape. Remember, the seat struts are 1/4 in. skinnier and 2 in. shorter than the backrest struts.

tip*
Cedar is soft, so when screwing the pieces together, finish driving the screws by hand to avoid setting their heads too deep.

Putting it all together

Cut all the pieces to the dimensions given in the Cutting List, using the templates for the legs and the top slat. Cut out the shapes with a jigsaw, then sand the pieces with a belt sander (Photo 5). Lay out the hand grip hole in the top slat (C), then cut it out using a jigsaw and spade bit (Photo 6). You'll need to rip the back and seat slats 2 in. wide using a table saw.

Lay out, countersink and drill all the screw holes for the slats and supports. Finish-sand all the pieces with 120-grit, then 150-grit sandpaper. Round over the sharp edges with the sandpaper.

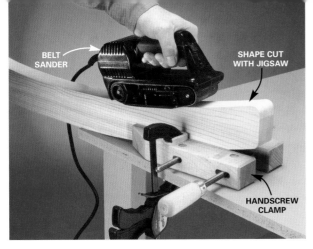

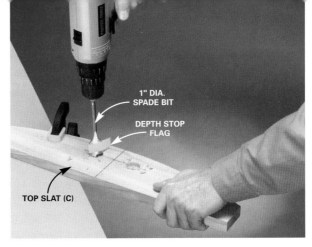

5 Sand the edges of the curved pieces with a belt sander. If you don't have a bench vise, you can support the legs with a handscrew clamp while you sand.

6 Drill the ends of the hand grip holes with a 1-in. dia. spade bit. Drill partway in from both sides so you won't tear out the wood.

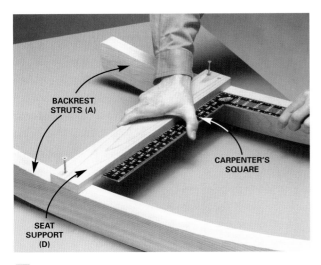

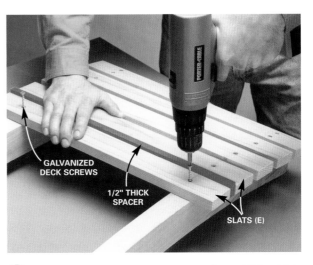

7 Use a carpenter's square to align the seat supports 90 degrees to the backrest struts, then glue and screw them in place. Use both glue and screws to attach the slats, too.

8 Attach the slats to the seat struts using a 1/2-in. thick spacer to align them. Finish driving the screws by hand to avoid setting their heads too deep.

Screw the two seat supports (D) and curved top slat to the backrest struts (Photo 7) using the spacing given in Figure A. Then attach the five slats to the backrest struts and six slats to the seat struts (Photo 8).

Finishing touches

Before applying the finish, unscrew the two seat supports and apply weather-resistant glue (like Titebond II or Gorilla Glue) to the joints, then rescrew the seat supports to the backrest struts. The glue will strengthen the joint. The chair relies primarily on these seat supports for strength.

Brush on two liberal coats of a penetrating exterior wood sealer (like Thompson's Water Seal). Let the first coat dry for 24 hours, then apply the second coat. After

an hour, wipe off any excess finish. Let the finish dry for a couple of days before using the chair. After a year or two, you'll want to recoat the chairs to keep them looking good. If you decide to paint the chairs instead, use an oil-based primer followed by a semigloss oil-based paint. Don't use a clear varnish; the sun will eventually break it down and you'll be refinishing every summer instead of relaxing.

Set up the chair by sliding the seat struts through the backrest struts and seat supports as shown in the photos on p. 74. Push the seat in all the way so the rear seat slat is firmly against the backrest struts. Then kick back and relax!

Simplest bench in the world

Built with two boards and a handful of screws.

One of the easiest ways to make a good garden even better is to set a comfortable bench in a secluded corner. Just having a place to sit transforms an ordinary patch of flowers into a quiet, contemplative refuge.

So when we were looking for a simple bench, we mimicked a useful design once used by Aldo Leopold, whom many consider the father of wildlife ecology. Leopold's writings have led many to discover what it means to live in harmony with the land. If this bench was good enough for him, it's definitely good enough for us!

A little research led us to this sturdy design we could build quickly with a few 2x8s, glue and screws. Best of all, it's amazingly comfortable, perfect for bird-watching—even for two people. Thanks, Aldo!

project at a glance

skill level
beginner

special tools
drill
circular saw

approximate cost
$15–$25

EASY FOR EVERYONE

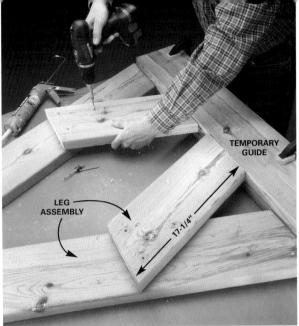

1 Mark one end of the 2x8 x 10 at a 22-1/2° angle with a speed square or protractor, then cut with a circular saw. Make a mark 36 in. away and repeat the cut at the same angle. Cut the remaining front leg and two back legs from the same piece. Cut the seat and the backrest from the 2x8 x 8.

2 Fasten the legs together. Stack and clamp the seat and backrest to the edge of the worktable as guides, and then align the legs against them. Spread adhesive on the front leg, set the rear leg in place, and fasten the legs together with three 2-1/2-in. screws.

shopping list

- 1 2x8 x 8 cedar, redwood or treated lumber (seat and backrest)
- 1 2x8 x 10 cedar, redwood or treated lumber (front and rear legs)
- Exterior construction adhesive
- 2-1/2" galvanized deck screws

building tips

To make a simple project even simpler, remember these tips:

- Be sure to assemble the legs (Photo 2) so they're mirror images of each other, and not facing the same direction.
- Use clamps or a helper to hold the legs upright when securing the seat.
- Predrill all your screw holes to prevent splitting the wood.

3 Attach the seat and backrest. Stand the two ends up, 42 in. apart, spread glue on the tops of the rear legs, and screw the seat in place. Lay the bench on the worktable and attach the backrest with glue and screws.

Leaning tower of shelves

This stylish but sturdy shelf unit will neatly hold your stuff—and you can build it in a day.

This shelf unit may look lightweight and easy to topple. But don't be fooled. It's a real workhorse. The 33-1/2 in. x 82-3/4 in. tower features five unique, tray-like shelves of different depths to hold a wide variety of items up to 13-1/4 in. tall. Despite its 10-degree lean, the unit is surprisingly sturdy, and its open design won't overpower a room.

project at a glance

skill level
intermediate

special tools
miter saw
finish nailer
iron

approximate cost
$60–$80

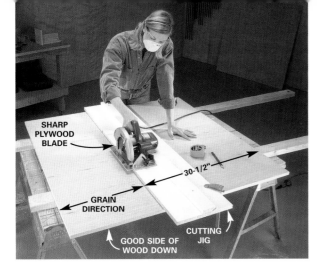

1 Cut 3/4-in. shelf plywood to width first, using a circular saw and a homemade jig for exact cuts. Use a sharp plywood blade and cut with the best side of the wood facing down to minimize splintering.

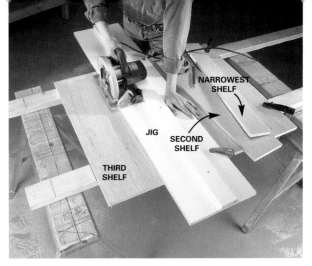

2 Cut the individual shelves, beginning with the narrowest, using the jig for perfectly straight cuts.

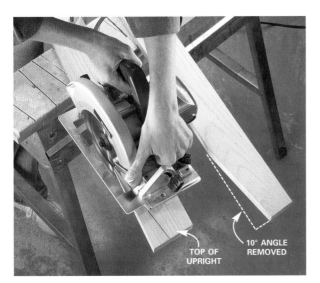

3 Cut both shelf uprights to length with a miter saw. Clamp to sawhorses. Mark the 10-degree angle at the top (dimensions in Figure B), then cut with a circular saw.

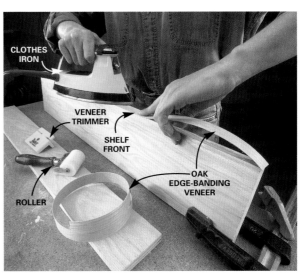

4 Iron edge-banding veneer to the front edge of all five shelves. Roll the entire surface to ensure a solid bond, and trim the edges.

Whether you choose to make this piece more functional, as in this office setting, or place it in a family room to showcase treasures, the basic construction is the same. You select the type of wood and stain or paint to dress it up or down to fit the look of any room.

All the materials can be purchased in home centers or lumberyards. The only special tools you'll need are a power miter box for crisp angle cuts and an air-powered brad nailer for quick assembly and almost invisible joints. And you'll have to rustle up an old clothes iron for applying oak edge-banding material. Once you've gathered all the material, you can build the shelf unit in one afternoon.

Buying the wood

We built our unit with red oak and oak veneer plywood and finished it with two coats of red oak stain.

One note when buying boards: Use a tape measure to check the "standard" dimensions of 1x3s and 1x4s. They sometimes vary in width and thickness. Also check the two full-length 1x4s you plan to use as the uprights to be sure they're straight, without warps or twists. And always examine the ends, edges and surface for blemishes or rough areas that won't easily sand out.

Cut plywood shelves first

Lay a couple of 2x4s across sawhorses (Photo 1) to cut the half sheet of 3/4-in. plywood cleanly and without

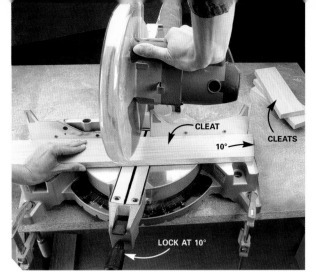

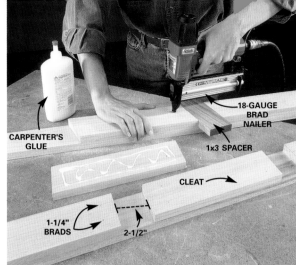

CLEAT
10°
CLEATS
LOCK AT 10°

18-GAUGE
BRAD
NAILER
CARPENTER'S
GLUE
1x3 SPACER
CLEAT
1-1/4"
BRADS
2-1/2"

5 To maintain accuracy, lock the miter box at 10 degrees, then cut all angled pieces—uprights, cleats and one end of shelf sides—without changing the table.

6 Glue and nail the shelf cleats to the uprights using a 1x3 spacer. Hold each cleat tight to the spacer.

pinching the saw blade. Since all five shelves are 30-1/2 in. wide, cut this width first, making sure the grain will run the long way across the shelves. Remember to wear safety glasses, earplugs and a dust mask. Make a homemade jig to fit your circular saw and clamp it to the plywood.

Next, cut all five shelf depths, starting with the smallest shelf (3-3/8 in.) first. Cut smallest to largest so you'll have enough wood to clamp the jig. Make sure you account for the width of your saw blade when you cut each shelf.

Now mark and cut the top of all four 1x4 uprights (the end that rests against the wall), according to Photo 3 and the two dimensions provided in Figure B. Use a sharp blade in your circular saw to prevent splintering. Then stow the sawhorses and move to the workbench.

*tip The beauty of this project is that any wood species will work. If you plan to paint it, select alder or aspen for the solid parts and birch for the plywood.

Select the best front of each plywood shelf, clamp it to the bench on edge and sand it smooth with 150-grit paper on a sanding block. Then preheat a clothes iron to the "cotton" setting and run it over the top of the edge-banding veneer, making sure the veneer extends beyond all edges (Photo 4). Roll it smooth immediately after heating. Let each shelf edge cool for a couple of minutes before trimming and sanding the edges.

Cut the uprights and shelf frame next

Now enter the miter saw, which you use to make all the 90-degree straight cuts first (five shelf backs and 10 shelf sides; see Cutting List). Remember that one end of each shelf side has a 10-degree cut, so we recommend first cutting them square at their exact length, then cutting the angle carefully so the long edge of each piece remains the same.

Next, rotate the miter saw table to the 10-degree mark and cut all the angle pieces. First cut the bottom of both uprights so each upright rests flat against the floor and wall (see Figure A). Then trim the top of the upright to match the bottom, being careful to maintain the 84-in. total length. Next, cut the cleats based on the Cutting List dimensions, which are measured edge to edge (Photo 5 and Figure A). Leave the top cleats long and cut them to exact fit during assembly. Then, to speed finishing, use an orbital sander with 150-grit sandpaper to smooth all pieces before assembly.

materials list

- One half sheet (4' x 4') of 3/4" oak plywood
- Three 8' oak 1x3s
- Four 8' oak 1x4s
- One package (25') of 7/8" oak iron-on veneer (Band-It brand, The Cloverdale Co., (800) 782-9731, www.band-itproducts.com, purchased at Home Depot)
- Veneer edge trimmer (Band-It brand; see above and click "Retail," "Related Products")
- Wood glue
- 1-1/4" brad nails
- Foam pads (1 pkg. of Ace brand 3/4" round, self-adhesive non-skid pads from Ace Hardware)

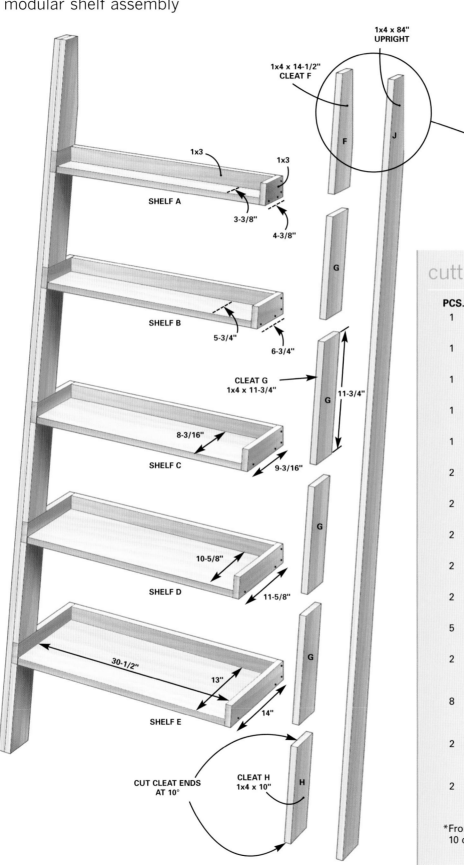

figure a
modular shelf assembly

1x4 x 14-1/2"
CLEAT F

1x4 x 84"
UPRIGHT

1x3

1x3

SHELF A

3-3/8"

4-3/8"

F

J

G

SHELF B

5-3/4"

6-3/4"

CLEAT G
1x4 x 11-3/4"

G

11-3/4"

8-3/16"

SHELF C

9-3/16"

G

10-5/8"

SHELF D

11-5/8"

G

30-1/2"

13"

SHELF E

14"

CUT CLEAT ENDS
AT 10°

CLEAT H
1x4 x 10"

H

figure b
top of upright

2-1/32"

8-3/8"

F
AND
J

10° ANGLE

cutting list

PCS.	SIZE & DESCRIPTION
1	3/4" x 3-3/8" x 30-1/2" oak plywood (shelf A base)
1	3/4" x 5-3/4" x 30-1/2" oak plywood (shelf B base)
1	3/4" x 8-3/16" x 30-1/2" oak plywood (shelf C base)
1	3/4" x 10-5/8" x 30-1/2" oak plywood (shelf D base)
1	3/4" x 13" x 30-1/2" oak plywood (shelf E base)
2	3/4" x 2-1/2" x 4-3/8" oak (shelf A sides)*
2	3/4" x 2-1/2" x 6-3/4" oak (shelf B sides)*
2	3/4" x 2-1/2" x 9-3/16" oak (shelf C sides)*
2	3/4" x 2-1/2" x 11-5/8" oak (shelf D sides)*
2	3/4" x 2-1/2" x 14" oak (shelf E sides)*
5	3/4" x 2-1/2" x 30-1/2" oak A - E (shelf backs)
2	3/4" x 3-1/2" x 14-1/2" oak shelf cleats F (cut with 10-degree angles)
8	3/4" x 3-1/2" x 11-3/4" oak shelf cleats G (cut with 10-degree angles)
2	3/4" x 3-1/2" x 10" oak shelf cleats H (cut with 10-degree angles)
2	3/4" x 3-1/2" x 84" oak uprights J (cut with 10-degree angles)

*Front part of side cut at 10 degrees

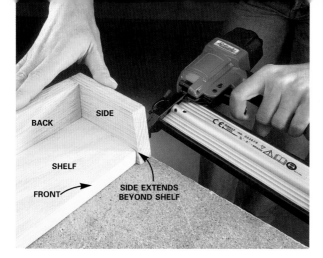

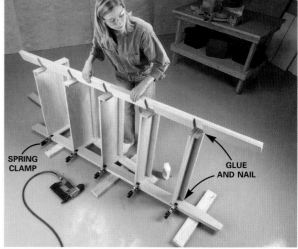

7 Glue and nail the shelf backs, then attach the sides to the plywood shelves. Position the sides to overlap the shelf base as shown.

8 Clamp the shelves into one upright. Spread glue in the shelf notches of the other upright, position it flush with the front of the shelves and nail. Flip the unit over and attach the other upright.

Assemble uprights first, then the shelves

To begin assembly, lay out both uprights and all cleats to ensure that the angles are correct so the shelves will be level when the unit is against the wall. Then glue and nail the first cleat flush with the base of each upright (using five or six 1-1/4 in. brads) on each cleat. Work your way upward using 1x3 spacers (Photo 6). Make sure the spacer is the exact same width as the shelf sides! Set these aside to dry.

For shelf assembly, first glue and nail on the shelf backs. Next, apply the sides with glue and nails (Photo 7).

For final assembly, lay one upright on 2x4s, then clamp on the shelves as shown in Photo 8. Apply the glue, position the second upright on top flush with the front edge of the shelves, then sink four 1-1/4 in. brads into each shelf from the upright side. Carefully turn the unit over and repeat the process to attach the second upright. Work quickly so the glue doesn't set. Lift the ladder shelf and place it upright against a straight wall. Check it with a framing square and flex it if necessary to square it up and to make sure that the uprights rest flat against the floor and wall (assuming your floor is level). Attach three bar clamps as shown in Photo 9 while the glue dries.

The shelf is highly stable as designed, but once you've stained or painted it, you can add self-adhesive foam gripping pads to the bottom of the uprights. And if you don't feel secure having it on a slippery floor, the unit's width is perfect for screwing the top of the uprights into wall studs.

9 Set the shelf unit against a straight wall, check for squareness and apply three bar clamps until the glue dries.

Successful wood stripping

You can do it safely and effectively.

L et's face it: Stripping wood is a drag. We approach the job knowing it's difficult and messy, but hoping we can reclaim a jewel from the muck. Knowing what to use and how to use it is essential to success. Here's a rundown of the three basic types of strippers and how to use them safely and effectively.

Safety first

Stripping chemicals range from hazardous to almost-safe. Some strippers require you to use less protection than others, but always err on the side of safety and follow these guidelines:

● Protect your body with long pants, a long-sleeve shirt and a solvent-proof apron.

● At a minimum, wear splash-proof goggles, not just safety glasses. Use a full face shield when you're working with caustic strippers. The lye will burn your skin and eyes.

● Wear long chemical-resistant gloves and turn back the ends into cuffs so that when you lift your arm, the stripper drips into the cuff, not onto your arm. (Take them off to scratch your nose!)

● Work only in areas with good ventilation, *preferably outdoors.* If you (or someone with a "fresh" nose)

smell fumes, *you need more ventilation.* Avoid working with chemical strippers in basements, since many fumes are heavier than air and sink to the floor, where they're hard to eliminate.

● Wear a respirator with new cartridges rated for use with organic solvents. Respirators are only secondary protection; you can't depend on them. Ventilation is the key.

project at a glance

skill level
beginner

special tools
respirator
goggles
protective
    clothing
putty knife

approximate cost
$10–$20 per
piece of furniture

Choosing a stripper

Slow and safe

SAFEST STRIPPER, made by 3M, can be used indoors without special ventilation or gloves (although if your skin is sensitive, you may want to wear them anyway). Safest Stripper is particularly effective on oil-based paint and polyurethane. However, it can take as long as 24 hours to soften a finish. Safest Stripper seems to pull oil-based finish out of the pores better than other strippers, so it's handy for woods like oak and ash. Because it's water-based, it will raise the wood grain and can loosen veneer.

Fast but hazardous strippers

REFINISHERS work only on plain lacquer or shellac. Read the label. They contain powerful solvents like acetone and toluene. Refinishers dissolve the finish instantly but are highly flammable. They're used differently than other strippers: Wearing gloves, goggles and respirator, soak steel wool or an abrasive pad with refinisher, scrub the surface and wipe off the finish as it liquefies. The finish will start melting almost immediately. Repeat until you are down to bare wood.

METHYLENE CHLORIDE (also called dichloromethane or DCM) strippers soften all finishes, including paint, in as little as 10 minutes. These strippers are identifiable by labels that say "extra heavy duty," "tuff-job," "super-strip" or the like, indicating that they contain a high percentage of methylene chloride. They work from the bottom up, so the finish comes off in sheets (Photo 1). Because they work by making the finish let go of the wood, you often need to use less of this stripper than other types. Work outdoors or in a very well ventilated area. As an added precaution, use a respirator with organic vapor cartridges.

Medium-fast, moderately hazardous strippers

SOLVENT MIXTURES may contain small amounts of methylene chloride mixed with other solvents, or new nonflammable stripping agents such as n-methyl-2-pyrrolidone (NMP) and gamma butyrolactone. You still must wear gloves and goggles, and most require ventilation. These strippers work from the top down (Photo 1). For many folks they represent a happy medium, since they are relatively safe yet relatively fast.

CAUSTIC STRIPPERS are strong alkalines such as lye. Peel Away 1 is one example of this type of stripper. Although water-based and nonflammable, they can seriously burn your skin and eyes, so wear goggles and gloves and be careful not to splash. Because caustic strippers are water-based, they raise the wood grain and can loosen joints and veneer. They also may darken the wood, so they're often used when the wood will be repainted. Unlike other strippers, they can't be left on too long, or the wood itself may get damaged.

1 Strippers made of solvent mixtures work from the top down (left side), melting the finish into a soft goo. Methylene chloride strippers work by penetrating the finish (right side) to break the bond between it and the wood.

2 Apply the stripper in a layer 1/8 to 1/4 in. thick. On vertical surfaces, semi-paste removers work best because they cling. Once the stripper is on, leave it alone and let it do the work.

Successful stripping

Some strippers, especially those called "refinishers," are highly flammable. If the container says the stripper is flammable, keep sparks and flames away from your work area. Be especially aware of gas pilot lights, electronic spark igniters, and even light switches and electrical plugs. If you use a fan to increase ventilation, position it so that you are between the fan and the open window or door. Have the fan push clean air toward you, and the vapors away from both you and the fan. That way you won't be drawing vapor-filled air through a spark-producing fan motor.

Choose a stripper

Except for "refinishers," which are only for shellac and lacquer, most strippers will remove just about any finish. Choose a stripper based on its speed and safety. A good rule of thumb: The safer it is, the slower it works. As shown in "Choosing a Stripper," you can choose fast and hazardous, moderately fast and moderately hazardous, or slow and relatively safe. Be aware that the safety requirements for each stripper may differ; read labels carefully.

Some modern finishes won't budge for any stripper, but they're rare. Occasionally, very old pieces may be covered by a thin, milk-based paint that also is resistant to normal strippers. However, it will come off with a caustic stripper.

Set up your work area

After choosing your stripper, gather your stripping paraphernalia (see "The Basic Equipment," below). Dismantle the piece as far as is practical and remove any hardware, making certain you label all the parts carefully for reassembly. You can make a numbered sketch for

The basic equipment

The basic equipment for safe stripping includes:

- A fan for ventilation, even in the garage with the overhead door open
- Long chemical-resistant gloves, with cuffs rolled back to keep goop from running down your arm
- Solvent-proof apron of heavy cloth, plastic or rubber
- Organic-cartridge respirator (with some strippers) and new cartridges
- Splash-proof goggles (if they're not part of the respirator)
- Tools for removing the gunk: a dull putty knife, scrub pads and brushes, wood shavings, string, wooden sticks and scrapers
- A big, sloppy old brush and a can or bowl for applying and holding the stripper
- Solvents for washing the stripped surface: water or alcohol, lacquer thinner and mineral spirits, depending on the stripper
- Plastic bags or sheeting to cover your piece while the stripper works.

3 Seal your work in a bag. If the piece is too big for a bag, cover it with a tent made of polyethylene sheeting. Put several layers of newspapers under the work to catch the drips.

4 Scoop off the finish using a putty knife with a dull edge and rounded corners.

complicated pieces, and number parts in hidden areas, such as inside the joints. You might even want to take "before" photos.

Put on the stripper

The key to easy stripping is to apply a lot of stripper, persuade it to stay on and give it plenty of time to work, without interruption. Many strippers contain a wax that will rise to the surface and form a crust to prevent the active solvent from evaporating. If you brush over the stripper after applying it, you disturb the crust and allow the solvent to evaporate. Also, for the wax to be effective, work in a temperature of about 70 degrees F.

Shake the can of stripper gently before use, then cover the cap with a rag or paper towel. Unscrew it slowly because sometimes the stripper spurts out. Apply the stripper in a thick layer (Photo 2) and try to keep the work horizontal so the stripper doesn't run.

The most effective way to keep the stripper wet and active is to seal the workpiece in plastic. You can use a leaf bag (Photo 3), or a tent of polyethylene film (available in rolls from your home center). Use duct tape to seal the plastic, keeping the tape on the outside. Do a dry run to make sure the plastic covers the piece completely.

For fast-acting methylene chloride strippers, an hour in the bag should do the trick. Allow two to three hours for the moderately fast strippers, and overnight for

3M's Safest Stripper. If you aren't sure, apply the stripper late in the day, bag your work, and leave it overnight.

The bag method works for all except caustic strippers, which you should check periodically, removing the gunk as soon as the wood comes clean to prevent possible

Special precautions for methylene chloride strippers

Methylene chloride, the main solvent in many "fast" strippers, can cause skin and lung irritation, exacerbate the symptoms of heart disease, and may cause cancer. If you have heart disease, are pregnant or are elderly, avoid using strippers that contain methylene chloride. Inhaling methylene chloride reduces the amount of oxygen in the blood and can trigger a medical emergency in people with heart disease. With methylene chloride strippers, you can't detect when an organic vapor respirator becomes ineffective, so rely on maximum ventilation when using them.

To minimize your risk, take the following precautions:

- **Work outdoors or in a well-ventilated indoor area and keep your exposure time short.**
- **Wear long gloves, an apron, shoe covers and a face mask to keep methylene chloride off your skin and clothes. Wash your hands and face with soap immediately after using the stripper.**
- **Since methylene chloride readily penetrates neoprene (rubber) gloves, wear only chemical-resistant gloves.**

5 Wood shavings help scrub sludge from turnings and carvings. Other useful tools include string for getting into cracks and turnings, plastic scrub brushes and pointed dowels for tight corners. The bag and newspaper act as a dropcloth and cleanup aid.

6 The wood is washed clean with the recommended solvent to remove any bits of paint and any remaining stripper. A final wash with one cup of ammonia in a quart of water, and then an over-night drying, is recommended.

damage to the wood. (It'll burn and darken it.) The other strippers can remain on the wood for long periods without damaging it.

Take it all off

Put on your goggles, gloves, apron and respirator, then take your project outside and remove it from the bag. Open the bag carefully. The finish should virtually fall off right down to the bare wood. Scoop it off (Photos 4 and 5), using whatever tool works without damaging the wood. If you're using a water-based stripper, don't use metal tools or steel wool; they can leave rust marks on the wood.

As you remove the sludge, spread it out on newspaper. The object is to let the sludge dry out before you dispose of it. If the stripper on your piece starts to dry before you get it off, add more stripper with your brush or pad. If the finish still doesn't come completely off, recoat the wood, tie up the bag and repeat the process. The idea is to let the stripper do the work. If you try to pry or scrape off leftover finish, you'll nick and gouge the wood.

Washing the wood

Before the wood has a chance to dry, wash off any last bits of paint or residue from the stripper. For methylene chloride strippers, apply a mix of equal parts of de-natured alcohol, mineral spirits and lacquer thinner with a nylon pad. For other strippers, use the solvent recommended on the container.

Finally, repeat the scrub with a solution of ammonia and water (Photo 6). This will remove silicone or other oils that can interfere with both solvent- and water-based finishes.

Note: If you're using a refinisher, neither wash is necessary. Apply your new finish directly to the stripped wood.

Cleaning up

Clean scrubbers, brushes, gloves and other tools in the remaining solvent wash. Spread your messy plastic, newspapers with finish gunk and solvent-soaked rags outside in the fresh air to dry, away from people and pets, to prevent spontaneous combustion. Let used solvent wash evaporate. This won't take long if you pour it onto a pile of wood shavings spread on newspaper or plastic someplace where there is no risk of fire.

Unless it includes lead paint, dry residue from household stripping projects is usually considered safe to throw out with the trash. Any residue containing lead paint, and all liquid residue, should be treated as hazardous waste. Contact local health, environmental or sanitation authorities for disposal instructions.

Stair-step plant display

Show off your favorite plants with this simple cedar stand.

We tend to buy plants first and worry about good spots for them later. So unfortunately, many of the prettiest plants get lost in the corners of a deck and sunroom and don't get the attention (or the light) they deserve.

To help solve this problem and to spotlight some favorite plants, we came up with this simple display stand. It's made from cedar 1x2s that are cut into just two lengths, stacked into squares and nailed together. We used western red cedar with the rough-sawed side exposed. You may have to check several suppliers to find a good selection of 1x2s. Assembly is simple and fast, because there's nothing to measure as you build—just keep everything square and use the wood pieces themselves for spacing and alignment.

project at a glance

skill level
beginner

special tools
power or hand
 miter saw
basic hand tools

approximate cost
$15–$20

Here's what you'll need

For supplies, you'll need seven 8-ft.-long cedar 1x2s, some exterior glue, like Titebond II, a few dozen 4d galvanized finish nails, and some 100- or 120-grit sandpaper. You'll also need a hammer, a tape measure and a framing square, plus a saw that can cut the 1x2s to a consistent length. A power miter saw is great for this (you can rent one) but you could also use a handsaw in a miter box. An exterior finish for the wood is attractive, but not really necessary.

Begin by trimming any rough or out-of-square ends from your 1x2s. Almost all the ends will show, so they need to look good. Cut the 1x2s into sixteen 20-in. pieces and twenty-seven 10-3/4-in. pieces. It's important that the two groups of pieces are consistent in length, so rather than measuring each one,

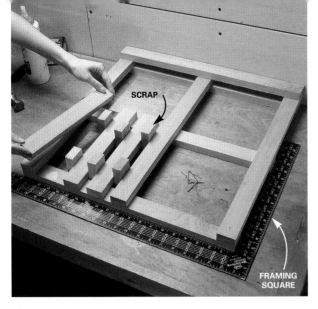

SCRAP

FRAMING SQUARE

1 Assemble the first two layers without nails or glue to get the spacing right and to make sure everything is square. Use scrap pieces of 1x2 as spacers. Once everything is square, glue and nail all the intersections.

2 Build up the stand "log-cabin style" until you get to the seventh layer, which has two platforms. When that's nailed down, continue until the 12th layer, which has the final platform.

clamp a "stop block" to your bench the appropriate distance from the blade of your saw, and push the 1x2 up against it for each cut.

How to build it

Begin making your stand by arranging the lowest two layers without nails or glue (Photo 1). Lay out the bottom three 20-in. pieces against a framing square, then lay three more 20-in. pieces and three 10-3/4-in. pieces on top of them as shown in Photo 1.

Adjust the spacing, using scrap pieces to create the gaps, and make sure everything is square. The second layer should have a plant platform in one corner and nothing in the other three. When everything looks good, nail the pieces together, using one nail and a dab of glue at every intersection. Keep the nails 3/4 in. away from the ends of the boards to prevent splitting.

Add five more layers each consisting of two long and one short piece, with glue and a nail at every overlap. Check the sides with the square as you go to keep them straight. At the seventh layer, add two more platforms, with the 10-3/4-in. pieces running perpendicular to the pieces on the first platform. Add another five layers, with just two 10-3/4-in. pieces per layer, then fill in the top layer to create the final display platform (Photo 2). When you're done nailing, sand all the outside edges of your stand and apply an exterior stain or preservative. Wait a few days for the finish to dry completely, then start moving in the plants!

figure a
exploded view

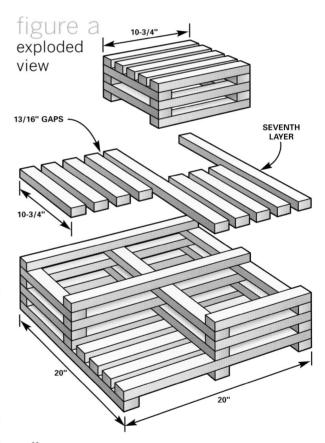

10-3/4"

13/16" GAPS

SEVENTH LAYER

10-3/4"

20"

20"

tip Always nail at least 3/4 in. in from the end, and if the wood still splits, predrill the nail holes using a bit the size of the nail or the nail itself with the head snipped off. Your boards may also differ in thickness from those shown, which were 13/16 in. thick. If so, simply adjust the spacing between the boards.

Fast furniture fixes

Make those nicks and scratches go away with just a few minutes' work.

Furniture looking a little shabby with all those little scratches and dings? You know, the vacuum cleaner bumps here and there, and the Hot Wheels hit-and-runs? Not to worry. We'll show you simple touch-up techniques that will make these minor eyesores disappear quickly and painlessly.

We're not talking about refinishing or even repairing here, which are different games altogether. This is about hiding flaws so only you will know they're there.

The procedures and materials shown in this article won't damage the original finish on your furniture if it was made in the last 50 years.

However, if the piece of furniture you're touching up is very old, or an antique, it may have a shellac finish. With shellac, you shouldn't attempt the scratch-removal process shown on p. 94. And if the piece is an antique, think twice about doing any touch-up, which could actually devalue it.

You can test for a shellac finish with a few drops of alcohol in an out-of-sight spot. Alcohol will dissolve shellac.

Think safety: Even though all the fluids and sprays we show here are everyday hardware-store products, most are both flammable and toxic. Read and follow the directions on the label. Don't use them in a room where there's a pilot light, or near open flames or in an unventilated space. If you'll be doing anything more than a few quick passes with the sprays shown here, work outdoors and wear a respirator mask with organic cartridges. And if you're pregnant, stay away from these materials altogether.

project at a glance

skill level
beginner

special tools
felt-tip markers
putty sticks

approximate cost
$5–$10

touch up scratches

1 Hide scratches with permanent-ink felt-tip markers. You can either use the furniture touch-up markers available at hardware stores and home centers, or, to get an exact match, buy markers at an art supply store that carries an array of colors (check the Yellow Pages). For thorough coverage, you may need to dab the ink onto the scratch, let it dry, then even out the color by stroking lightly across it with the tip. Keep in mind that colors tend to darken when they soak into wood fibers.

2 Touch up thin scratches with a fine-tip permanent marker. When filling in scratches, steady your hand against the furniture for accuracy; as much as possible, flow the ink only onto the scratch.

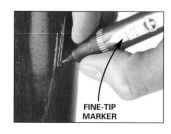

FINE-TIP MARKER

patch gouges

Fill in gouges with colored putty sticks, sold at most hardware stores and home centers. This putty works well for small holes and nicks but is somewhat trickier to use as a fill for larger damage, as shown here. Unlike hardening putties, it remains soft and somewhat flexible, so you have to shape it carefully. And it won't hold up under heavy wear.

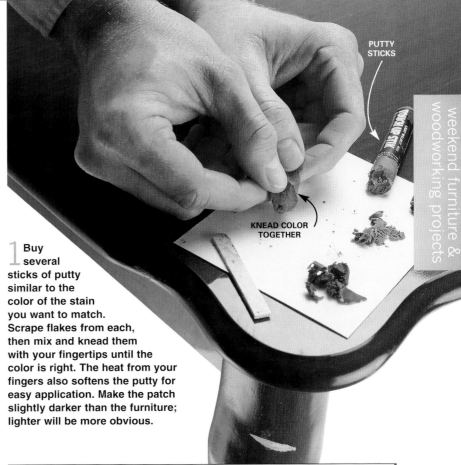

PUTTY STICKS

KNEAD COLOR TOGETHER

1 **Buy several sticks of putty similar to the color of the stain you want to match. Scrape flakes from each, then mix and knead them with your fingertips until the color is right. The heat from your fingers also softens the putty for easy application. Make the patch slightly darker than the furniture; lighter will be more obvious.**

2 **Press putty tightly into the gouge with a small flat stick, then flatten it and scrape away the excess with the stick's long edge. Round the end of the stick with sandpaper.**

3 **Wipe away any putty adhering to the wood around the gouge, and smooth the surface of the putty with a clean cloth. A thin, light-colored line will usually appear around the perimeter of the patch. Use a matching marker to color this line, as shown in Photo 2 on p. 92.**

4 **Spray the patch with two or three quick passes of shellac, then after it dries, a few quick passes of spray lacquer—either high gloss or satin, depending on your furniture's finish. Never apply lacquer or polyurethane/varnish directly over a putty patch; it will leave a permanently soft mess. Shellac will harden; however, the patch will remain somewhat pliable under the finish, so don't attempt this on a heavy-wear surface.**

wipe away scratches and recoat the surface

You can buff out fine scratches using very fine (0000) steel wool saturated with clear Danish oil. (You can also use ultra-fine automotive rubbing compound.) The process shown here only works for scratches in the finish itself, not scratches that are all the way into the stain or the wood.

0000 STEEL WOOL

1 Pour a generous amount of clear or neutral Danish oil onto a very fine steel wool pad. Rub the surface with the oil-saturated pad using your flat hand. Rub *with* the grain, never against it or at an angle to it. Continue rubbing until you remove enough of the clear surface finish to eliminate the scratches, *but be careful not to remove any of the stain below the clear finish.* Rub not only the scratched area but also the area around it in gradually decreasing amounts. Be careful not to rub edges or corners excessively; they wear through quickly.

2 Wipe away all the Danish oil with rags or paper towels, then thoroughly clean the entire surface with mineral spirits several times to make sure all the oil is removed. If any oil remains, the lacquer (Photo 3) won't adhere. Allow the surface to dry overnight before applying lacquer.

3 Spray the entire surface with clear lacquer. Move the spray can in one continuous, straight stroke, allowing the spray to extend beyond the edges in all directions. Wipe the nozzle with a rag after each stroke to prevent drips. Move with the grain, and make sure the angle of the spray remains the same all the way across. Keep the spray aimed away from other surfaces that you don't want coated, or mask them with newspaper.

CAUTION: RAGS AND STEEL WOOL SATURATED WITH DANISH OIL CAN SPONTANEOUSLY COMBUST IF LEFT BUNCHED UP. DRY THEM OUTDOORS, SPREAD OUT LOOSELY. WHEN THE OIL HAS DRIED, YOU CAN SAFELY THROW THE RAGS AND STEEL WOOL IN THE TRASH.

clean dirty, greasy, gummy surfaces

The results of a simple surface cleaning with mineral spirits may amaze you. Polish buildup and the dirt embedded in it muddy the finish but will wipe away. Don't use stronger solvents; they might dissolve the finish itself.

1 **Soak a coarse, absorbent, clean cloth with mineral spirits and wipe the finish. Keep applying and wiping until the cloth no longer picks up dirt. Then do a final wipe with a fresh, clean rag.**

2 **Clean crevices, grooves and carved areas with cotton swabs dipped in mineral spirits.**

5¢ sponge brushes

Need a quick touch-up brush? If you have any leftover self-adhering foam weatherstripping, you can save yourself a trip to the store. A short piece—1/2 in. thick x 3/4 in. wide—wrapped around the end of a thin strip of wood or a tongue depressor will work as well as store-bought foam brushes for small jobs. Foam weatherstripping is made from extra-porous foam, which holds a lot of paint and smoothly applies it to flat surfaces. It also smooshes down nicely when you're coating molding contours or painting in tight corners.

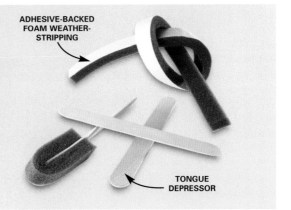

ADHESIVE-BACKED FOAM WEATHER-STRIPPING

TONGUE DEPRESSOR

Coat & mitten rack

Build this handsome project in just a few hours— you won't believe you got along without it!

This simple coat rack is designed to be easy to build with butt joints connected by screws that get hidden by wooden screw-hole buttons and wood plugs. The rack mounts easily to the wall with screws driven through the hidden hanging strip on the back. The five large Shaker pegs are great for holding hats, umbrellas and coats, and the hinged-hatch door at the top keeps the clutter of gloves and scarves from view.

You can build this project in a few hours, with an additional hour to apply a finish. Maple is an ideal wood for Shaker-style pieces, but any hardwood will do. Figure on spending about $65 for wood, hardware and varnish.

tip Be sure this project is screwed to the wall studs. Drill two holes into the hanging strip at stud locations and use 2-1/2 in. or longer wood screws.

project at a glance

skill level
beginner

special tools
jigsaw
drill
clamps

approximate cost
$65

figure a
shaker rack details

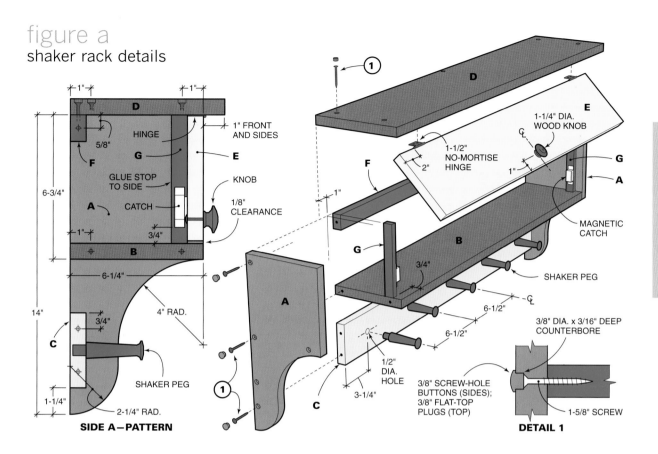

SIDE A—PATTERN

DETAIL 1

Cutting the pieces

Using a compass, transfer the pattern measurements in Figure A, above, and then cut the sides (A) with a jigsaw (Photo 1). Next cut the top (D) to length and rip the shelf (B) to the width given in the Cutting List, at right. Cut the hanging strip (F) and the peg strip (C) to the same length as the shelf (B). Now, using your spade bit, drill the 3/8-in. counterbore holes for the screw-hole buttons 3/16 in. deep into the outside of parts A (Figure A and Photo 2). Also drill the 3/8-in. counterbore holes in the top. These holes must be 3/8 in. deep.

Mark and drill the 1/2-in. holes for the Shaker pegs in the peg strip. Drill the holes for the Shaker pegs perfectly perpendicular to the peg strip to ensure they all project evenly when glued in place.

shopping list

ITEM	QTY.
1x8 x 12' maple (A, B, D, E)	1
1x4 x 6' maple (C, F, G)	1
1-1/2" no-mortise hinges*	1 pair
1-1/4" beech knob*	1
Narrow magnetic catch*	2
3-3/8" long Shaker pegs*	5
3/8" screw-hole buttons*	10
3/8" plugs*	5
3/8" spade bit	1
1/2" spade bit	1
1-5/8" wood screws	15
Carpenter's glue	1 pint
Danish oil	1 pint
150- and 220-grit sandpaper	

* Available from home centers or Rockler Woodworking and Hardware, (800) 279-4441, www.rockler.com.

cutting list

KEY	PCS.	SIZE & DESCRIPTION
A	2	3/4" x 6-1/4" x 14" maple sides
B	1	3/4" x 6-1/4" x 32-1/2" maple shelf
C	1	3/4" x 3-1/2" x 32-1/2" maple peg strip
D	1	3/4" x 7-1/4" x 36" maple top
E	1	3/4" x 5-13/16" x 32-5/16" maple hatch
F	1	3/4" x 1-1/4" x 32-1/2" maple hanging strip
G	2	3/4" x 1/2" x 6" maple hatch stops

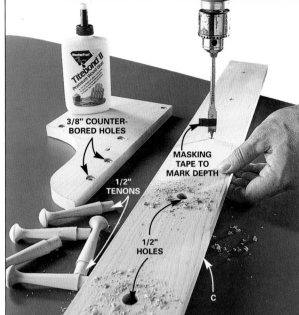

1 Cut the side pieces (A) using a jigsaw or band saw. Sand the curved edges smooth with a 1-1/2 in. drum sander attached to your drill.

2 Drill the 1/2-in. holes 5/8 in. deep for the 3-3/8 in. Shaker pegs and the 3/8-in. counterbore holes 3/16 in. deep for the screw-hole buttons in parts A.

Assembly

Lay the pieces on your workbench, as shown in Photo 3. Align the hanging strip (F), the shelf (B), and the peg strip (C) as shown and clamp the sides (A) to these parts. Predrill the holes with a combination pilot hole/coun-

tip * Sight down the edge of the peg strip to perfectly align each peg as the glue sets.

tersink bit using the center of the counterbore holes as a guide. Next, screw the sides to B, C and F. Mark and drill hinge mounting holes in the top (D), then fasten the top to the sides in the same manner.

Glue and clamp the hatch stops to the inside of parts A, as shown in Figure A, p. 97. To finish the assembly, cut the hatch (E) to size and install the hinges on the underside of part D and the top of the hatch. Now glue the buttons and plugs into their corresponding holes. Use only a small drop of glue for the buttons but be sure to apply a thin layer of glue completely around the plugs. This will swell the plugs for a tight fit. After the glue is dry, trim the wood plugs flush with the top.

Finishing

After assembly, lightly sand the entire piece with 220-grit sandpaper. Apply two coats of clear Danish oil or polyurethane to all the surfaces (remove the hinges and knobs). Once the finish is dry, add magnetic catches to the hatch stops (G).

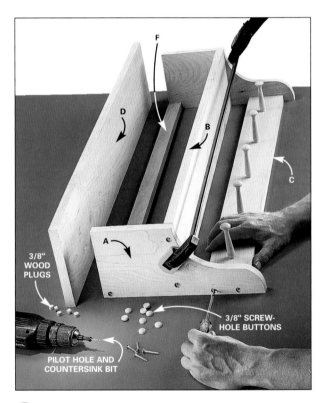

3 Assemble the shelf by clamping parts C, F and B to the sides. Drill pilot holes and screw the pieces together. The screws will be covered by the buttons and plugs.

weekend kitchen & bathroom projects

Cabinet facelift

Simple, attractive kitchen upgrades you can do yourself—without replacing your cabinets.

Take a look, a really close look. At first glance it may be hard to recognize, but the kitchen on the right is the same as the one in the photo below. The cabinet "boxes," the countertop, the layout, the flooring, the sink and the window haven't changed a whit. Better yet, once the materials were in hand, this transformation took place in just a few days—without putting the kitchen out of commission. The frosting on the cake? The total cost for upgrading the cabinets was $2,200 (not including the wall tile). With the average full-scale kitchen remodeling project costing more than $30,000 (and about one-third of that amount spent on cabinetry), you can see we got a big impact for a small cost.

project at a glance

skill level
intermediate

special tools
power miter saw
drill
basic hand tools

approximate cost
$2,200 for project shown (not incl. tile)

Whether you tackle one or all of these cabinet upgrades, you'll increase the visual appeal of your kitchen quickly, inexpensively and with minimum hassle.

BEFORE

AFTER

If you're pleased with the basic layout and function of your kitchen but want to update the look—and add a few new features—read on. We'll show you how paint, new cabinet doors and drawer fronts, moldings and a few accessories can transform your kitchen.

Most of the projects require only a drill, basic hand tools and intermediate DIY savvy, although a power miter saw and pneumatic finish nailer allow you to cut and install the crown molding faster.

Bear in mind, these upgrades won't fix cabinets that are falling apart, create more storage space or make your kitchen easier to navigate. But if you want to give your kitchen an inexpensive yet dramatic facelift, here's how.

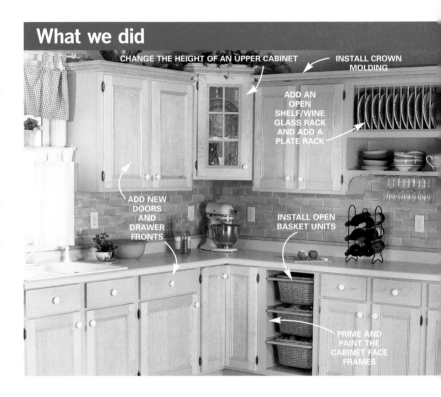

What we did

CHANGE THE HEIGHT OF AN UPPER CABINET

INSTALL CROWN MOLDING

ADD AN OPEN SHELF/WINE GLASS RACK AND ADD A PLATE RACK

ADD NEW DOORS AND DRAWER FRONTS

INSTALL OPEN BASKET UNITS

PRIME AND PAINT THE CABINET FACE FRAMES

Raise an upper cabinet

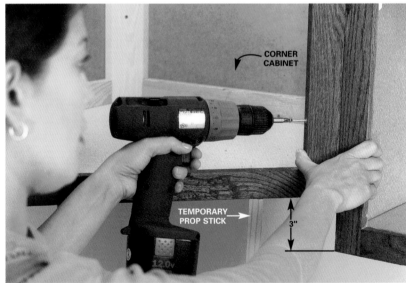

CORNER CABINET

TEMPORARY PROP STICK

3"

To break up the monotony of a row of cabinets, change the height of one or more upper cabinets. This provides more "headroom" for working and more space for lighting and appliances, while creating a more interesting and varied look.

In order to raise a cabinet, your cabinets must be the modular kind such that each cabinet is an independent "box" screwed to adjacent ones. Earlier "builder cabinets," with the entire row of cabinets built and installed as one unit, can't be easily

To raise a cabinet, remove the shelves and doors and then the screws securing it to the wall and cabinets on either side. Raise the cabinet, temporarily prop it in place, drill new pilot holes, then reinstall the screws.

separated. We elevated our corner cabinet 3 in., temporarily propped it up with scrap lumber, drilled pilot holes for new screws, then reattached it. A cabinet that's been in

place a long time may need a sharp rap with a hammer to free it from paint and grime that have "glued" it in place.

Paint your cabinet face frames

Proper preparation and sanding between coats are the keys to a smooth, durable paint job on your cabinet face frames.

Oil paints arguably create the smoothest surface, since they dry slowly and "self-level" as brush stroke marks fill in. However, this slow drying time means they're more vulnerable to dust. Cleanup is also more of a hassle. Latex paints dry quickly and may show brush strokes more, but additives like Floetrol (The Flood Co., 800-321-3444) improve "brushability."

After priming, paint the cabinets with a gloss or semigloss paint. Apply a thin first coat, let it dry, then lightly sand with 120- or 180-grit sandpaper. Wipe the surface, then apply a second coat. Two or three thin coats are better than one or two thick ones.

If you have a gas stove, turn off the gas for safety while using mineral spirits, shellac or oil paints, and provide plenty of ventilation.

SANDING BLOCK WITH 120-GRIT PAPER

PIGMENTED SHELLAC PRIMER

Clean the cabinet face frames with mineral spirits, then scrub them with household ammonia and rinse. Fill holes with spackling compound, then sand with 120-grit sandpaper. Vacuum the cabinets, then prime them with a pigmented shellac. Lightly sand the dried primer.

Add new doors and drawer fronts

We had a local cabinet shop make our new doors and drawer fronts the exact same dimensions as the old ones. We used the same hinges and mounting holes in the face frames to ensure the right fit. You can have your components made locally or by one of the companies listed in the Buyer's Guide, p. 106.

Existing drawer fronts can be attached in a number of different ways. We were able to simply pry off the old and screw on the new. If yours can't be removed, you'll need to use a circular saw to cut all four edges of the drawer front even with the edges of the drawer box, then apply the new drawer front directly over the old. This will make your drawers 3/4 in. longer; make certain your drawer hardware and cabinets can accommodate the extra length. If not, you may need to install new drawer hardware or new drawer boxes.

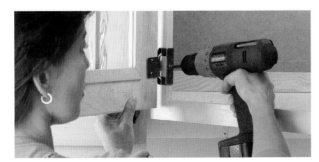

Mount the hinges to the doors, then mount the doors to the face frames using the existing screw holes. Most hinges allow for some up-and-down movement and tilt so the doors can be adjusted evenly.

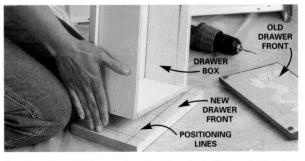

OLD DRAWER FRONT

DRAWER BOX

NEW DRAWER FRONT

POSITIONING LINES

Replace the old drawer fronts. We pried off the old front using a chisel and a flat bar, marked the position of the drawer box on the back of the new drawer front, then joined the two using carpenter's glue and screws.

Add an open shelf, wine glass rack and plate rack

If you have a short cabinet flanked by two taller cabinets, you can add this combination shelf/wine rack.

We cut the shelf to length, then added mounting strips on each end. We cut four 9-in. sections of wine glass molding from a 3-ft. length (see Buyer's Guide, p. 106), then glued and nailed them to the bottom of the pine shelf. We also cut curved brackets from each end of a 1x6 maple board and cut the center 1 in. wide to serve as shelf edging. Finally, we installed the unit by driving screws through the mounting strips and into the cabinets on each side.

To display your plates and keep them accessible and chip-free, build and install this plate rack. The total cost of materials? Under $10.

To create the two plate rack "ladders," measure the cabinet, then build each ladder so the finished height equals the height of the inside of the cabinet. The finished width should be equal to the width of the face frame opening. Drill 3/8-in. holes, 3/8 in. deep in 3/4-in. x 3/4-in. square dowels and space them every 1-1/2 in. Cut the dowels to length, add a drop of glue in each hole, insert the dowels, then use elastic cords or clamps to hold things

WINE GLASS BRACKETS

Build a shelf to fit snugly between the cabinets on each side. We used a jig-saw to create curved brackets, nailed wine glass brackets to the bottom of the shelf, then installed the entire unit as one piece.

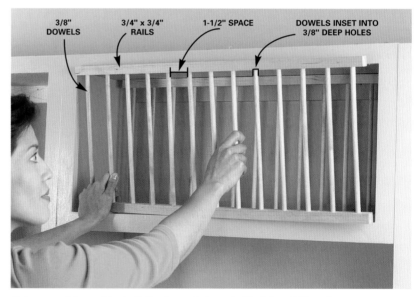

3/8" DOWELS   3/4" x 3/4" RAILS   1-1/2" SPACE   DOWELS INSET INTO 3/8" DEEP HOLES

Cut, assemble and install the two plate rack "ladders." Use short screws to secure the ladders in the cabinet opening. We set the rear ladder 4 in. away from the back of the cabinet and the front ladder snug against the back of the face frame.

together until the glue dries.

A drill press comes in handy, but you can get excellent results using the same tools we did: a cordless drill, a steady hand and a 3/8-in. drill bit with masking tape wrapped around it as a depth guide for the holes in the rails.

Install crown molding

Crown molding comes in many profiles and sizes; we installed rope molding (see Buyer's Guide, p. 106). If your face frames aren't wide enough on top to nail the molding to, nail strips of wood to the top edge to provide a nailing surface.

Raising the corner cabinet created a challenge where the moldings on each side butted into it. We held the upper part of the crown molding back a few inches, but extended the thin rope molding portion so it butted into the corner cabinet.

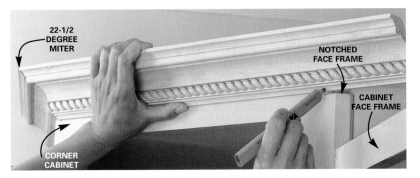

Position and mark each piece of crown molding as you work your way around the kitchen. Make small notches in the top corners of the face frames so the moldings lie flat against the sides of the cabinets when installed.

Cut crown molding by placing it upside down and securing it at the correct angle with a clamp and wood scrap.

Install open basket units

The "Base 18" baskets we installed (see Buyer's Guide, p. 106) came with two side tracks that could be cut narrower to accommodate cabinets ranging in width from 15-7/8 in. to 17-7/8 in. "Base 15" baskets fit cabinets with an inside width of 12-7/8 in. to 15-7/8 in. Measure carefully, cut the basket tracks to width, then install them as shown.

Remove cabinet hardware, then the rails where you want to create an open cabinet. A fine-tooth pull saw works well for removing dividers, since it lies flat against the cabinet frame as it cuts. Sand the area to create a smooth surface.

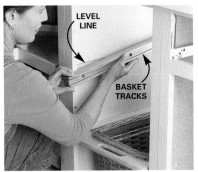

Cut the tracks to the proper width, then level them in both directions and screw them to the sides of the cabinet.

Buyer's Guide for Cabinet Facelift

All the products used in this project are readily available through catalogs, the Internet and specialty woodworking stores. Here are a few sources:

Cabinet doors and drawer fronts

A local cabinetmaker made our 13 maple doors and six drawer fronts for $1,500. Expect to pay about $20 per square foot for custom doors, slightly less for the drawer fronts. You could also have a company specializing in cabinet refacing measure and order the doors for you.

There are a variety of mail order sources you can explore:

- Custom Kitchen Cabinet and Refacing Co.: (888) 407-3322, www.reface.com
- Jackson Custom Woodworks: (866) 261-7643. www.jacksoncustom.com
- Kitchen Door Depot: (877) 399-5677, www.kitchendoordepot.com
- Rockler Custom Door and Drawer Front Program: (800) 279-4441, www.rockler.com

Crown molding, bun feet, baskets, wine glass molding

We ordered our maple rope crown molding (No. 53639, $77.99 per 8-ft. length), wicker baskets (No. 47527, $67.99 each), wine glass molding (No. 22210, $10.99 per 36-in. piece) and bun feet (No. 70410, $10.59 each) from Rockler (800-279-4441, www.rockler.com).

Outwater: (800-835-4400, www.outwater.com) and Woodworker's Supply: (800-645-9292, www.woodworker.com) sell similar items.

Miscellaneous

The porcelain pulls, dowels for the plate rack, primer and paint were bought at a home center.

We ordered the wall tile (Newport, Sage Green by Walker Zanger Ceramics, 877-504-0235, www.walkerzanger.com) from a local tile shop.

Thyme saver

Does your stew boil over every time you're distracted for five minutes looking for the right spice? Often spices are jammed into a drawer with only the tops visible. If you have this problem, take an hour to make this nifty rack that slips neatly into the drawer. Make it with leftover scraps of 1/4-in. and 1/2-in. plywood from my shop. Now spend less time cleaning the burners and more time stirring the pot!

EASY FOR EVERYONE

Swing-out wastebasket

Our hang-on-the-door swing-out wastebasket mounts on the inside of a vanity door with two plastic mirror clips. You can use any small wastebasket with a lipped edge, but the one we used is made by Rubbermaid. It's 10 in. wide, and will work on any vanity door more than 11 in. wide. This setup will work under your kitchen sink as well, using a larger wastebasket that will hold a grocery bag as a liner.

EASY FOR EVERYONE

project at a glance

skill level
beginner

special tools
drill

approximate cost
Less than $5

1 Mount two plastic mirror clips to the back of your vanity door. Make sure they're level with each other, and low enough so the wastebasket's top edge will just clear the door opening. Also, space the clips far enough apart to prevent the wastebasket from sliding from side to side. You'll probably need to use shorter screws than those in the clip package so they won't come through the other side of the door.

2 Clear out space inside the cabinet to allow room for the basket when doors are closed, then hang the wastebasket on the clips.

Replace a kitchen faucet

Just getting to it is the hard part.

nstalling a new kitchen faucet isn't tough at all. Actually, the directions that come with your new faucet are probably all you'll need to do that part of the job. Barring unforeseen problems, you could be washing up under the new faucet in an hour or so.

But what the directions *don't* mention are the bugaboos that can pop up while you're trying to get the old faucet out. You may be faced with bushwhacking your way through a dark, dank jungle of drainpipes, water lines, a garbage disposer and maybe more, just to access the faucet. Then, you'll be called on to perform pretzel-like contortions inside the sink cabinet to pull an old faucet with connections that may be so badly corroded you'll swear they're welded together. Here's what you need to know to get through the tough parts.

The right stuff

Chances are, you'll need to make more than one trip to the hardware store for parts, but to give yourself a fighting shot at completing the job with one-stop shopping, consult this list.

tip *Before disconnecting the drain lines, take a Polaroid or digital snapshot or make a sketch of the layout to help you put it all back together.*

● **Shutoff valves:** Before you shop for your new faucet (see "Selecting a Faucet," p. 112), take a look under the sink and make sure that there are shutoff valves feeding the faucet. If you don't have shutoff valves, add them. If you have them, confirm that they're in working order by turning on the hot and cold water at the faucet and shutting off the valves. If the faucet still drips, install new ones. Most likely you have 1/2-in. copper supply pipes. If so, add easy-to-install solderless "compression fitting" valves (Photos 9 and 10) to your shopping list. But if not, buy whichever valve type is compatible with your pipes.

● **Supply tubes:** Next, measure the existing supply tubes and buy new stainless steel-sleeved ones (Photo 9). They're designed to give rupture-free service for years and can easily be routed around obstacles without kinking.

● **Basin wrench:** Also buy a basin wrench ($15; Photo 4). This weird little wrench is made specifically for removing and installing those hard-to-reach fasteners that clamp older faucet assemblies to the sink. (Newer faucets have plastic wing nuts that can usually be loosened and tightened by hand.) A basin wrench's spring-loaded jaws pivot so you can either loosen or tighten nuts in tight spaces. If you need to remove drain lines to access the faucet, get a pipe wrench or a slip-joint pliers (Photo 1). For cutting copper tubes, buy a conventional tubing cutter. But if your copper supply lines are within a few inches of the back of the cabinet, buy a

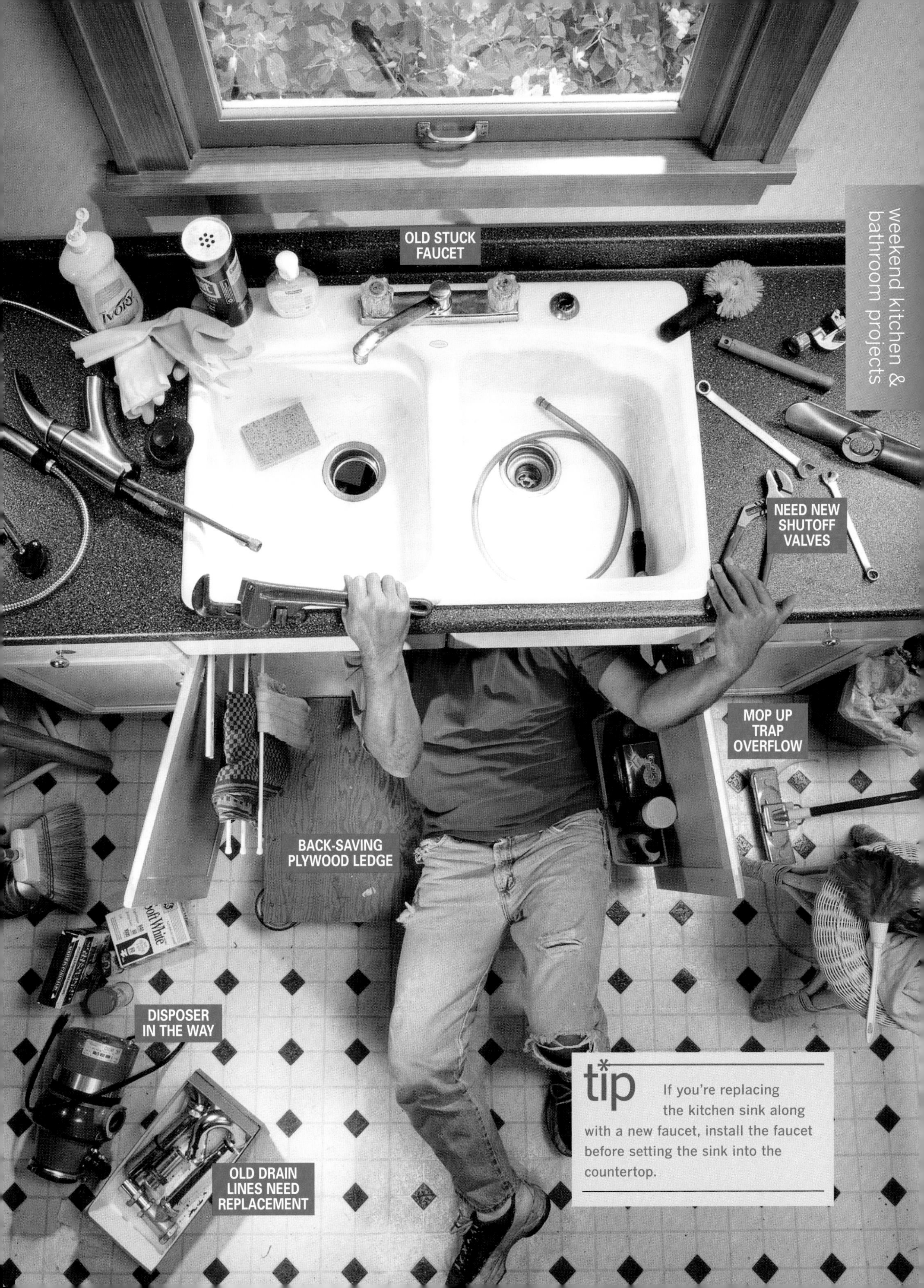

OLD STUCK
FAUCET

NEED NEW
SHUTOFF
VALVES

MOP UP
TRAP
OVERFLOW

BACK-SAVING
PLYWOOD LEDGE

DISPOSER
IN THE WAY

OLD DRAIN
LINES NEED
REPLACEMENT

tip* If you're replacing
the kitchen sink along
with a new faucet, install the faucet
before setting the sink into the
countertop.

DISHWASHER DISCHARGE HOSE

P-TRAP

WATER SUPPLY LINES (SHUTOFF VALVES MISSING)

CUSHIONED PAINT CAN

RETAINING RING

1 **Disconnect the drain lines and P-traps if they block your access to the faucet and water supply pipes. (Place a bucket or coffee can under the P-trap to dump residual water after you pull it free.)**

2 **Unplug the garbage disposer, or shut off the circuit breaker in the main service panel if the disposer is directly wired. Disconnect the dishwasher discharge line and place a 1-gal. paint can under the garbage disposer with some rags on top to cushion the disposer when it drops free. Release the disposer by tapping the retaining ring with a hammer in a counterclockwise direction.**

special mini tube cutter (Photo 3). You'll also need a set of open-end wrenches for disconnecting and hooking up the water lines.

Getting at it

After you pull out all of the cleansers, buckets and old vases from under the sink, go ahead and lie under there and see if you can easily access the faucet. If so, go right to Photo 3. If not, it's time to start dismantling the things blocking your path.

Most likely, the main obstacles will be the pipes and P-traps that drain the sinks. Don't be afraid to pull them out, but more importantly, don't be afraid to replace them with new ones. If you have older, chrome-plated drain lines, the pipe walls may be so corroded that they'll

tip Prop up a scrap of plywood on some 1-qt. paint cans in front of the cabinet. You'll be much more comfortable lying under the sink. Otherwise, the edge of the cabinet would be digging into your back (see photo, p. 109).

crush in the jaws of a pipe wrench or slip-joint pliers. After you remove them, throw all the parts in a box for matching them exactly at the store later. If you have plastic drain parts, be careful during removal—you'll probably be able to reuse them.

Sometimes a garbage disposer can be a 20-lb. roadblock. Don't be discouraged—it's easier than you think to remove it and then reinstall it after the faucet is in (Photo 2). Unplug it and pull it out of the cabinet to get it out of the way. If it's hard-wired, shut off the circuit breaker that controls the disposer, disconnect the disposer from the sink and set it aside inside the cabinet with the electrical cable still attached.

tip Plan on replacing your faucet during store hours. Chances are better than 50/50 you'll need at least one more part.

Disconnecting the old faucet

The first step in removing the old faucet is to disconnect the water supply lines (Photo 3). If there are no shutoff valves and the water pipes are hooked up directly to the

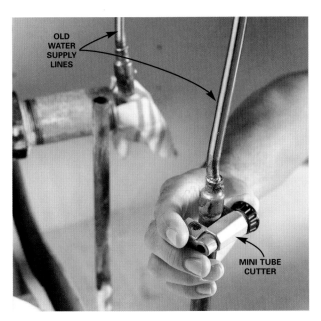

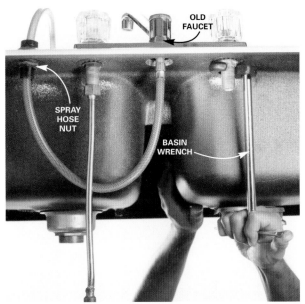

3 Shut off the water below the sink if you have valves, or shut off the main water supply valve if your old faucet is plumbed directly without valves. Open the kitchen faucet and another lower faucet to bleed off any pressure and to drain the water. If you're installing or replacing valves, cut the water lines directly below the fittings with a tube cutter or hacksaw.

4 Reach up behind the sink, fit the basin wrench jaws onto the tailpiece nuts and turn counterclockwise to loosen. Then disconnect the spray nozzle hose, remove the faucet and clean the sink area under the old faucet flange.

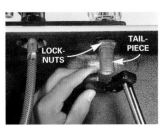

5 Follow any manufacturer's preassembly instructions and place the optional flange (see Photo 8) over the faucet opening. Finger-tighten the flange nuts underneath the sink and check the alignment of the flange, faucet and sink hole from above.

6 Check the operation of the faucet and handle to confirm you're not putting it in backward, and thread the feeder lines through the flange and sink holes. Then slip on the faucet washer, and thread on and tighten the faucet-mounting nut from below, gently spreading the faucet supply tubes if necessary to gain tool clearance (sometimes manufacturers provide a special tool for this).

FLANGE NUT

7 Hand-tighten, then snug up the flange nuts with an open-end wrench. You can only turn the wrench about a one-sixth revolution at a time.

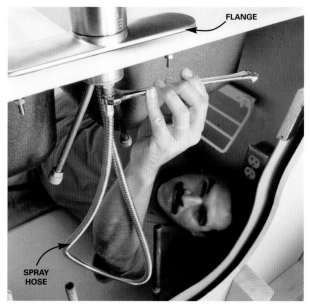

FLANGE

SPRAY HOSE

8 Thread the spray nozzle line through the faucet body, then thread the spray hose fitting onto the faucet supply tube and tighten it. Pull the nozzle out of the faucet to make sure the hose under the sink operates freely, then attach the counterweight following the manufacturer's instructions.

faucet supply lines, or if you're replacing defective valves, turn off the main water supply valve to the house and cut off the pipes (Photo 3) below the connections with a hacksaw or tube cutter. Make sure new valves are closed before turning the water back on to the house. Once the water lines are disconnected, use the basin wrench to loosen the old faucet and remove it (Photo 4).

When all else fails. . .

Sometimes, in spite of all your best efforts, it's simply impossible to loosen the old faucet nuts. Calm down! Try soaking the threads with penetrating oil and try again. If that doesn't do it, it's time to pull out all the stops and pull the sink so you can get at the nuts. It's not that tough to do. Loosen the screws on the bottom of the sink rim for a clamp-down sink, or cut the caulk between a drop-in sink and countertop with a utility knife and lift out the sink. Then you'll be able to go after those nuts with a locking pliers or a pipe wrench to free the old faucet.

Follow the manufacturer's directions to mount the new faucet, then remount the sink (with the new faucet) and hook up the water lines as we show.

Selecting a faucet

When you're buying a faucet (as with most other things), you get what you pay for. Faucets that cost less than $100 may be made of chrome-plated plastic parts with seals and valves that wear. They're OK for light-duty use but won't stand up long in a frequently used kitchen sink. Faucets that cost more than $100 generally have solid brass bodies with durable plating and washerless controls that'll give leak-free service for many, many years. Some even come with a lifetime warranty. Quality continues to improve up to about $200. Spend more than $200 and you're mostly paying for style and finish. Stick with brand name products so replacement parts will be easier to find—in the unlikely event you'll ever need them.

tip* With most faucets, only three of the four holes are covered, so you'll either need to get a blank insert or use the extra hole for a liquid soap or instant hot water dispenser. Plan to do the installation while you're under the sink with everything torn apart.

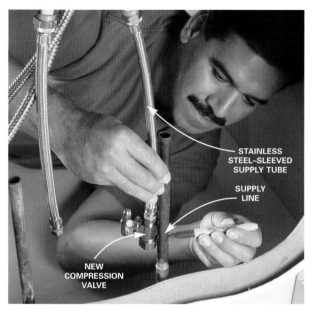

STAINLESS STEEL-SLEEVED SUPPLY TUBE

SUPPLY LINE

NEW COMPRESSION VALVE

9 Tighten the new valves onto the supply tubes and mark the feeder lines just above the compression nuts on the valves for cut-off.

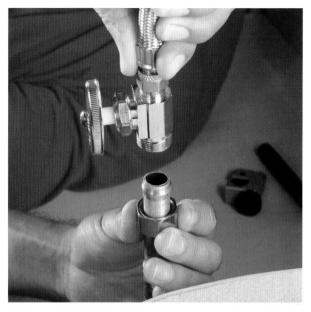

10 Clean the copper tubing with fine sandpaper, then slip the nut, compression ring and valve body over the pipe and tighten. Close the valve, turn on the main water valve and check for leaks. Place a bucket under the faucet and turn the faucet on to check for leaks. Re-assemble the garbage disposer, P-traps and drain lines.

Unclog a kitchen faucet aerator

If you get weak water flow when you turn on your faucet—whether it's brand new or ten years old—don't assume your water pressure has suddenly gone bad. You could simply have a filter screen, or aerator, that's clogged. Remove the aerator as shown in the photo, rinse it out and reinstall it. If it's corroded or worn, take it to a home center and pick up a new one ($3 to $5). Most stores have a slick gauge you can screw your old aerator onto to determine which replacement to buy. If you can't find a replacement for your aerator, soak the parts in vinegar overnight, scrub them with an old toothbrush and reinsert into the faucet (make sure to reassemble the parts in the same order you removed them).

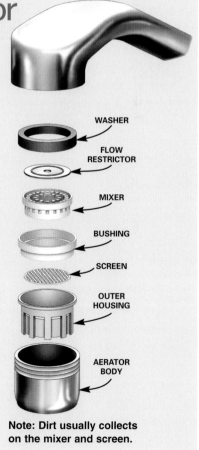

WASHER

FLOW RESTRICTOR

MIXER

BUSHING

SCREEN

OUTER HOUSING

AERATOR BODY

Note: Dirt usually collects on the mixer and screen.

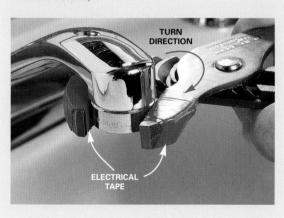

TURN DIRECTION

ELECTRICAL TAPE

Wrap the jaws of a pliers with tape to keep them from scratching the aerator. Unscrew the aerator body from the faucet and remove all the internal components. Clean and reassemble.

Space-saving cabinet

Built to nest between wall studs.

Built into the wall, between the studs, our unobtrusive cabinet extends only 2-1/4 in. into the room. Yet it can hold a small warehouse of supplies—canned goods, cereal, paper towels, six-packs of soda. Or brooms, cleaning products, mops and more. And you can build it in a weekend for less than $150.

Install it on an inside wall in the kitchen, bathroom, hallway or on any inside wall where you have drywall, and two studs that are 16 in. on-center. The stud cavities must be free of insulation, ductwork, electrical and plumbing lines. Installing the cabinet in a plaster wall, though possible, would be trickier: Cutting plaster straight is difficult, plus you'd need to add a back to the cabinet to cover the rough plaster-and-lath back wall.

The cabinet's case and shelves are made from No. 2 pine 1x6s (actual size: 3/4 x 5-1/2 in.). There's no need to cut these pieces to width, only to length. Doors are cut from 3/4-in. MDF (medium-density fiberboard). MDF is sold by some, but not all, home cen-

project at a glance

skill level
intermediate

special tools
circular saw
router
drill

approximate cost
$125–$150

materials list

- 56' No. 2 1x6 pine
- 16' No. 2 1x2 pine
- 4x8 sheet of 3/4" MDF (medium-density fiberboard)
- 56 plug-in shelf supports
- 2 piano hinges, 1-1/2" x 72" long
- 4 magnetic door catches
- 2 door pulls
- 1 tube of paintable caulk
- 1 tube of construction adhesive
- 2" and 1-5/8" No. 6 Phillips head screws
- small piece of pegboard
- paint

figure a space-saving cabinet

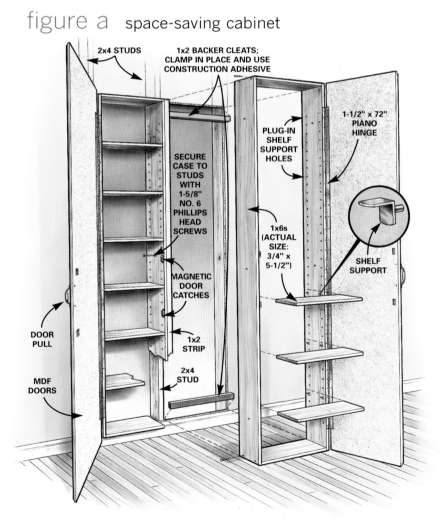

2x4 STUDS

1x2 BACKER CLEATS; CLAMP IN PLACE AND USE CONSTRUCTION ADHESIVE

1-1/2" x 72" PIANO HINGE

PLUG-IN SHELF SUPPORT HOLES

SECURE CASE TO STUDS WITH 1-5/8" NO. 6 PHILLIPS HEAD SCREWS

1x6s (ACTUAL SIZE: 3/4" x 5-1/2")

SHELF SUPPORT

MAGNETIC DOOR CATCHES

DOOR PULL

1x2 STRIP

2x4 STUD

MDF DOORS

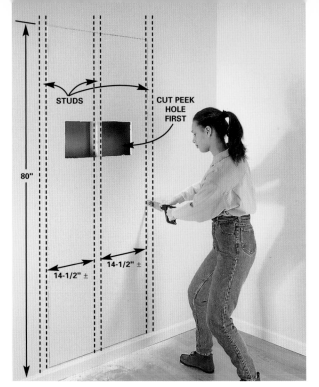

1 Mark and cut an opening in the drywall between the two studs. Hold a small saw flat against the inner edges of the studs, then cut across the top and bottom. Cut carefully so you won't have to make drywall repairs later. Before you begin the main cuts, make a smaller peek hole, just large enough to see that there are no obstructions within the two stud cavities. If the location isn't usable, you can easily patch the small hole. After the full opening is cut, check the studs to see if they are unevenly spaced, bowed or out of plumb; if so, you'll have to slightly reduce the width of the two cabinet cases and use shims when placing them so they're exactly vertical. Once you've determined the exact width of your cabinet cases, cut your 1x6 pieces to length.

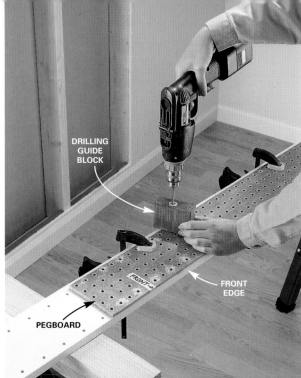

2 Drill holes for the plug-in shelf supports in the inner 1x6 sides of the case. Use pegboard, clamped in place and aligned with the *front edge*, to position the holes accurately (we drilled every other hole). Space the holes exactly the same on all four of the sides, so your shelves will be level. Tip: The drilling guide block, cut from a piece of 2x4, keeps the drill bit exactly vertical (drill the guide hole in the block as straight as possible, aligning it carefully by eye). The block also serves as a stop to prevent the bit from coming through the other side.

ters, so call around. Almost any home center will special-order it if they don't stock it. We don't recommend plywood or particleboard for doors this long; both are less stable than MDF, and could warp.

The step-by-step photos and descriptions, and the detailed drawing, provide all the information you need to build and install the cabinet. And on p. 114 you'll find a list of all the necessary materials. We painted our cabinet white, both inside and out. You could paint it the same color as the walls, so that it's hardly noticeable in the room.

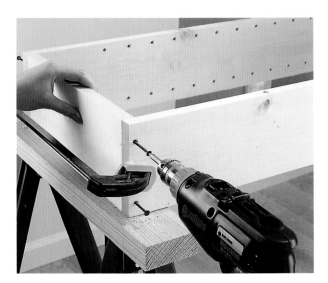

3 Assemble the two cases with 2-in. No. 6 Phillips head screws. Drill pilot holes, and countersink the screwheads to keep the wood from splitting. No glue is needed.

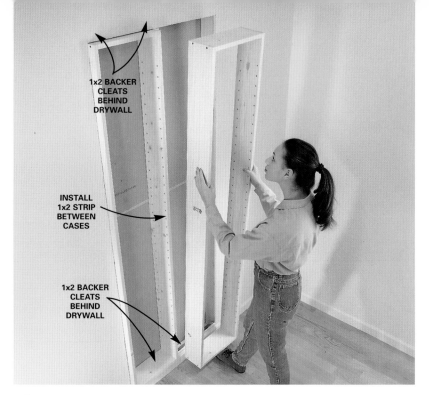

1x2 BACKER CLEATS BEHIND DRYWALL

INSTALL 1x2 STRIP BETWEEN CASES

1x2 BACKER CLEATS BEHIND DRYWALL

1/4" RADIUS COVE BIT

4 Mount the two cases in the openings between the studs. Use shims if necessary to get them level and plumb. Then slide a 1x2 strip (the same width as the thickness of the center stud) between the two cases, flush with the leading edge, as shown in Figure A, p. 114. Clamp the strip and cases together, then screw them together with 1-5/8 in. No. 6 Phillips head screws. Next, press the back edges of the cases securely against the rear drywall, and secure them to the studs with 1-5/8 in. screws. Note the 1x2 backer cleats, shown here and in Figure A; they help support the cut drywall edges at the top and bottom of the openings. Clamp these four cleats in place to the back side of the drywall with construction adhesive and allow the adhesive to dry before installing the cases in the openings.

5 Rout finished edges on the doors, after cutting them to size (cut them on a table saw or with a circular saw using a clamped-in-place straight-edge guide). We used a 1/4-in.-radius cove bit in a router to form the edges, but you could use a simple round-over bit. Sand the edges after routing.

6 Hang the doors using 1-1/2 in. wide x 72-in. long piano hinges. Getting the doors aligned can be frustrating, but here's a trouble-free method: First, mount both hinges on the case edges flush with the inside edges of the case, using only three screws. Next, set the doors in place, against the closed hinges. Prop the doors to exactly the right height with a stack of books under each door. Get a uniform 1/16-in. spacing between the two doors. Next, using a fine-tip marker, mark the position of the outside door edge on the exposed barrel of the hinge. Open one door, sliding the supporting books along under it; line up the door edge with the mark on the hinge barrel, then mark two screw hole locations on the inside of the door, as shown. Predrill small pilot holes, and install the two screws. Do the same with the other door, then check the alignment. Fine-tune the screw positions on the doors if necessary, then install the rest of the screws with a small Phillips head bit in your drill/driver.

MARK SCREW HOLE LOCATIONS IN TWO PLACES

1-1/2" x 72" PIANO HINGE

PROP DOORS TO EXACT HEIGHT WITH STACKED BOOKS

PAINTABLE CAULK

7 Caulk the joint where the drywall and case adjoin using a paintable caulk, and smooth it with your finger or a small putty knife. After priming and painting the cabinet parts and the back wall, mount the shelf supports and shelves, and install door pulls and magnetic door catches.

space-saving cabinet **117**

Open shelves

A simple way to spice up your kitchen.

Converting a few of your wall cabinets to open shelving is a great way to create display space for dishes or to keep cookbooks and cooking supplies within easy reach. Anyone handy with a paint brush can complete this project in a leisurely weekend. Don't forget to order the glass shelves about a week before you need them.

You'll need a screwdriver, hammer and tape measure as well as basic painting equipment like a paint brush, putty knife, masking tape, and sandpaper or sanding sponge. Use a drill with a 9/32-in. bit to drill holes for the metal sleeves (Photo 3).

Some cabinets, like those shown here, are easy to convert by simply removing the doors and ordering glass shelves. Others may require a little carpentry work, like removing a fixed shelf. Take a close look inside the cabinet to see whether there are hidden challenges. If it looks good, remove the doors and carefully measure for shelves. Measure from one side of the cabinet to the other and from front to back. Deduct 1/8 in. from these measurements to arrive at the glass size. Look in the Yellow Pages under "Glass" to find a company that will cut the glass and polish all of the edges. Ask the glass salesperson what thickness you need for strength and safety. Longer spans require thicker glass.

project at a glance

skill level
beginner

special tools
drill
basic painting
  tools and
  hand tools

approximate cost
$40–$50 per
cabinet

While you're waiting for the glass to arrive, paint the cabinet interiors. Choose a color that matches or complements a floor or wall color. Preparation is the key to a long-lasting, perfectly smooth paint job. Photos 1 and 2 show the painting steps. If you're painting over Melamine or another hard, shiny surface, make sure to thoroughly roughen the surface with 80-grit sandpaper and prime with shellac before brushing or spraying on the coats of paint.

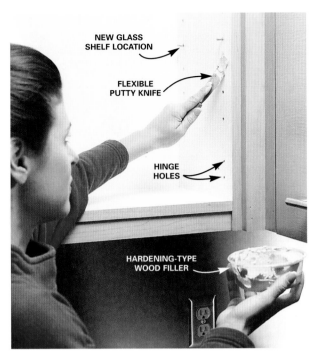

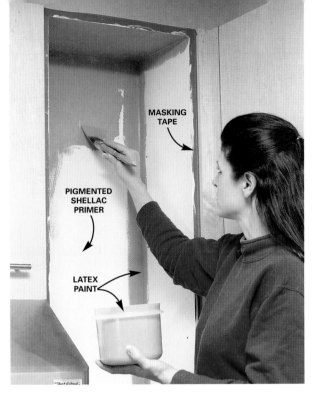

1 Remove the cabinet doors and hinges. Fill all extra shelf bracket or hinge holes with a hardening-type wood filler. Allow this to harden, sand it smooth, and apply a coat of lightweight surfacing compound to fill low spots left after the wood filler shrinks. Let the second coat dry. Then sand the entire cabinet interior with 80-grit paper to provide a "rough" surface for the paint to grab.

2 Paint the cabinet interior. Use masking tape to protect unpainted areas. Prime the interior with white pig- mented shellac (BIN is one brand) to keep the filler from showing through and to provide a binder for the final coats of paint. Sand the primer lightly with a fine sanding sponge after it dries. Remove the dust with a vacuum cleaner and brush on the final coats of latex or oil paint.

tip   If you're applying acrylic paint, add a conditioner such as Floetrol to your paint first. It will help eliminate roller and brush marks and give your cabinets a smoother finish. You can use up to one quart of Floetrol per gallon of paint. For more information go to www.flood.com.

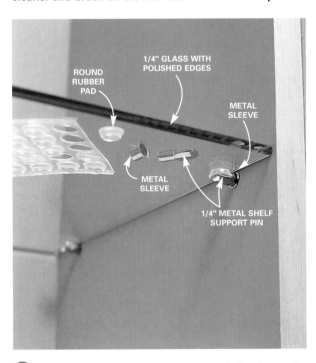

Photo 3 shows the hardware we used to support the glass shelves. If you don't have holes for the shelf pins, use a tape measure and square to mark the hole locations and bore 9/32-in. holes to accept the metal reinforcing sleeves. The shelf pins, sleeves and round rubber pads are available from Rockler Woodworking and Hardware, www.rockler.com.

3 Support glass shelves with metal shelf pins inserted into holes drilled in the cabinet sides. To prevent the pins from enlarging the holes, drill 9/32-in. holes and tap in metal sleeves. Then insert the metal shelf support pins in the sleeves and apply a self-adhesive round rubber pad to each pin to keep the glass shelves from sliding off.

Warm bathroom floors

Under-tile heat is easy to install and cheap to operate, and your feet will love it!

You finished that long, hot shower. You're squeaky clean and cozy warm—until you step onto the tile floor. Then you get another sensation—ice-cold feet. The solution isn't to banish tile from bathrooms—it's too durable, water resistant and easy to clean to do that. The answer is to warm up that tile from below with electric resistance heat.

Lots of pros, few cons

This in-the-floor heating system consists of one thin continuous cable heating element woven into a mat that you install under the tile. This makes it a project best done when overhauling or changing the floor covering of an existing room or when adding a new room. It can be installed as supplemental heat to take the chill out of the floor or as space heat to warm the entire bathroom in moderate climates. It's also a great project for warming entryway and kitchen floors.

The benefits?

- It's easy to install. You embed a cable-laced mat in the mortar when you lay the tile. If you're not comfortable with the wiring portion, hire an electrician.
- It's safe. Once the heating system is installed, it's nearly impossible to damage. The GFCI-protected thermostat instantly cuts power in the event of a short or other problem.
- It's inexpensive to operate. At 12 watts per square foot, our 30-sq.-ft. mat drew 360 watts of power—about the equivalent of an electric blanket or large TV. If you operate it only during the high-traffic morning and evening hours, this translates into 25¢ to $1 per day, depending on your location, electrical costs and the season.

project at a glance

skill level
intermediate to advanced

special tools
electrical tester
trowel
hot-melt glue gun

approximate cost
$15–$25 per sq. ft. plus cost of tile materials

- It takes up zero space. Got a big, clunky radiator? Remove it and gain valuable square footage by installing this stuff.
- It's versatile. If your existing furnace or boiler doesn't have enough oomph to heat a newly remodeled or added space, floor heat can do the job.
- It's really, really comfortable. When your feet are warm, your entire body feels warm. You'll find yourself reading and playing games with your kids on the bathroom floor.

The downside? It can't be retrofitted under existing tile floors, the total initial cost of materials is about $15 to $25 per square foot, and you'll most likely need to run new wiring from the main circuit panel to the bathroom.

Where to find electrical power

For a heated floor area less than 20 sq. ft., you could (in most cases) draw power from an adjacent GFCI-protected outlet without overloading the circuit. (If the thermostat you purchase is already GFCI protected like ours, you can use any outlet. In any case, the mat must be GFCI protected.) But a larger mat on an existing circuit—a circuit that might also accommodate a 2,000-watt hair dryer—can cause overloads and nuisance circuit breaker trips. For our larger mat, we elected to install a dedicated circuit with its own wiring and circuit breaker. Both 120-volt and 240-volt mats are available.

A programmable thermostat that turns the mat on during busy times, then off when you're sleeping or away, costs more initially but will save energy and money in the long run.

HEATING MAT

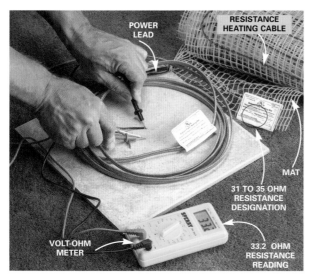

POWER LEAD

RESISTANCE HEATING CABLE

MAT

31 TO 35 OHM RESISTANCE DESIGNATION

VOLT-OHM METER

33.2 OHM RESISTANCE READING

1 Test the heating cable for manufacturing or shipping damage with a volt-ohm meter. The resistance reading on the mat label (in our case, 31-35) and the resistance registered by the meter (in our case, 33.2) should be within 10 percent of each other. If not, see the manufacturer's instructions. Digital volt-ohm meters like the one shown cost less than $30 and are easy to operate.

CEMENT BOARD SCREWS

SUBFLOOR

THIN-SET MORTAR

CEMENT BOARD

2 Install cement board over the existing subfloor. Trowel on a layer of thin-set mortar, then secure the cement board with cement board screws. Cover the seams with mesh fiberglass tape and thin-set to create a "unibody" floor. Snap chalk lines on the floor to mark the tile layout.

Special-order your custom-size mat

A number of companies offer electric resistance floor warming systems. We ordered our electric mat, thermostat and installation materials from Watts Radiant (888-432-8932; www.suntouch.net). We sent them the required detailed drawing of the bathroom floor plan and location of fixtures. In two days, they faxed back a proposed mat layout and bid. The mats come in 12-, 24- and 30-in. widths and increments of 5 ft. in length (10 sq. ft. minimum). When in doubt, the company will specify a mat smaller than you need since the mat cable can't be cut. A good instructional video comes with the materials. A few common mat sizes are beginning to be available at some home centers.

When you receive the mat, use a volt-ohm meter (Photo 1) to obtain a resistance reading to make sure it wasn't damaged during manufacturing or shipping.

Prep your floor as you would for any tiling job. Install 1/2-in. cement backer board, securing it to the existing subfloor with mortar and cement board screws (Photo 2). Tape and mortar the seams to create a solid, continuous surface. Snap tile layout lines on the floor once the mortar has dried.

Test-fit the mat to avoid glitches

Before proceeding with the actual installation, do a test layout (Photo 3). Follow these basic guidelines:

- Install the mat up to the area where the vanity cabinet or pedestal sink will sit, but not under it; that can cause excessive heat buildup.
- Keep the mat 4 in. away from walls, showers and tubs.
- Keep the mat at least 4 in. away from the toilet wax ring.
- Keep the blue heating cable at least 2 in. away from itself (Photo 5). Never overlap the cable.
- Don't leave large gaps between the mats. Your feet will be able to tell!
- If your mat is undersized, give priority to the areas where you'll be standing barefoot most often!

Following your preliminary layout, mark the path of the thick "power lead" between the mat and wall cavity (Photo 4) and chisel a shallow trench into the floor. Notch the bottom plate to accommodate the two conduits that will contain the power lead and the wires for the thermostat-sensing bulb.

tip Make sure no screw- or nailheads protrude above the cement board. A sharp edge can damage the cable.

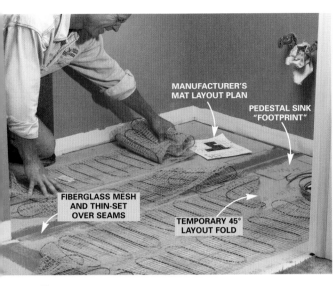

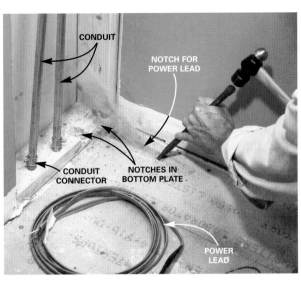

3 Test-fit the mat, keeping the cable 4 in. from fixtures and walls and 2 in. from one another. Give priority to those areas where you'll stand barefooted most. You MUST NOT cut or cross the cable, so make sure the mat fits.

4 Chisel a groove in the cement board for the enlarged portion of the power lead to nestle into. Notch the bottom plate of the wall to provide a pathway for the power lead, thermostat wires and conduit.

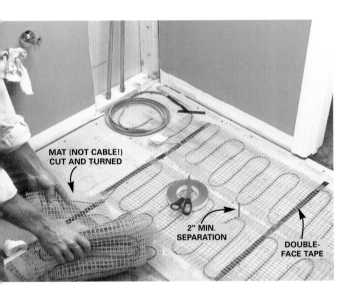

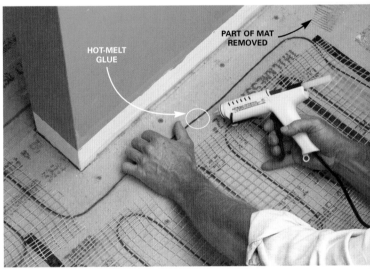

5 Install the mat, securing it lightly to the floor with double-face tape. Cut the mat (NEVER THE CABLE), then reverse direction at walls.

6 Secure individual cables to the floor using small blobs of hot-melt glue. Carefully cut and remove the orange mesh to free the cable. Do this to work around angles, obstacles and sections where full-width mats won't fit. Do not overlap the cable. When the entire mat is fitted and installed, press it firmly into the tape and hot-melt glue any loose ends or humps in the mat. Perform a resistance test (shown in Photo 1) to check for damage.

Glue and tape the mat in place

Install the mat, securing it lightly to the cement board with double-face tape (Photo 5). To make turns, cut the mat between two loops in the cable, then flip the mat and run it the opposite direction. Never, ever cut, nick or stress the cable itself. Where the full-width mat won't fit, or where you encounter angles or jogs, carefully cut the mat from around the cable, and hot-melt glue the cable

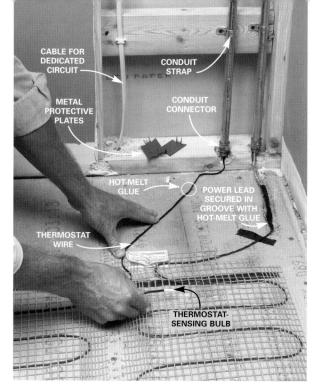

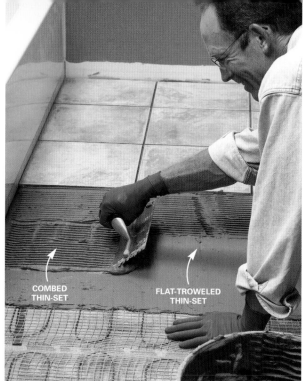

7 Fish the power lead and thermostat wires through two 58-in. lengths of conduit and connect the tops of the conduit to a 4 x 4-in. electrical box. Position the lower end of the conduits in the notches and secure the electrical box to the studs. Weave the thermostat wire through the mesh so the sensing bulb is an equal distance between wires and 12 in. into the warming area. Use hot-melt glue to secure the thermostat wires to the floor and the power lead in the groove. Cover the notches in the bottom plate with protective metal plates. Do another resistance test.

8 Apply the mortar, first pressing it firmly into the mesh and floor with the flat side of the trowel, then combing it with the notched side. Try to "float" the trowel just above the cable. Use care not to snag the mesh or nick the cable.

to the floor (Photo 6). Continue using the full mat again when you can.

Install the entire mat complete with cuts, flips and turns to make sure it fits the space right, make any final adjustments, then press the mat firmly into the tape. Use hot-melt glue to additionally secure the mat. Don't leave any humps or loose edges; you'll snag them with your notched trowel when you're applying the thin-set mortar.

If you're not going to tile right away, lay thick corrugated cardboard over the mat to protect the cable. You'll be glad you did when your kid walks in wearing baseball cleats.

Wiring setup

Install conduit connectors to both ends of two pieces of 58-in. long 1/2-in. electrical metal tubing (EMT). Fish the power lead cable through one length of conduit. Hot-melt glue the power lead into the groove. Fish the thermostat wires through a second piece of conduit,

then weave it 12 in. into the mat, keeping it equidistant from the cable on each side (Photo 7).

Secure the two lengths of conduit to a 4 x 4-in. metal electrical box. Secure this box to the studs so the lower ends of the conduits nestle into the notches you made in the bottom plate (Photo 7). Secure metal protective plates over the notches in the bottom plate to protect the wires and cable where they pass through.

Install the wiring from the area of the main circuit breaker panel (or nearby outlet) to the area of the wall cavity where the thermostat will be located. Don't do any actual wiring in the main panel yet.

tip

The No. 1 goof that people make is slamming the edge of their trowel on the floor to knock excess thin-set loose. This can result in cutting or nicking of the cable.

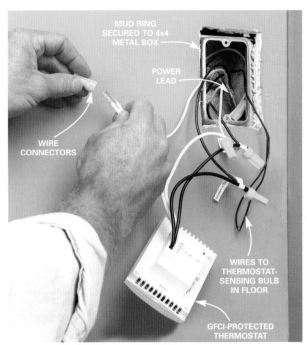

MUD RING
SECURED TO 4x4
METAL BOX

POWER
LEAD

WIRE
CONNECTORS

WIRES TO
THERMOSTAT-
SENSING BULB
IN FLOOR

GFCI-PROTECTED
THERMOSTAT

9 **Lay the tile using the chalked lines as your guide. Wiggle and tap the tiles firmly into place to create a level surface.** Readjust previously laid tiles so they remain in line and properly spaced; the thick mortar bed used to cover the cable and mesh allows for more movement than a standard tile installation. Grout the tile once the thin-set has properly set.

10 **Wire the thermostat according to the manufacturer's instructions.** Our thermostat had individual pigtails for securing the wires from the power lead and the cable running from the main panel. Have your electrician make the final connections in the main circuit panel. Power up the system for 10 or 15 minutes to ensure that the floor heat functions, then turn it off and keep it off for two to four weeks while the mastic and grout cure and harden.

Install the tile

Select tile that's at least 6 in. square so each tile will span two or more sections of cable. Smaller tiles are more likely to conform to the minor hills and valleys of the cable when you tamp them in place, creating a wavy surface.

Spread the mortar over a 5- to 10-sq.-ft. area of floor. Use the flat side of the trowel to press the mortar firmly through the mat and into contact with the cement board. You can establish a flat, uniform layer by lightly floating the trowel across the tops of the cable. Then use the notched side to comb the mortar to create ridges (Photo 8); a 3/8 x 1/4-in. trowel works well for most tiles. Again, lightly skim your trowel over the cable. The sheathing on the cable is tough, but you still need to avoid any "sawing" type action or jabs with the trowel. It takes a little trial and error to get a flat layer.

Place the tile, then tap it firmly into place with a rubber mallet. Do two resistance tests (Photo 1) while installing the tile to ensure you haven't damaged the cable. (If the resistance test fails, see the manufacturer's instructions to find the problem.) Once the mortar has dried, grout the joints.

Final steps

The instructions that came with the mat and thermostat were so darn good we felt comfortable completing the wiring of the thermostat and mat. We left installing the new circuit breaker and final connections in the main circuit panel to a licensed electrician. We suggest you do the same. Once the wiring is complete, energize the system for a few minutes to make certain the controls work and the resistance cable heats. Don't put the system into full operation until the thin-set and grout have had time to properly cure and harden—usually two to four weeks.

Then call the family together and play a game of Scrabble on your cozy, warm bathroom floor.

Door-mounted spice & lid racks

An easy project providing easy access.

These simple racks will help transform those chaotic gangs of spice bottles and pan lids into orderly regiments. We show you how to build only the spice rack; the lid rack uses the same steps but without the shelves. Each spice rack can hold 20 to 30 bottles, and each lid rack two to six lids, depending on the height and width of your cabinet doors. Before building, measure your spice bottles and lids to determine the spacing of your shelves and dowels. Here are other key measurements and clearances to keep an eye on:

Existing shelf depth. If the existing cabinet shelves are full depth, narrow them by about 2 in. to accommodate each door-mounted rack. Shelves that are permanently affixed in grooves in the cabinet sides will need to be cut in place with a jigsaw. Adjustable shelves can be removed, cut along the back side with a circular saw or table saw, then replaced. You may need to move brackets or add holes to remount narrowed shelves.

Spice rack depth and positioning. Make certain the new rack won't hit the cabinet frame when the door swings. We found that fitting the rack between the two 2-in. wide vertical stiles (Photo 1) gave us adequate room.

tip* Use high-gloss polyurethane for natural wood, high-gloss enamel for painted wood. These finishes are more "scrubbable."

If your doors are solid wood or laminate, hold in place a scrap of wood the same depth as the spice rack (2-1/2 in. was the depth we used) and swing the door. Move it away from the door edge until it no longer makes contact with the cabinet frame, then mark the door. This will determine the overall width of your spice rack.

We used soft, easy-to-nail pine and basswood for both the spice and the lid racks. If you're using a harder wood, like maple or oak, position the pieces, then predrill holes through the side pieces and into the shelf ends. This will prevent splitting and make nailing easier. Install your shelves one at a time so you don't have to balance and juggle multiple pieces as you work. Always nail on a flat, solid surface.

project at a glance

skill level
beginner

special tools
jigsaw
drill

approximate cost
Less than $10

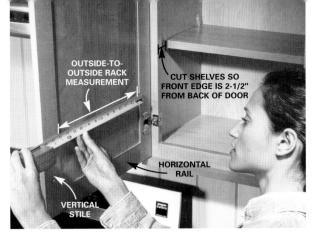

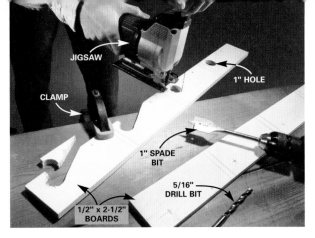

1 Measure the distance between the two vertical stiles and the two horizontal rails to determine the outside dimensions of your spice rack. Cut existing shelves back 2 in. so they don't interfere with the rack when the door is closed.

2 Transfer the dimensions from Figure A onto 1/2 x 2-1/2 in. side boards. Cut out the sides of the spice rack. Drill 1-in. holes to create the circular shape, then finish the cutout with a jigsaw. Drill 5/16-in. holes for the dowels. Sand the edges and surfaces smooth.

figure a
swing-out spice rack
Dimensions will vary according to the size of your cabinet doors

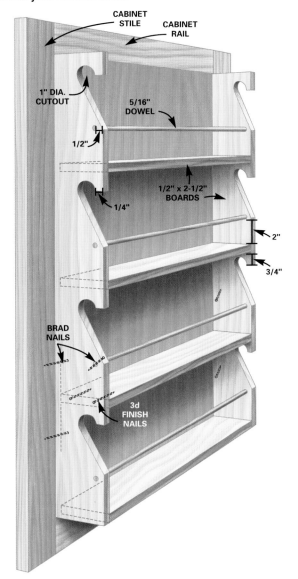

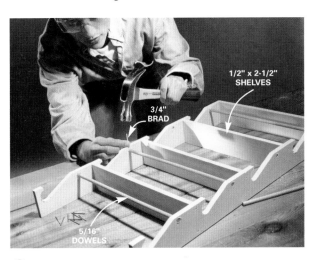

3 Glue and nail the shelves in place one at a time, using 3d finish nails. Then use 3/4-in. brads to pin the dowels in place. Sink all nailheads using a nail set. Apply polyurethane or other finish to match the cabinets.

4 Clamp the finished rack to the door, then drill angled pilot holes through the rack and into the door every 8 in. Secure with brad nails (remove the door for this step if you find you need a more solid surface for hammering). Use carpenter's glue for a more permanent installation.

Hand-held shower head

EASY FOR EVERYONE

Functional and luxurious.

A detachable hand-held shower head with an adjustable, pulsating spray gives you the luxury of all-over-the-body water massage, plus it's great for washing the kids, the dog and the tub and shower walls. The new head simply screws on in place of the old.

project at a glance

skill level
beginner

special tools
wrench
pliers

approximate cost
$35–$75

1 Remove your old shower head with a pliers. Use a small wrench or another pliers to keep the shower arm from turning. Pad the wrench teeth with a folded piece of cloth so they won't mar the shower arm.

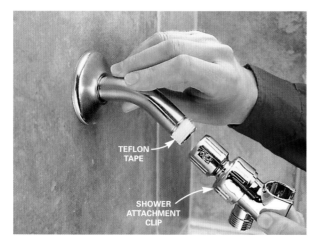

2 Mount the shower attachment clip to the shower arm after cleaning off the old threads and wrapping them (clockwise) with Teflon plumber's tape. Tighten with a pliers using a folded cloth to protect the finish.

3 Screw the shower hose to the attachment clip and tighten with a pliers. In most cases, you won't need Teflon tape on these threads, but check the instructions that came with your new shower head.

5 section

weekend wall, flooring & interior projects

Rag-rolled walls

Add a touch of classical artistry to your favorite room.

Are you bored by the prospect of just rolling another ordinary coat of paint on your walls? Try the sponge-applied, parchment glaze that we show here. The subdued color and subtle texture mark the room as something special, and showcase your furniture, wall hangings and floor coverings.

Called by various names—rag rolling, glazing, faux finishing, sponge painting—the application techniques vary. The technique we show here involves applying thinned-down paints (glazes) with a sponge, then patterning this wet glaze with a cheesecloth and dry brush.

You don't need to be a pro to get great results, but you do need to practice a bit before you start. Do this on large sheets of inexpensive drawing paper, scrap drywall, or the walls in your laundry room.

SELF-ADHESIVE MASKING PAPER

BASE COLOR

1 Apply self-adhesive masking paper to trim, pressing it tightly in place to avoid paint seepage. Also cover windows and large woodwork with plastic or dropcloth, as shown in Photo 6. Mask off the ceiling if it's smooth; if it's textured, you'll just have to work carefully.

2 Roll on a base color of eggshell (semigloss) latex paint. The semigloss finish will allow you to wipe the glaze off a section and start over if you don't like the way it turns out. Allow the base color to dry overnight before applying the glaze.

MIXING CONTAINER NO. 1

MIXING CONTAINER NO. 2

SAMPLE BOARD

MINERAL SPIRITS

MIXING CONTAINER NO. 3

4'

4'

3 Mix the three glaze colors in three mixing containers. All the glaze colors are oil-based, so they dry slowly, allowing time to manipulate the wet glaze on the wall. Note the sample board in the background. We made this before applying the base coat (Photo 2) to be sure we had the colors we wanted, and also to test our three glaze mixes against.

4 Pour each glaze mixture into a tray, and begin by brushing the two darker colors onto the corners of one wall. Make alternate dashes—each about 6 to 10 in. long—in the corner with these two colors. Start in the least conspicuous corner of the room. As you can see in Photo 6, you'll want the corners a bit darker than the rest of the wall for the proper effect. Brush about 4 ft. up and 4 ft. across, since you're going to want to complete an area of about this size before moving on to the next area. That's about as much as you can comfortably reach with just arm movement.

CAUTION: OIL-BASED PAINTS AND MINERAL SPIRITS ARE BOTH FLAMMABLE AND TOXIC. USE THEM IN A WELL-VENTILATED ROOM AND FOLLOW ALL THE SAFETY PRECAUTIONS ON THE LABEL. TAKE CARE TO PREVENT SPONTANEOUS COMBUSTION OF SATURATED RAGS. WHEN YOU'RE DONE, DON'T BALL THEM UP. INSTEAD, HANG THEM OUT IN THE OPEN UNTIL COMPLETELY DRY, THEN DISPOSE OF THEM.

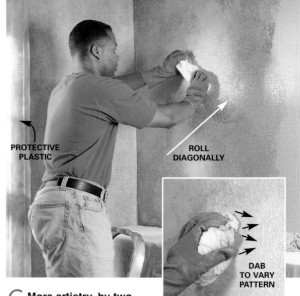

DAB
TO VARY
PATTERN

PROTECTIVE
PLASTIC

ROLL
DIAGONALLY

5 Here's where some artistry begins. Using a different sponge for each color, dip the sponges into the glaze and dab each of them randomly on the wall within your irregularly shaped, 4 x 4-ft. working area. Cover about one-third of the area with each color. Some overlapping of colors, and an occasional drip, run or drag is OK, but avoid a pattern of geometric shapes. However, throughout the work, try to maintain the same arm movements, so that the room will have a consistent directional pattern to it. Don't be shy about applying the glaze. If you don't like what you've done, you can wipe the whole mess off and start over again.

6 More artistry, by two alternating methods: First, as shown above, roll a 5-ft. strip of cheesecloth into a loosely gathered hotdog shape about a foot long. Using both hands, roll the cheesecloth diagonally up the wall to spread and texture the glaze. Be careful not to drag the cloth.

Second, after every two or three passes with the roll, loosely wad up the cheesecloth and dab at the glaze to vary the pattern, as shown in inset photo, above. Avoid geometric patterns, and think clouds.

Avoid rolling or dabbing all the way to the edges of the section you're working on; you want the edges to remain wet to link up with your next work section. When the cheesecloth starts getting saturated, start a new piece.

As a general rule, you can expect the sponged glaze/rag rolling technique to cost you two or three times as much as ordinary painting, and take you about twice as long.

As you move from area to area, don't allow the adjoining area edges to dry before you get back to them—keep a wet edge, or you'll have a visible seam, which will destroy the effect. *The oil-based glaze will give you about 30 minutes of working time.* So, from this point on, you need to work quickly without stopping, and have all your materials at hand to complete the whole room, including strips of cheesecloth cut about 5 ft. long for Step 6. If the phone rings, ignore it. If you must stop, finish the wall and stop at a corner.

● **Sponges and supplies:** You'll need three sponges. By far the best sponges to use are the large-size natural kind shown in Photos 4 and 5, but they can cost more than $20 each. If that stuns you, large artificial sponges will also work, but you'll have to be a bit more clever about how you hold them when applying the glaze.

● **Other supplies:** You'll also need mineral spirits, three mixing containers, four brushes, a roller, three paint trays, and about 10 sq. yds. of tight-weave (90-grade) cheesecloth.

DAB WITH
DRY BRUSH

7 With a dry, soft brush, dab at the corners where you can't get at the wet glaze with the cheesecloth. Blend the corner textures smoothly together, keeping them slightly darker than the walls. Also dab any areas of the wall that need attention, altering the glaze to suit your fancy and disguise obvious sponge or cheesecloth marks. Wipe the brush bristles clean with a dry rag after every 8 or 10 dabs.

tip* Think of cloud shapes as you dab on the glaze. The results you want look something like what's shown in Photo 6. Wear rubber gloves; this can get a bit sloppy.

Quick and easy touch-ups

Need a handy container for small touch-up jobs? Use the plastic measuring cup that comes with powdered laundry detergent. The handle makes for easy holding while you dip and swipe your brush, and the cup is disposable to boot.

Handy Hints®

Belt-mounted tape dispenser

Use your belt as a close-at-hand tape dispenser. Slide a roll of tape onto the belt and loosely refasten it. Pull tape off as needed.

Using swatches

When you choose room colors, you can select them all from the families of colors on a single paint swatch; select one for the trim, one for the walls and one for the ceiling. As a rule of thumb, if your ceilings are less that 9 ft. tall, paint them two shades lighter than the walls. If they're taller, paint them two shades darker. For the trim, select a color within the same family.

Simple stenciling

Beautiful walls from an ancient art.

Stenciling is a traditional decorative technique that perfectly complements a Craftsman-style room. And it's perfectly easy to learn, too. If you can handle a paint brush and a tape measure, you can quickly master the techniques for applying an attractive, simple border. And with a little practice, you can tackle complex patterns using multiple stencils and colors— and even create your own designs.

The key tools are a special stenciling brush ($10; Photo 2) and the stencil and paint. A wide variety of each are available at craft and art supply stores. You can also find stencil patterns at bookstores or on the Internet, or even buy stencil blanks and cut your own with an X-Acto knife. We bought our stencil, a pattern called

project at a glance

skill level
beginner

special tools
stenciling brush
masking tape

approximate cost
$50–$100
depending on
cost of stencil

EASY FOR EVERYONE

Ginkgo Frieze, from www.fairoak.com for $42. Match the brush size to the area being filled within the stencil. We used a 1/2-in., medium-size brush, which is a good, all-purpose size. You can use almost any paint—artist acrylics, wall paints or the special stenciling paints sold at craft and art supply stores. We used artist acrylic paint for our stencil.

Plan the layout

Position your stencil on the wall at the desired height and mark the alignment holes or top edge. Then snap a light, horizontal chalk line around the room at that height. We used blue chalk for photo clarity, but make sure that whatever color you use wipes off easily. Or use faint pencil marks, which can be easily removed or covered later.

The key to a good layout is to avoid awkward pattern breaks at doors, windows and corners. To work out the best spacing, measure the stencil pattern and mark the actual repetitions on the wall. Vary the spacing slightly as needed to make the pattern fall in a pleasing way. Or if your stencil has multiple figures, you can alter the spacing between them, as we did here. Start your layout at the most prominent part of the room and make compromises in less visible areas. Draw vertical lines at the pattern center points to make positioning easier.

Dab on the paint

Tape the stencil pattern up on the alignment marks (Photo 1) and put a small quantity of paint on a paper plate. Push the stenciling brush into the paint just enough to coat the tips of the bristles, then pat off the excess on a dry cloth or newspaper, making sure the paint spreads to all the bristles as you do so (Photo 2). The brush should be almost dry— remember, it's easier to add paint than it is to take it away.

Lightly dab on the paint (Photo 3). Hold the stencil pattern with your free hand to keep it still and flat. Don't worry about getting paint on the stencil, but avoid wiping or stabbing too hard around the edges. You can cover the cutout completely or work for shading effects. Cover

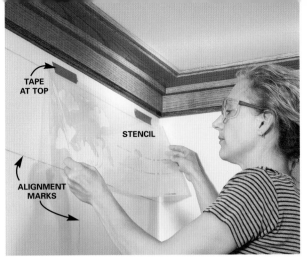

1 Snap lines on the wall to align with the alignment marks on your stencil. Tape the stencil in place along the top edge with removable masking tape.

2 Dab the special stenciling brush into the paint, then pat off the bristles on a dry cloth. Leave the brush almost dry.

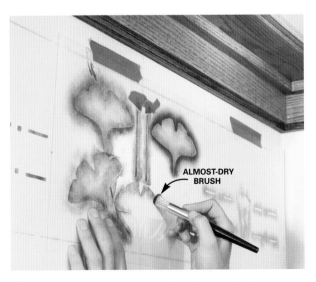

3 Apply the paint to the stencil with light dabbing and swirling motions until the stencil area is covered. Work in from the edges, brushing toward the center.

simple stenciling **135**

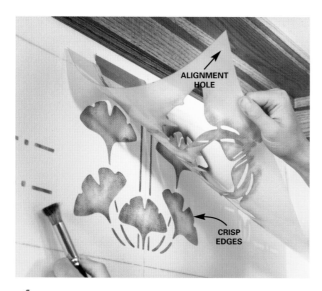

ALIGNMENT HOLE

CRISP EDGES

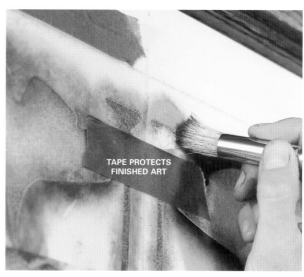

TAPE PROTECTS FINISHED ART

4 Lift the stencil up on the tape hinges and check for paint drips and for clear, sharp edges. Lay the stencil back down and touch up if necessary.

5 Allow the first color to dry, then tape the stencil up on the same marks and apply the second color. Cover nearby areas of the stencil to avoid getting paint in them.

nearby cutouts with masking tape so you don't accidentally get paint in them (Photo 5).

Mistakes are easy to correct. You can lift the stencil (Photo 4) and wipe off any paint that's smeared under the edge with a damp paper towel, or touch it up later with wall paint. If you wipe some of the stenciled area away, just lay the stencil down again and touch up.

Our stencil design called for two colors, so we masked off the cutout where the second color would go, stenciled on the first color all the way around the room, then went back and added the second color, following our original alignment marks (Photo 5). Additional colors and even additional stencil patterns can be added in this manner.

Fix that loose seam in a vinyl floor

Two sure-fire methods.

EASY FOR EVERYONE

If you have an open seam in your vinyl floor, don't procrastinate. Foot traffic can wreck the vinyl's exposed edges, making a good-looking repair impossible. Worse, water can seep into the opening, leading to subfloor damage. Start by inspecting the seam. Press the loose edges down to make sure they'll still join to form a tight seam.

If the seam closes neatly, you can make a nearly invisible repair using "multipurpose" vinyl adhesive ($5) and a seam sealing kit ($12). Vacuum out any grit under the vinyl—even a tiny grain of sand can create a pimple on the vinyl's surface. Curl the vinyl back as you vacuum, but be careful not to kink or crack it. If the vinyl is too stiff to bend, soften it with heat from a hair dryer. You can leave most of the old adhesive alone, but scrape away loose spots. A putty knife bent in a vise makes a good scraper. It's also a handy adhesive applicator (Photo 1). After you spread the adhesive, rub down the

BENT PUTTY KNIFE

seam with a block of wood. Use a wet rag to wipe away any adhesive that squeezes out of the joint. Then lay wax paper over the seam, followed by a scrap of plywood. Weigh down the plywood with stacks of books or buckets of water. Leave the weights in place for at least 10 hours. Then apply the seam sealant (Photo 2). Sealant is available in gloss and satin versions to match your floor's sheen.

If the edges are damaged or the seam won't close neatly, the best repair is a metal transition strip (below right) that completely hides the seam. Transition strips ($5 to $15) are available at home centers and hardware stores in various styles, lengths and finishes.

project at a glance

skill level
beginner

special tools
putty knife

approximate cost
$20

Method 1

SEAM SEALANT

STRAIGHTEDGE

1 Protect the floor with masking tape and apply an even coat of adhesive. Then lay wax paper over the seam and press it down with a board and weights overnight.

2 Apply a bead of seam sealant over the seam. Hold a straightedge about 1/4 in. away from the seam to guide the applicator nozzle, but don't get sealant on the straightedge.

Method 2

TRANSITION STRIP

DAMAGED SEAM

Use a metal transition strip to cover a seam that has damaged edges. Cut the strip to length with a hacksaw, then nail or screw it into place.

Wallpaper simplified

A pro shows you how to handle common problems with ease.

If you want to change the entire character of a room fast, hang wallpaper. You can change a dull room into a dramatic personal statement in less than a weekend, and you don't need a bunch of expensive tools to do the job. In fact, you can buy all the tools you'll need for less than $40.

This kind of transformation does require patience, careful planning and familiarity with key techniques. We asked a professional hanger to demonstrate every technique you'll need, start to finish, and to show you how to save time and avoid a heap of frustration.

The techniques we show apply to 90 percent of papers you'll find at wallpaper stores. We won't cover the specialty papers (such as grass cloth, foil, fabric and ones that require pretrimming). We recommend you master the basics before taking on these papers. Nor will we address removing old paper.

With our instructions, you can successfully wallpaper a room even if you haven't done it before. Start with a simple bedroom or dining room, a space that doesn't require a lot of fitting and trimming. With experience, you can tackle tougher rooms like kitchens and baths.

Selecting wallpaper

For your first time papering, we recommend that you buy from a paint and wallcovering store. The staff can advise you on the best primers, paste and tools for the particular paper you select. They'll answer any questions unique to your situation. Tell the salesperson where you'll be using the paper, and ask what features you'll need to meet the demands of the room. Prices average $20 to $50 per roll, but some specialty papers can cost as much as $100 a roll.

Our paper (see style numbers, p. 143) cost $40 a roll and took three weeks to arrive. We used 11 rolls for our 12 x 12-ft. room.

Selection tips:

- If your room has crooked walls (check them with a level and a long, straight board), consider a paper with a random pattern so the crooked corners aren't so noticeable.
- Big prints and dark colors will make a room feel cozy, but make sure the room is large enough to view the pattern from a comfortable distance.
- Small prints and light colors make a room feel larger.
- Once you get your paper, unroll it and inspect it for flaws. Save the run and dye lot numbers for ordering matching paper in the future.
- Read and follow the hanging instructions of the paper you've selected. Pros always do. Fail to follow instructions and you could void the paper's warranty. Or worse yet, it could fall off the wall. See p. 143 for more buying details.

Prepare the walls

It's far easier to paper a room if it's empty. If it isn't possible to remove all the furniture in the room, move it to the center and cover it with plastic. Turn off the electrical power to the switches and outlets at the service panel and remove the cover plates. Place a canvas dropcloth over the floor to catch any dripping primer or paste (plastic dropcloths are too slippery).

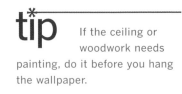

tip If the ceiling or woodwork needs painting, do it before you hang the wallpaper.

Scan the wall with a utility light to highlight any imperfections, and fill or sand them down. Don't cheat on this step; some papers can actually accentuate cracks and bumps in a wall. If a wall is in really rough shape, ask the salesperson about "liner paper." Hang it like wallpaper over the wall to smooth it out. Then apply your wall-

1 Repair any dings or cracks in the walls with joint compound and drywall tape. Sand the repairs smooth. Mask off trim and apply an acrylic undercoat (sizing) over all surfaces to be wallpapered. Cut in the edges and corners with a brush. Allow it to dry overnight or the time specified on the label before applying the wallcovering.

Gather your tools and set up your workstation

Pros use a special table made of basswood because it's a good surface to cut on and easy on razor blades. Rent one from a wallpaper store ($20 per day), or substitute a 36-in. hollow-core door or a 3 x 6-ft. piece of 3/4-in. plywood resting on a pair of sawhorses. Soften the plywood edges with sandpaper so you don't accidentally tear your paper.

You can buy all the specialty tools you need at a wall-covering store or home center. Purchase a vinyl smoother ($2; Photo 8), a snap-off razor with an extra pack of blades ($7; Photo 9), a seam roller ($2; Photo 11) and two 6-in. broad knives ($5 each; Photo 9). You may already have the other items you need: a 6-ft. step-ladder, a 5-gallon bucket, a paint roller and 3/8-in. nap roller cover, a sharp scissors, a 4-ft. level, a 10-ft. or longer tape measure and a sponge.

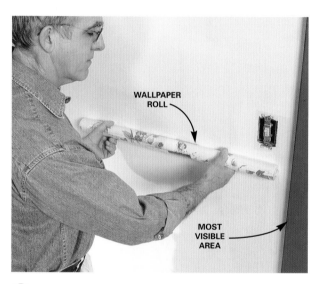

2 Mark the position of each sheet with a pencil, using the roll of wallpaper as a guide. Start your first sheet in the most visible corner and work around the room in both directions to the least noticeable corner. Adjust your starting point to avoid narrow strips (less than 2 in.) along windows, doors or corners.

paper over it. Consider a heavyweight vinyl- or fabric-backed commercial paper with a dull background if your walls are lightly textured. Otherwise, skim-coat or sand them smooth.

Wash the walls down with TSP (trisodium phosphate), or a TSP substitute, to dissolve grease, oils and other dirt, then rinse with clean water. Next apply a 100 percent acrylic prewallcovering primer/ sizer, which is available at wallpaper stores for about $20 a gallon (Photo 1). This gives you more working time to slide the paper into position. The primer also helps control

shrinking, which could result in seams opening up, and allows you to remove the paper more easily when it's time for a change. Prewall primer dries fast and is difficult to remove, so wash your brushes quickly and don't get it on your hands.

tip* If you're hanging a dark paper, have the wall-covering store tint the primer the dominant color of the paper to disguise gaps at the edges or seams.

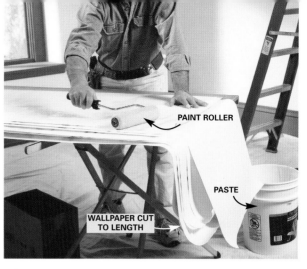

3 Draw a light plumb line with a pencil from ceiling to floor at your starting point, using a 4-ft. level as a guide. Measure the height of the wall and add a total of 4 in. for trimming the paper at the top and bottom. Cut strips from the roll to your measurement length with scissors.

4 Place the cut strips face down on the worktable. Paste the bottom half of a sheet evenly with a 3/8-in. nap roller, dipping it in a 5-gallon bucket with paste in it. Cover the edges by laying the upcoming strips under the one you're pasting; excess paste will be rolled onto the upcoming sheets. This will keep your worktable clean.

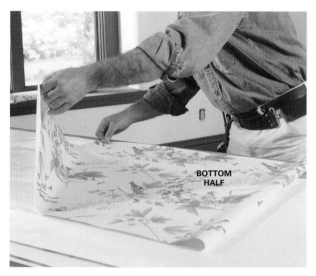

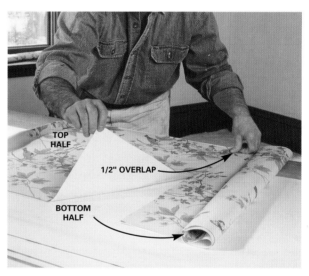

5 "Book" the bottom half of the paper by folding the pasted faces together. Align the edges to keep the paste from drying out.

6 Roll up the bottom half loosely, slide the top half onto the table and spread more paste. Book the top half over so it overlaps the bottom edge by 1/2 in. Roll it up and allow the entire sheet to rest for the time specified by the manufacturer, about 10 minutes.

Plan carefully to avoid wrestling with tiny strips

Planning the sheet layout will let you visualize all your cuts and allow you to make adjustments to the beginning and end points. Ideally, you would hang your first sheet, come full circle and the pattern would match perfectly. That's not going to happen. Put that final joint where it's least visible. Your goals are to have the patterns match at corners where they're most noticeable and avoid hanging strips less than a few inches wide. Narrow strips can be tricky (and frustrating) to hang.

Start your trial layout at the most visible corner of the room—across from a door in our case—and work around the room in both directions, meeting at the least visible spot. Use a roll of paper to roughly space how the sheets will align on the wall (Photo 2). If your layout leaves strips less than 2 in. wide against a door or into a corner, adjust your starting point by about 6 in. Our first layout left

tip A pattern mismatch will always occur somewhere in the room, so plan it where it's least visible.

7 **Align the top half of the paper's edge to the plumb line, overlapping the ceiling molding by a few inches. Let the other edge hang loose to make positioning easier.**

8 **Pull a vinyl smoother across the paper. Move up and down along the plumbed edge, then diagonally away from it, to work out bubbles and wrinkles. Align and flatten the bottom half the same way.**

a tiny strip along a door, so we shifted it over to overlap the trim. The sheets now meet in an inconspicuous corner behind the door.

A good level gets you started straight

More often than not, the corners of the room and the door and window molding will be a little crooked or out of plumb. Taking the time to set a plumb line with a level to start your first sheet and near each corner will provide consistent reference points to align the wallpaper on each wall. This makes hanging a whole lot easier (Photo 3).

Pros will cut all the full-length strips needed for a room before they start pasting. For your first time, we recommend cutting only two or three sheets ahead. Measure the height of the wall and add a few inches to the top and bottom, enough extra to shift the pattern up and down for the best position.

tip To line up sheets, focus your eyes on a dominant element and the rest of the pattern will line up.

9 **Trim the overhanging paper with a sharp razor knife, using a 6-in. broad knife as a guide. Slide the broad knife across while leaving the tip of the razor in the paper until the cut is complete. Press just hard enough to cut through the wallcovering, not the drywall behind it.**

An even paste job and proper booking ensure tight seams

If your paper requires paste, use the type that's recommended in the instructions or by your supplier. Premixed is easiest. We're using "clear hang" premixed adhesive. It took 2 gallons of paste for our 12 x 12-ft. room with 9-ft. high walls. Many papers come prepasted. Roll these into a tray of water to activate the paste. Your supplier may recommend a special activator for certain prepasted papers to guarantee they'll stick to the wall.

Paste the back evenly (Photo 4). Roll it perpendicular to the long edge to move paste to the edges, then back and forth the long way again till the paste is evenly spread.

The strips of paper need time to "relax," that is, expand slightly because of the moisture in the paste. Booking the paper (Photos 5 and 6) keeps the paste from

Crucial details for buying wallpaper

The back of the wallpaper sample tells about ordering, durability and the essential hanging details you need to know. If the sample doesn't have this information, ask the salesperson about each of the following categories.

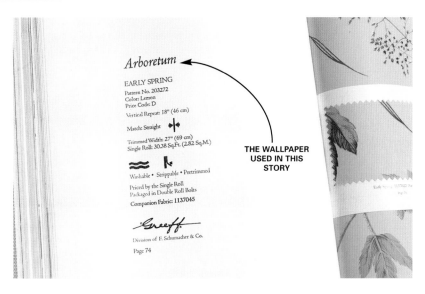

Arboretum

EARLY SPRING
Pattern No. 203272
Color: Lemon
Price Code: D
Vertical Repeat: 18" (46 cm)

Match: Straight

Trimmed Width: 27" (69 cm)
Single Roll: 30.38 Sq.Ft. (2.82 Sq.M.)

Washable • Strippable • Pretrimmed

Priced by the Single Roll
Packaged in Double Roll Bolts
Companion Fabric: 1137045

Greeff

Division of F. Schumacher & Co.

Page 74

THE WALLPAPER USED IN THIS STORY

Vertical repeat
The repeat is the length of the image before it shows itself again. Repeats can range from none, for a covering without a pattern, to more than 36 in. Order extra paper for repeats more than 24 in.; you'll waste a lot when matching the pattern.

Match
The match is how the patterns align sheet to sheet. Our straight match requires shifting the pattern to have all the birds at the same distance from the ceiling.

With a random match, you don't have to fuss with lining up patterns from sheet to sheet. This is the easiest pattern to hang.

You align the pattern of a drop match halfway down the repeat. With drop matches, plan the dominant elements so you don't slice them off at the ceiling.

Single roll/double roll
Look for the square foot coverage to calculate how many rolls you'll need to cover a room. In double-roll bolts, the paper is twice as long as on a single roll. Compared with a single roll, this provides more usable square footage of paper. Add up the area of the walls (minus doors and windows) and divide by the number of square feet listed on the roll. Round up your calculation to the nearest roll. Order at least one extra roll, two if you've got a lot of tricky cuts or angles. The worst thing that can happen when wallpapering is to run out of paper!

Washable
Washability is the degree of cleaning a paper can take before showing wear. If a paper isn't washable, use it only in areas that aren't subject to a lot of abuse.

Pretrimmed
Most wallpapers are pretrimmed, which means the edges are perfectly cut and all ready for hanging. Don't store or drop pretrimmed papers on the ends because you'll mar the edges. Untrimmed papers require a good straightedge and experience to cut. Stick with a pretrimmed paper for your first hanging experience.

---

drying out while the paper adjusts. This is a critical step: If the paper doesn't sit long enough, it could shrink on the wall, resulting in open seams, blisters or curling. Set a timer to remind you when a sheet is ready. You can let a sheet sit for a little longer than the booking time but never less.

Plan ahead. Paste two or three sheets in a row if you're working on a blank wall that requires full sheets. Paste only one if you're coming up on a tricky window or corner that'll take some time to fit.

You'll see the payoff when you hang the first sheet

After the booking time is up, unroll your sheet and carry it to the wall. Gently unfold the top half. Standing on a stepladder, align the sheet to your plumb line (Photo 7). Leave the bottom half booked to keep the paste from drying out while you're positioning the top. Even though it might seem easier to butt the paper right up to the ceiling, don't try it. You'll get a much better fit and professional look by leaving it long and then trimming it off

SEAM

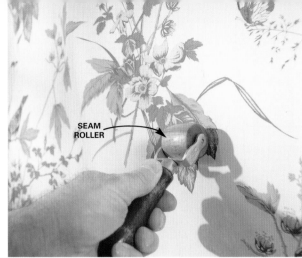

SEAM ROLLER

10 Loosely set one edge of the second sheet on the wall and align the pattern to the first. Precisely butt the second sheet to the first, leaving the other edge loose.

11 Press the edge to the wall with a seam roller, then work out the wrinkles with the smoother. Set the top half first, then unfold and set the bottom half. Wipe off any paste from the surface with a clean, damp sponge.

later (Photo 9). Once the paper is aligned, work out wrinkles with a vinyl smoother (Photo 8). If you have a wrinkle that's not smoothing out, pull one edge of the paper away from the wall, keeping the plumbed edge in place, and reset. Finish the top half while you're on the ladder, then come down and unfold, align, smooth and trim the bottom half.

Trim the paper in place to ensure a perfect fit

For straight, clean cuts, trim off the overlap by guiding the blade against a broad knife (Photo 9). Keep your blade sharp. The most common novice mistake is to try to economize on razor blades. A dull blade will tear the paper. Advance a new blade after every few cuts (after every one if you're using heavyweight paper).

Pick a leaf, branch or other element to help align the second sheet (Photo 10). Gently slide it into position to align the pattern and seam, but don't stretch the paper or it could shrink later. With some papers, the pattern may not perfectly align the full length of the sheet. Align these at eye level where it's most noticeable.

Go over the seam with the smoother, roll it with a

tip Our consultant noticed that the pattern repeated twice across the width of our paper. To avoid a mismatched corner, he held up a second sheet, found where the pattern aligned and cut a strip lengthwise. If your paper doesn't allow this, hang a full sheet—only **your** eyes will notice the mismatch.

seam roller (Photo 11), then smooth out the rest of the sheet. Wipe down the paper at the edges with a sponge dampened with clean water after completing each sheet.

Corners

Corners are never perfectly straight. Always end the paper at an inside corner and start the next strip along a new plumb line (Photos 12 and 13). A perfectly concealed seam at the corner involves a three-step process:
1. Wrap the first sheet around the corner and trim it off, leaving 1/4 in.
2. Set the next strip to a new plumb line so it completely overlaps the 1/4-in. wrap.
3. Trim off the paper that wrapped over at the corner. (Cut through the top piece only.)

There will always be a pattern mismatch at the corners. Keep it slight by starting out of the corner with the cut-off piece you came into it with. Photo 12 shows a way to cut this piece by guiding the razor with a broad knife with cardboard taped to one side to create the 1/4-in. wrap. If the strip you cut off is less than 2 in., discard it and start the wall with a new strip.

If you're using a vinyl or vinyl-coated paper, use a vinyl-to-vinyl adhesive on the overlap. Regular paste won't hold. Use this adhesive any time you're putting a paper over a vinyl or vinyl-coated paper—on borders, for instance.

If an outside corner is perfectly plumb and straight (check it with your level and a long, straight board), you can wrap the paper around it and keep hanging. If not,

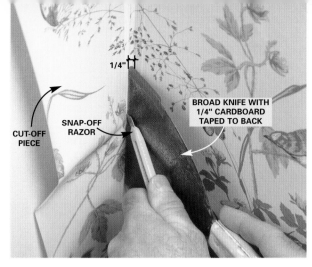

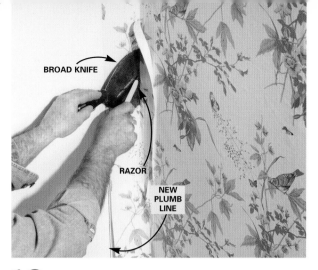

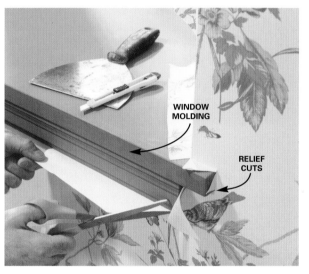

12 Wrap the paper around the corner, leaving the wrapped side loose and smoothing out the other. Trim off the paper with a sharp razor knife, leaving 1/4 in. wrapped around the corner. Guide the cut with a broad knife built up on one side with 1/4-in. thick cardboard taped to the knife. Book the cut-off piece for later use.

13 Measure the width of the cut-off piece at its narrowest spot and draw a plumb line with your level at that distance from the corner. (Careful, the corner won't be perfectly plumb or straight.) Hang the cut-off piece along the plumb line, wrapping the excess around the corner. Smooth it out. Trim through the overlapping sheet at the corner so the seam follows the corner.

14 Wrap the paper around an outside corner and trim it off, leaving 1/2 in. wrapped. Set a new plumb line if you're continuing on a long wall. Overlap the next piece, holding it 1/8 in. away from the corner.

15 Trim the paper around window and door moldings by pressing it to the edge of the molding and making relief cuts with scissors and a razor until it lies flat to the wall. Using the razor, trim off the excess paper following the contour of the moldings. Guide your cuts with the broad knife on straight sections.

fit it like an inside corner (Photo 14). If the corner is prone to a lot of abuse, install corner protectors ($2 to $3) from a home center.

Cutting around trim and other obstacles

Don't try to cut an opening for a window or door with the wallpaper on your worktable. Instead, align the seam and smooth out as much of the sheet as possible up to the molding. Relief cuts (Photo 15) will allow the paper to lie flat on the wall. Make these gradually so you don't overcut. Trim tight against the molding with the razor. Cut freehand along the contours and guide the razor with a broad knife on straight areas. Slit an "X" over electrical boxes and trim off the excess paper.

CAUTION: THE POWER MUST BE OFF WHEN YOU ARE TRIMMING AROUND ELECTRICAL BOXES.

Urethane chair rail

Attractive, lightweight and easy to install.

project at a glance

skill level
beginner to intermediate

special tools
hand miter box and saw
basic hand tools

approximate cost
$2 per lineal ft.

Urethane moldings are both lightweight and easy to apply, making them a great alternative to wood molding. In this story, we used them for chair rail and window trim.

One manufacturer recommends cutting the molding about 1/4 in. overlong for long runs (12 to 16 ft.) to help make up for seasonal wall expansion. It'll compress slightly and snap into place. Shorter lengths to 8 ft. should be cut about 1/8 in. overlong and anything less than 4 ft. should be cut to fit. The company also recommends butting crosscut ends together when splicing long lengths instead of bevel-cutting moldings at mid-wall joints. The molding is applied just like wood molding

tip*

To widen your miter box as shown in Photo 1 on p. 147, use a hammer to tap the sides free of the original base. Drill pilot holes and screw the sides to the new base. With the wider base, you'll be able to crosscut and bevel-cut the moldings. However, the other miter operations won't be possible, since the precut slots will no longer line up. This won't be a problem for cutting the moldings we show here.

except that it cuts and nails easier.

Set the molding into your miter box (screw the miter box down to your sawhorse or worktable) and cut it on your mark with slow, steady strokes as you hold the molding firmly with your other hand. Support long ends with additional sawhorses. Don't bother coping joints in corners; just lay the molding on its back side and cut at 45 degrees for inside and outside corners. Nails alone won't do—you must use the polyurethane adhesive caulk to bond it to the wall surface to make up for its low density.

Fill nail holes with spackling compound and then wipe the surface clean with a damp rag (Photo 4). This process will take two coats. Sand urethane molding as little as possible because unlike wood, the factory finish on the urethane molding is thin. Because you'll be painting the molding, you can touch up joints with acrylic caulk and wipe the excess away with a damp rag. You can save yourself a lot of time by prepainting the molding and then touching it up after you've cut and installed it.

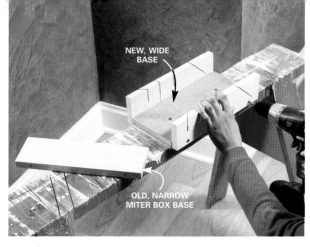

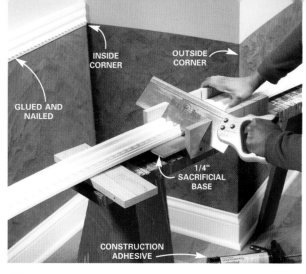

1 Hand miter boxes and fine-tooth hand saws are best for cutting urethane moldings. The moldings, however, are often wider than the miter box bed. Widen the bed by removing the screws on the side of the box and adding a wider base.

2 Measure the length, then cut the moldings with 45-degree bevel cuts in the corners and glue the back sides and joints with polyurethane molding adhesive.

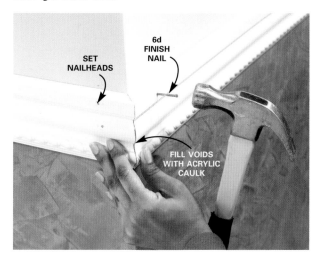

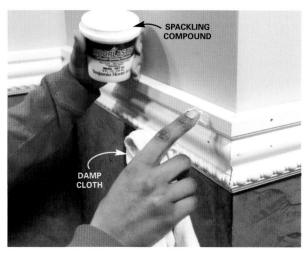

3 Glue and nail the moldings to the wall. Make small reference marks along the wall with your level to make sure you keep the molding straight as you nail. Set the nails with a nail set.

4 Fill the nail holes with spackling compound and the joints with acrylic caulk, then wipe with a slightly damp cloth. You'll need a second application once the spackling compound and caulk are dry. Wipe smooth or lightly sand, then paint.

Buying urethane moldings

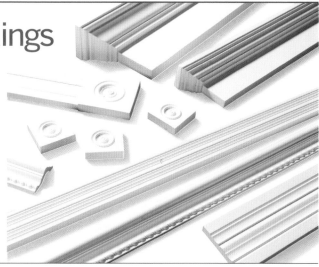

Home centers and lumberyards carry a limited selection of urethane moldings. They come in a wide variety of preprimed profiles and sizes for windows, doors, crown moldings and decorative panels. They're expensive but cost less than decorative wood moldings with the same profiles. To see all your options, go to the help desk. There you can order moldings to suit your taste. The moldings shown here are only a small sample.

For more information on urethane molding options, call (800) 446-3040, or go to www.fypon.com. Also, visit www.focalpointap.com or call (800) 662-5550 to find a dealer in your area.

Snap-together wood flooring

No glue, no nails, and you can do it in a weekend.

Here's a wood floor that's so easy to install you can complete an average-size room in a weekend. The joints just snap together. Simple carpentry skills and a few basic tools are all you need to cut the floorboards and notch them around corners.

In this article, we'll show you how to prepare your room and lay the snap-together flooring. The flooring we're using is similar to snap-together laminate floors except that it has a surface layer of real wood. The 5/16-in. thick flooring has specially shaped tongues and grooves

that interlock to form a strong tight joint without glue or nails. Once assembled, the entire floor "floats" in one large sheet. You leave a small expansion space all around the edges so the floor can expand and contract with humidity changes.

Wood veneer floors cost $6 to $15 per sq. ft., depending on the species and thickness of the top wood layer. Most home centers sell a few types of snap-together floors, but you'll find a better selection and expert advice

at your local flooring retailer. You can also buy flooring online.

Before you go shopping, draw a sketch of your room with dimensions. Make note of transitions to other types of flooring and other features like stair landings and exterior doors. Ask your salesperson for help choosing the right transition moldings for these areas.

You'll need a few special tools in addition to basic hand tools like a tape measure, square and utility knife. We purchased an installation kit from the manufacturer ($40) that included plastic shims, a tapping block and a last-board puller, but if you're handy you could fabricate these tools. You'll also need a circular saw and a jigsaw to cut the flooring, and a miter box to cut the shoe molding. A table saw and power miter saw would make your job easier but aren't necessary.

tip*

A pull saw works great to undercut doorjambs and casing (Photo 3). It's difficult to get close enough to the floor with a standard handsaw.

NO. 15 BUILDING PAPER

8' STRAIGHTEDGE

MARK LOW SPOT

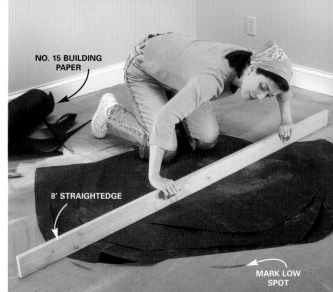

DUCT TAPE

4-MIL PLASTIC

CONCRETE FLOOR

1 Test for excess moisture in concrete floors by sealing the edges of a 3-ft. square of plastic sheeting to the floor with duct tape. Wait 24 hours before you peel back the plastic to check for moisture. Water droplets on the plastic or darkened concrete indicate a possible problem with excess moisture. Ask your flooring supplier for advice before installing a wood floor.

2 Check for low spots in the floor with an 8-ft. straight-edge and mark their perimeter with a pencil. Fill depressions less than 1/4 in. deep with layers of building paper. Fill deeper depressions with a hardening-type floor filler available from flooring stores.

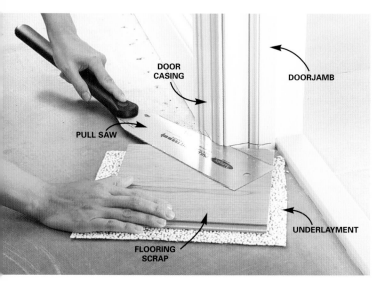

DOOR CASING

DOORJAMB

PULL SAW

UNDERLAYMENT

FLOORING SCRAP

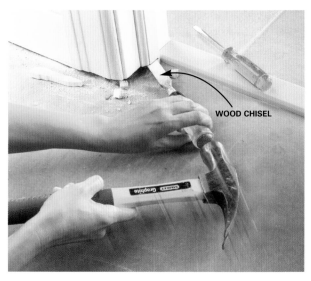

WOOD CHISEL

3 Undercut doorjambs and casings (door moldings) to make space for the flooring to slip underneath. Guide the saw with a scrap of flooring stacked on a piece of underlayment.

4 Break and pry out the cutoff chunks of jamb and cas-ing with a screwdriver. Use a sharp chisel or utility knife to complete the cut in areas the saw couldn't reach.

Make sure your floor is dry

Don't lay this type of floor over damp concrete or damp crawlspaces. Check all concrete for excess moisture. As a starting point, use the plastic mat test shown in Photo 1. Even though some manufacturers allow it, professional installers we spoke to advised against installing floating floors in kitchens, full or three-quarter baths, or entry-ways, all areas where they might be subjected to standing water.

Prepare your room for new flooring

You have to make sure the existing floor is smooth and flat before installing a floating floor on top. Clear the old floor, then smooth it by scraping off lumps and sweeping it. Check the floor with an 8-ft. straightedge and mark high spots and depressions. Sand or grind down ridges and fill low spots (Photo 2). Most manufacturers recom-mend no more than 1/8-in. variation in flatness over an 8-ft. length.

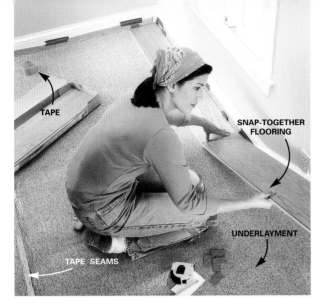

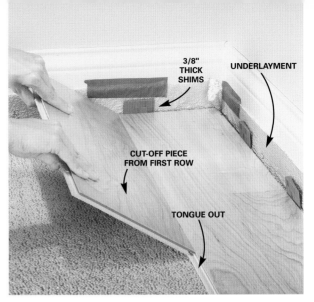

5 Unroll the underlayment and lap it up the baseboards or walls 2 in. Temporarily secure the edges with masking tape. Butt the sheets together and seal the seams with the tape recommended by the manufacturer. Cut the first row of boards narrower if necessary to ensure that the last row of flooring will be at least 2 in. wide. Then start the installation by locking the ends of the first row of flooring together. Measure and cut the last piece to fit, allowing the 3/8-in. expansion space.

6 Start the second row with the leftover cutoff piece from the first row, making sure the end joints are off-set at least 12 in. from the end joints in the first row. With the board held at about a 45-degree angle, engage the tongue in the groove. Push in while you rotate the starter piece down toward the floor. The click indicates the pieces have locked together. The joint between boards should draw tight.

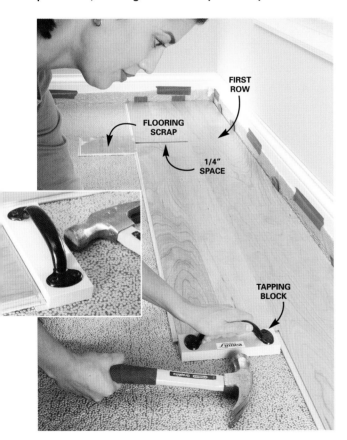

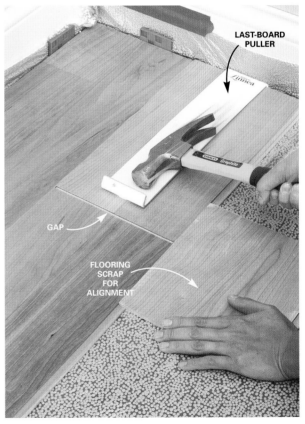

7 Leave a 1/4-in. space between the next full piece of flooring and the previous piece. Snap this piece into the first row. Snap a scrap of flooring across the ends being joined to hold them in alignment while you tap them together. Place the tapping block against the end of the floor piece and tap it with a hammer to close the gap.

8 Close a gap at the end of the row by hooking the last-board puller tool over the end of the plank and tapping it with a hammer to pull the end joints together.

REMOVE BUMP ON TONGUE

9 Plan ahead when you get near a doorjamb. Usually you have to slide the next piece of flooring under the jamb rather than tilt and snap it into place. To accomplish this, you must slice off the locking section of the tongue from the preceding row with a sharp utility knife before installing it.

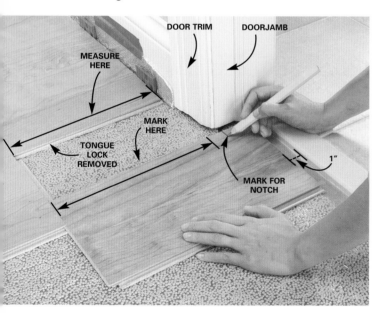

DOOR TRIM   DOORJAMB

MEASURE HERE

MARK HERE

TONGUE LOCK REMOVED

MARK FOR NOTCH

1"

10 Cut the plank to be notched to length, allowing a 1-in. space for the future transition piece. Align the end with the end of the last plank laid and mark 3/8 in. inside the jamb to make sure the flooring extends under the door trim.

tip If you have wood floors, fix squeaks and tighten loose boards by screwing them to the joists with deck screws before you install your new flooring.

Allowing the floor to expand and contract freely is critical. Leave at least a 3/8-in. expansion space along the edges. You can hide the gap under the baseboards or leave the baseboards in place and cover the gap with shoe molding or quarter round as we did. Cover the expansion space at openings or transitions to other types of flooring with special transition moldings (Photo 13). Buy these from the dealer.

Finally, saw off the bottoms of doorjambs and trim to allow for the flooring to slide underneath (Photo 3). Leaving an expansion gap at exterior doors presents a unique challenge. In older houses, you could carefully remove the threshold and notch it to allow the flooring to slide underneath. For most newer exterior doors, you can butt a square-nosed transition piece against the threshold.

Floating floors must be installed over a thin cushioning pad called underlayment (Photo 5). Underlayment is usually sold in rolls and costs 25¢ to 50¢ per sq. ft. Ask your flooring dealer to suggest the best one for your situation. Some types combine a vapor barrier and padding. Install this type over concrete or other floors where moisture might be a problem. Others reduce sound transmission.

Take extra care when installing underlayment that includes a vapor barrier. Lap the edges up the wall and carefully seal all the seams as recommended by the manufacturer. Keep a roll of tape handy to patch accidental rips and tears as you install the floor.

After the first few rows, installing the floor is a snap

You may have to cut your first row of flooring narrower to make sure the last row is at least 2 in. wide. To figure this, measure across the room and divide by the width of the exposed face on the flooring. The number remaining is the width of the last row. If the remainder is less than 2, cut the first row narrower to make this last row wider. Then continue the installation as shown in Photos 6 – 8.

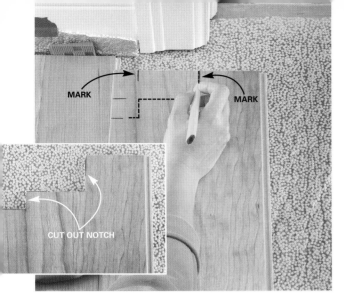

MARK MARK

CUT OUT NOTCH

SPECIAL GLUE

GLUE TONGUE

TAP IN

11 Align the flooring lengthwise and mark for the notches in the other direction, allowing for the floor to slide under the doorjamb about 3/8 in. Connect the marks with a square and cut out the notch with a jigsaw.

12 Apply a thin bead of the manufacturer's recommended glue along the edge where the portion of the tongue was removed. Slide the notched piece of flooring into place and tighten the glued edge by pounding on the special tapping block.

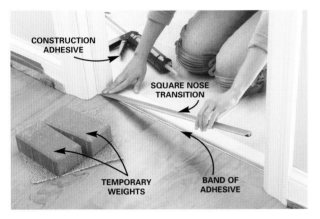

CONSTRUCTION ADHESIVE

SQUARE NOSE TRANSITION

TEMPORARY WEIGHTS

BAND OF ADHESIVE

NAIL SET

4D FINISH NAILS

13 Cut a transition molding, in this case a square nose transition, to fit between the doorstops or jambs. Spread a bead of construction adhesive only on the area of the floor that will be in contact with the transition piece. Set the transition in place and weight it down overnight.

14 Complete the flooring project by trimming off the protruding underlayment with a utility knife and installing shoe molding. Predrill 1/16-in. holes through the shoe. Then nail the shoe molding to the baseboard with 4d finish nails. Set and fill the nails. Do not nail the shoe molding down into the flooring.

You can't use the same tilt-and-snap installation technique where the flooring fits under doorjambs. You have to slide the flooring together instead. Photos 9 – 12 show how. If the opening requires a transition molding, cut the flooring short to leave space for it (Photo 13).

Complete the floor by cutting the last row to the correct width to fit against the wall. Make sure to leave the required expansion space. Finally, reinstall the baseboards if you removed them, or install new quarter-round or shoe molding to cover the expansion space (Photo 14).

Buyer's Guide

Here are some of the manufacturers that currently offer snap-together wood veneer floors. Many others are in the process of converting their glue-together floating floors to the snap-together system. Check with your local flooring supplier for current offerings.

- Alloc: (800) 362-5562, www.alloc.com
- Award: (888) 862-9273, www.awardfloors.com
- BHK: (800) 663-4176, www.BHKuniclic.com
- Kahrs: (800) 800-KAHR, www.kahrs.com
- wicanders: (410) 553-6062, www.wicanders.com

Hang a ceiling fan

It's easier than you think, even on an angled ceiling.

You don't have to be a "Casablanca" aficionado to appreciate the elegance a ceiling fan can bring to your home. And you can enjoy a fan all year long as it creates a welcome breeze in the summer and circulates warm air in the winter.

Ceiling fans (technically called paddle fans) used to be frustrating to install, to say the least. Most of the time you had to wing it because specialty hanging systems were poorly developed or nonexistent. Now most manufacturers have designed versatile mounting systems that take the hassle out of installation. When you add in the improved, stronger ceiling boxes, you'll find that just about any ceiling fan can go up quick and easy on any ceiling, sloped or flat.

In this article, we'll illustrate crystal-clear instructions that go beyond the basic set included with the fan. We'll also show you how to avoid common pitfalls like putting on parts in the wrong order and forgetting to slip shrouds on ahead of time. Some mistakes are more serious than these. Standard electrical boxes or blades hung too low can be downright dangerous.

Expect to spend at least $150 for a high-quality fan (see "Buying a Ceiling Fan," p. 157) and a bit more for accessories like electronic controls, fancy light packages and furniture-grade paddles.

Put up a new fan in a leisurely Saturday afternoon

If everything goes well, you can put up a ceiling fan in a couple of hours, including cleanup. In most cases, the whole job will take only a hammer, a screwdriver, a 3/8-in. nut driver and a wire stripper.

Most of the time, the wires that fed a previous ceiling light fixture are adequate for hooking up a new fan. If you have a wiring arrangement that's different from ours and you are unfamiliar with wiring techniques, consult

project at a glance

skill level
intermediate

special tools
wire stripper
basic hand tools

approximate cost
$100–$300

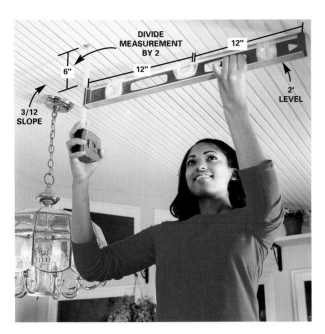

1 Determine the ceiling slope by holding a 2-ft. level against the ceiling and measuring the vertical distance from the level to the ceiling. Divide that number by 2 to get the drop over 12 in. of horizontal run, 3/12 slope in our case. See the chart on p. 158 to determine the minimum downrod length for the blade diameter you'd like.

2 Shut off the power at the main panel and remove the light fixture. Knock the existing electrical box free of the framing with a hammer and a block of wood, then pull the electrical cable free of the old box and through the ceiling hole. Leave the old box in the ceiling cavity unless you can easily remove it through the hole.

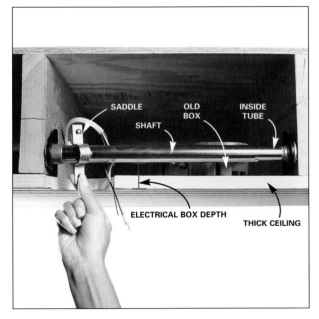

3 Feed the fan brace up into the hole, rest the flat edge of the feet against the ceiling and center the shaft over the hole. If your ceiling is more than 1/2 in. thick, as ours was, rotate the feet and position the rod the depth of the box from the ceiling. Rotate the shaft to secure the brace to the framing. Snap the metal saddle over the shaft so it's centered over the hole.

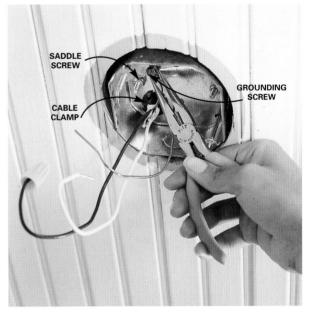

4 Feed the existing wire through the cable clamp in the top of the new metal box, slip the box over the saddle screws, and tighten the nuts to clamp the box to the shaft with a nut driver or a deep-well socket. Crimp a loop of grounding wire three-quarters around the grounding screw and tighten the screw.

HANGER BRACKET

5 Position the hanger bracket so that the opening in the bracket is on the uphill side of the sloped ceiling. Then screw it into the box with the special screws provided with the fan brace.

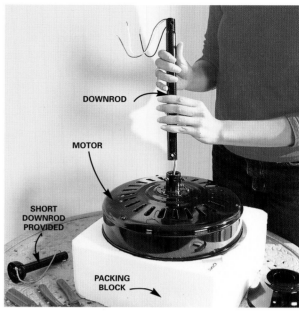

DOWNROD

MOTOR

SHORT DOWNROD PROVIDED

PACKING BLOCK

6 Place the motor right side up, thread the wire through the downrod and insert the downrod into the mounting collar.

an electrician or building inspector for help.

Follow the photo series for basic installation steps that apply to more than 95 percent of all fans. There may be small variations, particularly when it comes to the light and blade mountings, so you'll still need to consult the instructions provided with your fan. As with any other electrical work, you may need an electrical permit from your local building department before starting the job. The inspector will tell you when to call for an inspection.

Replace electrical boxes with specially designed paddle fan braces

Before starting any work, shut off the circuit breaker that feeds the switch and light fixture. If there's a working bulb in the fixture, turn it on. Then you'll know you have the right breaker when the bulb goes out. Check the wires with a voltage tester to make sure they're off after removing the fixture and when changing the wall switch.

The next step is to remove the existing plastic or metal electrical box and install a "fan brace" that's designed to hold ceiling fans. Few conventional boxes are strong enough to support a ceiling fan, so don't even think about trying to hang your fan from an existing box. Instead, buy a fan brace (about $15) when you purchase

your fan. You can choose braces that fasten with screws if the framing is accessible from the attic or if it's new construction. Otherwise, pick a brace that's designed to slip through the ceiling hole and through the electrical box. These braces (Photo 3) adjust to fit between the framing members in your ceiling; you simply rotate the shaft to anchor them to the framing.

Most existing electrical boxes are fastened to the framing with nails, making them easy to pound out with a hammer and a block of wood (Photo 2). After you free the cable, just leave the old box in the cavity (Photo 3) rather than struggling to work the box through the ceiling hole. Then pull the cable through the hole and slip the fan brace through the opening and secure it, following the directions that came with the brace. Little feet on the ends of braces keep them the correct distance from the back side of 1/2-in. thick ceilings so the new electrical box will be flush with the surface. If you have a thicker ceiling (like ours), rotate the ends to achieve the correct spacing.

tip Before you blast out the box, bend back the plastic clamps or loosen the metal cable clamps so it'll be easier to pull the electrical cable free after the box is loosened.

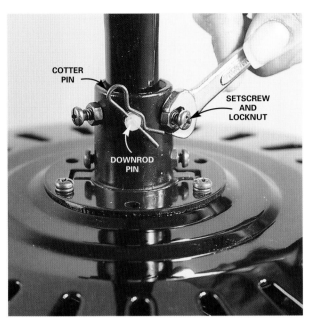

COTTER PIN

SETSCREW AND LOCKNUT

DOWNROD PIN

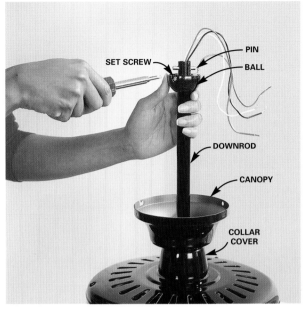

SET SCREW

PIN

BALL

DOWNROD

CANOPY

COLLAR COVER

7 Slip the downrod pin through the collar and tube, lock it into place with the cotter pin, and tighten the screws and locknuts.

8 Slip the collar cover, then the canopy over the down-rod. Slide the ball over the downrod and push the pin through both sets of holes, then lift the ball over the pin and tighten the set screw.

Buying a ceiling fan

If you haven't walked under a large fan display yet, hold onto your hat. You'll be overwhelmed by the selection of colors, styles and accessories, especially if you visit a ceiling fan store. If you intend to use your fan regularly, invest in a model in the $150-plus category. You'll get a quieter, more efficient, more durable unit. If you spend beyond that amount, you're usually paying for light packages, radio-actuated remote and wall controls, style, and design (fancier motor castings, inlays, blade adornments or glasswork). If you spend less, you're likely to get a less efficient, less durable, noisier unit with fewer color, blade and electronic choices.

Choose the blade diameter that best suits the room visually and make sure the unit will fit under the ceiling without jeopardizing beehive hairdos. (See p. 159 for height requirements.) Bigger rooms call for wider fan blade diameters. The bigger fan will not only look better but also move more air.

Most ceiling fans are designed for heated, enclosed spaces. If you're putting a fan in a screen room, a gazebo or other damp area, the building code requires you to use a "damp-rated" fan. These fans have corrosion-resistant stainless steel or plastic parts that can stand up to high humidity and condensation. If you live in a coastal area with corrosive sea air, or if you're putting a fan in a particularly wet environment like a greenhouse or an enclosed pool area, you should choose a "wet-rated" fan.

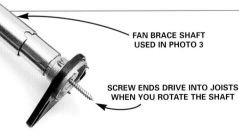

FLAT FOOT FOR 1/2" THICK CEILING

FAN BRACE SHAFT USED IN PHOTO 3

SCREW ENDS DRIVE INTO JOISTS WHEN YOU ROTATE THE SHAFT

Buyer's Guide

- Hampton Bay Fan and Lighting Co., 2455 Paces Ferry Road N.W., Atlanta, GA 30339; (770) 433-8211, www.homedepot.com

- Hunter Fan Co., 2500 Frisco Ave., Memphis, TN 38114; (800) 448-6837, www.hunterfan.com

- Regency Ceiling Fans, www.regencyfan.com.

9 Lift the assembly over the open side of the bracket and lower it into place. Rotate the motor until the ball slot locks into place over the tab on the bracket.

10 Connect the bare ground wire from the box to the green ground wire on the bracket with a wire connector. Connect the white neutral wire from the motor to the neutral wire from the box. Connect the blue and black wire from the motor to the black hot wire from the box and neatly fold them into the box.

New electronic controls save you from running additional wiring

Since most fan installations are retrofits into existing electrical boxes, there's usually a single electrical cable connecting the fixture to a single wall switch. You can leave the switch and use it to turn the fan on and off, then use the pull chains on the fan to control fan speed and lights. A second option is to install electronic controls. Higher-quality fans give you the option of adding a radio receiver kit for about $75. The receiver accepts signals from a special wall switch (included in the kit) to control the fan and light separately without additional wiring. The receiver also accepts signals from a handheld remote, so you can operate multiple fans and fine-tune fan speed and light intensity from your La-Z-Boy. Electronic switches are matched to fans by flipping code toggles in the controls and the fan, just like with your garage door opener. Installing an electronic switch (Photo 12) is

tip*

Tighten the locknuts firmly. Loose nuts are the most common cause of wobbly fans.

a snap. The receiver drops right into the fan housing and plugs into the bottom of the motor.

If the old light is fed by two three-way switches instead of a single switch, the control options are a little more complicated. You have three choices:

1. Leave the existing switches in place and turn one of them on. Then use a remote to control the fan and lights.
2. Use the existing switches and control the fan and lights independently with pull chains.
3. Disable one of the three-way switches and rewire the other one to receive a wall-mounted electronic control. Sorting out all the wires is complex. You'll need an electrician's help for this.

Minimum downrod length (in inches) for angled ceilings

Blade Dia.	Ceiling Slope						
	3/12	4/12	5/12	6/12	8/12*	10/12*	12/12*
27 in.	6	6	6	12	18	24	36
36 in.	6	6	6	12	18	24	36
44 in.	6	6	12	12	24	30	42
52 in.	6	12	18	18	24	30	42
56 in.	12	12	18	24	30	36	48

* Also requires slope adapting kit.

11 Screw the fan blades to their brackets and screw the brackets to the bottom of the motor. It's easiest to hold the screw in the bracket with the screwdriver while you lift the blade assembly into position. Then drive in the screw.

12 Place the radio receiver into the switch housing/light pod assembly and connect the light pod wires according to the manufacturer's instructions. Note the settings on the receiver's code toggles so you can dial in the same settings on the electronic controls at the wall switch. Now loosen the screws in the switch-housing hub halfway. Plug the motor wiring into the receptacle on the receiver and twist the switch housing into place on the hub. Retighten the screws.

Fan height requirements

Manufacturers generally require that fan blades be at least 7 ft. above the floor. Since most fan and motor assemblies are less than 12 in. high, they'll fit under a standard 8-ft. ceiling with the proper clearance.

Angled ceilings require that you install downrods (also called extension tubes or downtubes) that will lower the motor and fan blades so they'll clear a sloped ceiling surface. The more space between the ceiling and the fan, the better. The fan will have more air to draw from, and you'll feel more air movement because the blades are closer to you.

Most fans come with a short downrod designed for mounting on 8-ft. ceilings. If your ceiling's less than 8 ft., you'll need to remove the rod provided and flush-mount the fan. But if you have a higher or sloped ceiling, purchase a longer downrod.

OPTIONAL
REMOTE CONTROL

13 Check and reset (if necessary) the code toggles on the wall-mounted electronic switch to match the ones on the receiver. Remove the existing wall switch and connect the two black wires on the new switch to the ones that were connected to the old switch with wire connectors. Screw the switch into the box and install the cover plate.

New wallpaper border

A simple way to add spark to a room.

EASY FOR EVERYONE

Most wallpaper borders are inexpensive, go up fast and offer instant transformation; now that's a project hard to beat. Home centers and paint stores stock dozens of styles and can special order hundreds more. Whatever you choose, remember these key things:

● Apply sizing to the wall where you'll be installing your border. (Photo 1). The border will stick better and be easier to remove later on.

● If you're going to paint, do it beforehand, then wait at least 3 days for the paint to cure before installing your border.

● Some borders look best snug to the ceiling or crown molding, others a few inches down. To get a sense of

project at a glance

skill level
beginner

special tools
sponge
razor knife

approximate cost
$20–$30 for a
12x12-ft. room

what looks best, pin up a small section at various heights and take a look.

● Start and end installing your border in an inconspicuous spot; usually an out of the way corner. Chances are the pattern won't match by the time you circle the room.

● Cut sections of border the length of each wall plus 1/4-inch. Overlap the borders this 1/4-inch at the corners.

● Four hands are better than two when installing long borders. Cut a deal with the neighbors: You'll help with theirs if they help with yours.

tip If you're installing your border tight to a "popcorn textured" ceiling, run a flat blade screwdriver around the edge first to remove any loose texture and create a small flat trough.

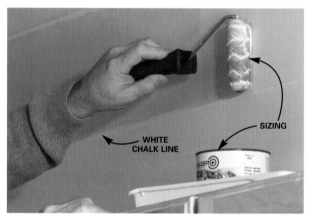

WHITE CHALK LINE — SIZING

1 Measure down from the ceiling the height of the border, then use a chalkbox with white chalk to snap lines around the room (white chalk brushes away the easiest). Apply sizing above this line. Watch out for runs and drips; some sizings dry to a glossy sheen.

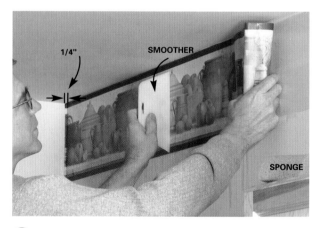

BORDER BOOKED STICKY SIDE TO STICKY SIDE

BORDER ROLLED STICKY SIDE OUT

2 Reroll the pre-pasted border sticky-side-out, immerse the roll in the water tray, then "book" it sticky side to sticky side as you remove it. Set the border aside for a few minutes while the paste activates.

1/4"   SMOOTHER   SPONGE

3 Install the border, pressing it flat with a smoother. Start by creasing one end sharply into an inside corner with 1/4-inch lapping onto the adjacent wall. Use a sponge to remove excess paste from the border and wall.

6 section

weekend home care & repair projects

Fast & easy lamp fixes

You can fix almost any lamp—and make it safe as well.

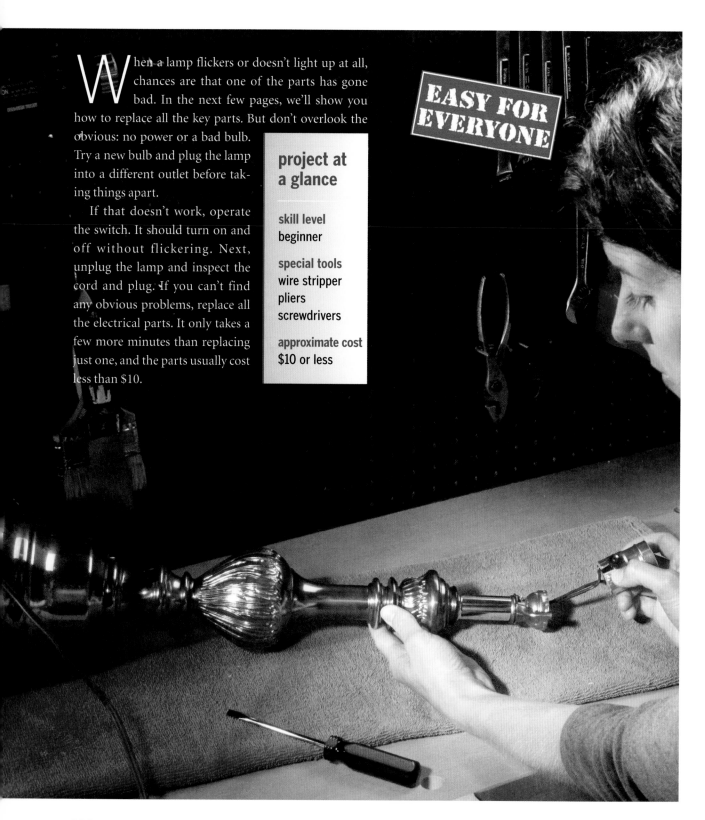

When a lamp flickers or doesn't light up at all, chances are that one of the parts has gone bad. In the next few pages, we'll show you how to replace all the key parts. But don't overlook the obvious: no power or a bad bulb. Try a new bulb and plug the lamp into a different outlet before taking things apart.

If that doesn't work, operate the switch. It should turn on and off without flickering. Next, unplug the lamp and inspect the cord and plug. If you can't find any obvious problems, replace all the electrical parts. It only takes a few more minutes than replacing just one, and the parts usually cost less than $10.

EASY FOR EVERYONE

project at a glance

skill level
beginner

special tools
wire stripper
pliers
screwdrivers

approximate cost
$10 or less

Replace a faulty socket

A lamp socket itself can go bad, but more often it's the switch inside the socket. Either way, the solution is replacement. A new socket costs about $5. Regardless of the existing switch type, you can choose a push-through switch, a pull chain, a turn knob or a three-way turn knob that provides two brightness levels. You can also choose a socket without a switch and install a switched cord instead.

The old socket shell is supposed to pop out of its base with a squeeze and a tug, but you might have to pry it out with a screwdriver (Photo 1). The socket base can be stubborn too. It's screwed onto a threaded tube that runs down through the lamp's body. When you try to unscrew it, you might unscrew the nut at the other end of the tube instead. This will allow the parts of the lamp body to come apart, but that isn't a big problem. Just use a pliers to twist the base off the tube (Photo 2), reassemble the lamp body and screw on the new socket base to hold it all together.

When you connect the new socket, don't reuse the bare ends of the wires. Some of the tiny strands of wire are probably broken. Cut them off and strip away 1/2 in. of insulation with a wire stripper (Photo 3). Using a wire stripper is almost foolproof, as long as you choose the correct pair of notches to bite through the wire's insulation. Most wire strippers are sized for solid wire, rather than the slightly larger stranded wire used in lamp cords. You can get around this problem by using the next larger pair of notches. Since most lamp wires are 18 gauge, start with the notches labeled 16. If the stripper won't remove the insulation, use smaller notches. If the stripper removes strands of wire, cut off an inch of cord and start over using larger notches.

When you connect the wires to the new socket, the neutral wire must connect to the silver screw (Photo 4). To identify the neutral wire, start at the plug. The wider

SOCKET SHELL

BASE

SET SCREW

1 Pry the socket shell out of its base. Cut the wires to remove the socket. Then loosen the setscrew so you can unscrew the socket base.

THREADED TUBE

BASE

2 Unscrew the socket base from the threaded tube. If the base won't spin off by hand, grab the tube and the base with a pliers to spin it free. Then screw on the new base and tighten the setscrew.

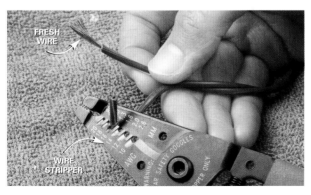

FRESH WIRE

WIRE STRIPPER

3 Strip off 1/2 in. of insulation with a wire stripper and twist the wire strands together. If you pull off any wire strands while stripping, cut back the cord and start over.

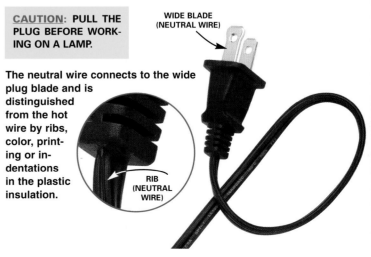

CAUTION: PULL THE PLUG BEFORE WORKING ON A LAMP.

The neutral wire connects to the wide plug blade and is distinguished from the hot wire by ribs, color, printing or indentations in the plastic insulation.

WIDE BLADE (NEUTRAL WIRE)

RIB (NEUTRAL WIRE)

4 Tie an underwriter's knot in the cord. Then connect the wires by wrapping them clockwise around the screws and tightening. Connect the neutral wire to the silver screw.

5 Pull the excess cord down through the lamp. Slip the insulation sleeve and socket shell over the socket and snap the shell into the base.

plug blade is connected to the neutral wire, and you'll find that the neutral wire is distinguished from the "hot" wire (photo, p. 163). The two wires may be different colors, there may be printing on one

or the other, or there may be tiny ribs or indentations in the plastic covering the neutral wire. If your old plug blades are of equal width, replace the plug and cord along with the socket.

An underwriter's knot prevents the wires from pulling out of the screw terminals when the cord is tugged.

Replace a cracked cord

1 Cut the old cord at the socket and pull it out. Push a grommet into the cord hole and screw a bushing onto the tube, if they're missing.

2 Feed the new cord through the threaded tube and socket base. Connect the cord to the socket as shown on p. 163.

The insulation on cords becomes stiff and brittle as it ages. Eventually, it cracks and might even flake off the wire, creating a shock and fire hazard. Don't try to solve this problem with electrical tape. Replace the cord. Cord replacement is also the best fix for a bad cord-mounted switch. You can buy a cord that has a switch attached.

Save yourself some time by buying a cord that's already connected to a plug ($3). Lamp cord sold at home centers and hardware stores is usually 18 gauge. That's large enough to handle 840 watts of lighting. If you have one of those rare lamps that uses bulbs totaling more than 840 watts, have it fixed at a lamp repair shop.

Make sure the cord is protected by a screw-on bushing where it enters the threaded tube and by a plastic or rubber grommet through the lamp body (Photo 1). Without a bushing or grommet, sharp edges can cut into the cord's insulation. If you can't find a bushing or grommet the right size at a home center or hardware store, see "Lamp Part Sources," p. 165.

To replace the cord, you'll take most of the socket replacement steps shown in the first part of this article. Remove the socket from its base, cut the old cord and pull it out. Feed the cord up through the threaded tube in the lamp's body (Photo 2). Then connect the new cord to the socket. Most cords come with the ends already stripped, so you won't even need a wire stripper.

Replace a problem plug

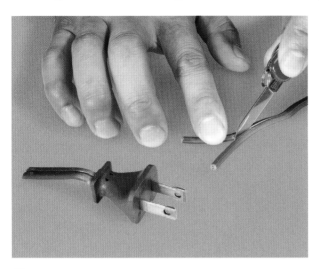

1 Cut the cord a couple of inches from the plug. Then split about an inch of cord with a pocketknife and strip off 3/4 in. of insulation.

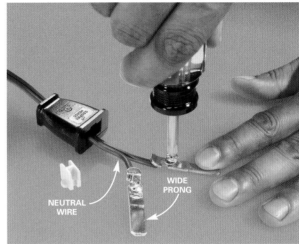

NEUTRAL WIRE

WIDE PRONG

2 Wrap the wires clockwise around the terminal screws of the new plug and tighten. The neutral wire must connect to the wider prong.

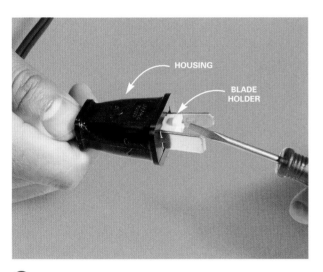

HOUSING

BLADE HOLDER

3 Slip the blades into the housing and push the blade holder into place.

Lamp part sources

Home centers and hardware stores carry basic lamp parts like sockets, cords and plugs. For hard-to-find parts and a wider selection of basic parts, visit a lamp repair shop (in the Yellow Pages under "Lamps & Shades, Repair") or these Web sites:

- www.grandbrass.com. Shop online and order online or by phone: (212) 226-2567

- www.paxtonhardware.com. Shop online and order by phone: (800) 241-9741

Plugs on lamp cords often have a weak point where the cord enters the plug. Pulling and flexing can break the wires at this point, leaving you with a lamp that flickers when you jiggle the cord. The cure is to replace the plug. To do this safely, choose a polarized plug ($5). A polarized plug has one blade that's wider than the other so it fits into an outlet only one way (photo, p. 163). Before you buy a plug, take a close look at the cord. Along with other labeling, you should find "SPT-1" or "SPT-2." This refers to the thickness of the cord's sheathing, and the plug you buy must have the same listing so it will fit over the sheathing. If you can't find the SPT listing, replace the entire cord as shown on p. 164.

The plug you buy may not look exactly like the one shown here, but installing it will be similar. Be sure to read the manufacturer's instructions. When you split the two halves of the cord (Photo 1), be careful not to expose any wire. If you do, cut back the cord and start over. Strip the wire ends (see Photo 3, p. 163) and make connections (Photo 2). The neutral wire must connect to the wider blade. See p. 163 for help in identifying the neutral wire. If you're not able to identify it, replace the entire cord.

Repair washing machine leaks

Fix the most common leaks yourself and avoid that $75 service call.

When the washing machine starts leaking water all over the floor, you face a tough choice. Either call a service technician to fix the problem or purchase a new machine. Both decisions are expensive. Most service technicians charge $50 to $100 just to walk in the door and diagnose the problem, and labor expenses can quickly accumulate. After receiving the final bill, you may even wish you'd replaced the machine!

This article will help you avoid the service call by showing you how to diagnose and fix the most common washing machine leaks. We cover hose, pump and tub leaks, but there may be additional problem areas specific to your brand of machine.

There are two types of washing machines: belt drive and direct drive. If you open up the cabinet and don't find any belts, then you've got a direct-drive machine. Repairs are similar for both machines, but generally easier on the direct-drive unit. The following photos are from a belt-drive washing machine. If you have a direct drive, refer to your owner's manual or diagrams (see "Buying Parts," p. 168) for brand-specific details.

tip* Make sure the water on the floor isn't the result of a plugged floor drain. It happens!

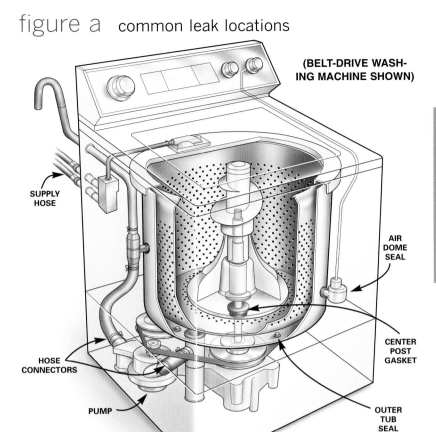

figure a   common leak locations

(BELT-DRIVE WASHING MACHINE SHOWN)

SUPPLY HOSE

HOSE CONNECTORS

PUMP

AIR DOME SEAL

CENTER POST GASKET

OUTER TUB SEAL

First, replace leaky supply hoses

HOSE WASHER

C

RUSTY OLD HOSE

Turn off the water main or shutoff valve and unscrew the supply hoses from the back of the machine with an adjustable pliers. Pry out the old hose washers with a flat-blade screwdriver. Install new gaskets in both hoses and reconnect the supply lines.

NEW NO-BURST HOSE

NEW HOSE WASHER

The first step is to locate the source of the leak. Empty the washing machine, move it away from the wall and start the fill cycle. Look for drips around the water supply hose connection at the back of the machine while it fills with water. Shut off the water and replace any old, heavily corroded or rusted hoses with new ones (photo, left). If the hoses are in good shape, replace the internal washers only. Special no-burst hoses ($10), regular hoses ($6) and new hose washers ($2 per 10-pack) are available at home centers and hardware stores.

Second, replace leaky internal hoses

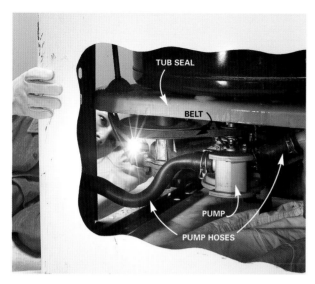

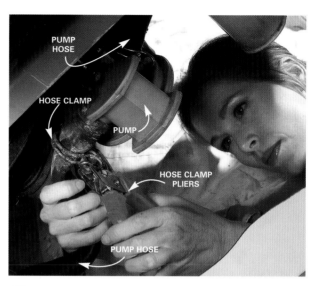

1 Unscrew the access panel from the back of the machine or open the cabinet. Look for leaks while the machine fills with water. If you don't see any, advance the machine to the agitate cycle and check again.

2 Squeeze the hose clamp together, slide it down the hose and pull off the hose. Keep a bucket or pan handy so you can catch any residual water left in the hoses. Replace the hose with an identical part and new worm-drive clamps (bottom of page).

Buying parts

Washing machine parts are available at appliance parts distributors. (Look in the Yellow Pages under "Appliance Parts.") Try to find a parts supplier with a well-informed staff, ideally ex–repair technicians, who can provide diagrams and help diagnose any problems specific to your brand of machine. A great Internet source is www.searspartsdirect.com. Enter your model number to access exploded-view diagrams and a thorough parts list for easy online ordering.

You'll need the brand and model number for proper part identification. Model numbers are usually stamped on a small metal plate (photo above) located under the tub lid or on the side or back of the machine. Copy down all the plate information and take it along to the parts distributor.

If the supply hoses aren't leaking, open the cabinet and inspect the internal components. Belt-drive machines typically have a rear access panel that unscrews. Access direct-drive machines by removing the two screws on the outside of the control panel and flipping up the lid. Then pry up the cabinet clips and pull off the entire cabinet. With the cabinet open, restart the fill cycle to check for internal leaks (Photo 1). Look for additional clues like rust and calcium deposits. Most often you'll find the leaks in the spots we show in Figure A.

Hoses tend to leak around a worn-out spring clamp. First try to remove the spring clamp with an adjustable

CAUTION: UNPLUG THE MACHINE BEFORE PERFORMING ANY REPAIRS.

pliers. If you can't get it, you'll need a special $15 hose clamp pliers (Photo 2) available from your local parts supplier. Replace the old spring clamp with a new worm-drive clamp (photo below). If the hose itself is cracked and leaking, remove it and take it to the appliance parts supplier for a replacement.

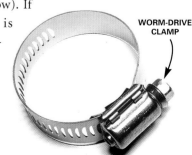

WORM-DRIVE CLAMP

Third, replace a leaky pump

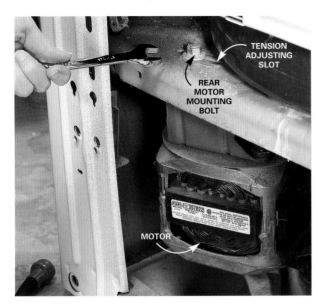

1 Loosen the two motor mounting bolts to relieve tension on the belt. One will be at the rear of the cabinet and the other is nearby.

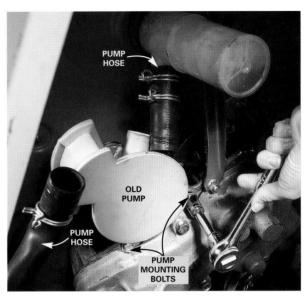

2 Disconnect the pump hoses. Then unscrew the pump mounting bolts, tip the pump pulley away from the belt and wiggle the pump loose. Direct-drive pumps will simply unscrew or unclip.

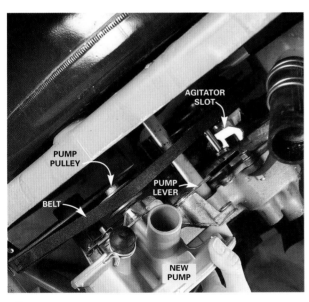

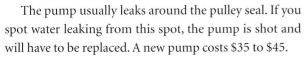

3 Install the new pump by sliding the pump lever into the agitator slot and aligning the belt with the pump pulley. Line up the bolt holes and firmly tighten the mounting bolts. Reconnect all hoses and clamps.

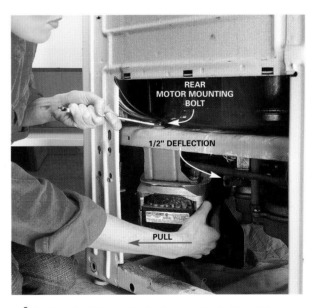

4 Pull against the motor to tension the belt and then tighten the rear motor mounting bolt. The belt should deflect about 1/2 in. when you push against it. Then tighten the mounting bolt located on the opposite side of the motor.

The pump usually leaks around the pulley seal. If you spot water leaking from this spot, the pump is shot and will have to be replaced. A new pump costs $35 to $45.

To replace the pump, work from underneath the machine. Unplug the machine and tip it up against the wall. Block up the front with a car jack or 2x4s so it can't tip over while you reach underneath. Replace the pump as shown in Photos 1 – 4. If the belt is darkened from burning or is worn down to the threads, replace it, too.

Fourth, replace worn-out tub fittings

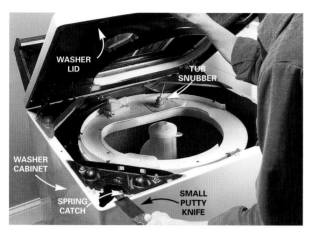

1 Slide a small putty knife between the washer lid and the cabinet. Push the putty knife against the spring catch while lifting up on the lid. Release both catches and fold the lid back.

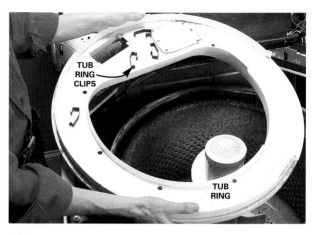

2 Pop off the tub ring clips, lift the tub ring out of the cabinet and set it aside.

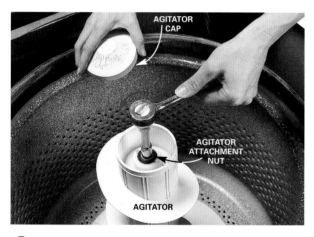

3 Twist or pry the cap off the agitator. Then unscrew the attachment nut and pull the agitator up and off the drive shaft.

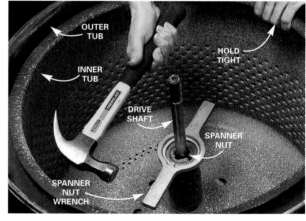

4 Hold the inner tub tight to the outer tub. Rap the special spanner wrench to break the spanner nut free. Remove the spanner nut.

5 Lift the inner tub up and off the drive shaft. You might have to wiggle it back and forth to help work it loose.

The most challenging repair is fixing a leaking tub fitting, whether it's the air dome seal ($5), the center post gasket ($8) or the tub seals ($15 to $20). (See Figure A and photos for locations.) Before proceeding, make sure that telltale drips are coming from around the tub. The details of this repair vary by brand and model. The details we show are for most Whirlpool and Kenmore belt drives. Study a schematic drawing or consult a parts specialist if your machine is different from what we show.

You'll need a special $15 spanner wrench (Photo 4) to remove the tub and replace the tub fittings on this type of machine. It's available at your local appliance parts supplier. Follow Photos 1 – 5 to access the tub fit-

6 Unscrew the old leaky tub seals from the outer tub. Later, install the new tub seals, making sure the metal washer is on top of the rubber washer.

NEW TUB SEAL

7 Tap up on the drive block with a hammer to break it loose from the drive shaft. Pull off the drive block and set it aside. Lift the outer tub from the cabinet, twisting it back and forth to work it loose.

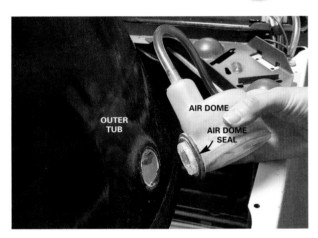

8 Twist the air dome a quarter turn and pull it free from the outer tub. Pry off the old air dome seal and replace it with a new one.

NEW AIR DOME SEAL

9 Squeeze the center post gasket together and pull it from the bottom of the outer tub. Install a new center post gasket and reassemble the machine.

NEW CENTER POST GASKET

tings. You can open the top of many machines by releasing the spring catches (Photo 1). However, on others you have to unscrew several screws and lift off the entire cabinet. Look in your owner's manual or at a parts diagram. (See the manufacturer's Web site or the site listed in "Buying Parts" on p. 168.) You'll have to unscrew the water inlet and the tub snubber (Photo 1) before unclipping the ring (Photo 2). Fastening systems for these vary by brand, as do attachment methods for the agitator (Photo 3) and inner tub (Photo 4).

There are four tub seals that secure the outer tub to the cabinet, each consisting of a bolt with a rubber and metal washer. Rust often develops around one of the tub

seals, causing a tub leak. A new tub seal kit will come with four new bolts and oversized rubber and metal washers that will seal small leaks (Photo 6). But if the tub is completely rusted through around the bolt, it's time to buy a new washing machine. Replace all four tub seals as shown in Photo 6.

If the leaking occurs only when the machine is agitating, a bad center post gasket ("doughnut") is the culprit. Remove the outer tub to replace the center post gasket (Photos 8 and 9). While you're at it, replace the air dome seal as well (Photo 8). Reassemble the washing machine and run a test cycle.

Trouble-free gutters

Install strong, sleek-looking gutters with off-the-shelf parts.

project at a glance

skill level
intermediate

special tools
duckbill and
 offset tin snips
crimper
pop rivet gun

approximate cost
$2–3 per
linear ft.

Almost all home centers and full-service hardware stores sell gutter systems that are designed primarily for easy installation. But with just a little bit more work, you can use these same parts to put together gutters and downspouts that are stronger and better looking too. We'll show you how to minimize joints; assemble strong, sleek-looking seams; and add roof flashing to keep water flowing into the gutters

where it belongs, all with off-the-shelf metal gutter parts.

If you're comfortable with basic hand tools, assembling and installing gutters shouldn't present any great challenge, but the job isn't for everyone. It requires that you know how to safely work from ladders (good balance and staying within your reach) and are comfortable doing it. Rent scaffolding for second-floor gutter work because it's much more stable than a ladder.

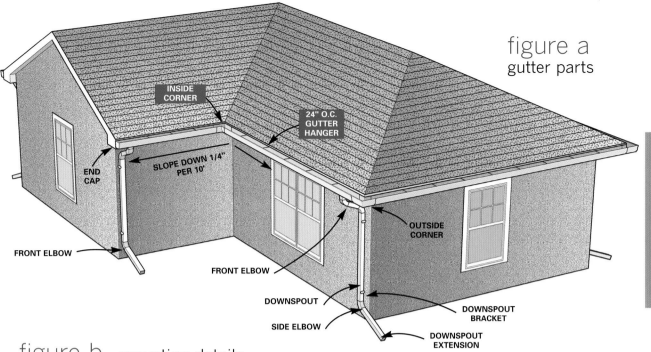

figure a
gutter parts

INSIDE CORNER

24" O.C. GUTTER HANGER

END CAP

SLOPE DOWN 1/4" PER 10'

OUTSIDE CORNER

FRONT ELBOW

FRONT ELBOW

DOWNSPOUT

SIDE ELBOW

DOWNSPOUT BRACKET

DOWNSPOUT EXTENSION

figure b mounting details

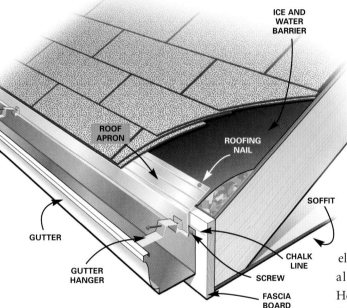

ICE AND WATER BARRIER

ROOF APRON

ROOFING NAIL

SOFFIT

GUTTER

GUTTER HANGER

CHALK LINE

SCREW

FASCIA BOARD

Evaluate and plan the project

Installing your own gutters can save you as much as $5 per linear foot over professionally installed gutters, but there are a few pitfalls to watch out for. Inspect the fascia and soffit (Figure B) for signs of rotted wood, which will need to be replaced before you put up the gutters. Many houses have a trim board or crown molding nailed to the fascia just under the shingles. You'll have to either remove this as we did or add a continuous strip of wood under it to create a flat plane for the gutters. In either case, prime and paint bare wood before you hang the gutters.

Draw a sketch and measure your house

Figure A shows an example of a gutter system for a typical house. Record the length of the gutter runs and mark the downspout locations. Then count up the inside and outside corners and end caps (note whether they are right or left ends). Measure the height of downspouts and add 4 ft. to each for the extension away from the house at the bottom. Each downspout requires three elbows. There are two types of elbows that turn either to the front or side of the downspout. Most installations require only front elbows, but occasionally you may need a side elbow, usually to turn the downspout extension sideways. Here are a few planning tips:

- Locate downspouts in unobstructed areas where water can be directed away from the house. Avoid locations with obstacles like electric meters, hose bibs or sidewalks.

- Place your downspouts in inconspicuous locations if possible.

- Install oversized 3 x 4-in. downspouts on gutters that drain large roof areas or if you live in an area with torrential rains.

- Slope long gutter runs (40 ft. or more) down both directions from the middle and put a downspout on each end.

- Buy special roof hanger mounting straps for houses without fascia boards or for fascias that aren't vertical.

1 Cut the front and back sides with a tin snips. Bend the gutter and cut the bottom.

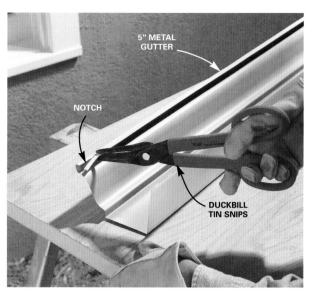

2 Cut a 2-in. long notch in the front lip of the gutter with a tin snips to join a gutter section with an inside or outside corner piece. (Cut a 4-in.-long notch to overlap and splice together gutter sections.)

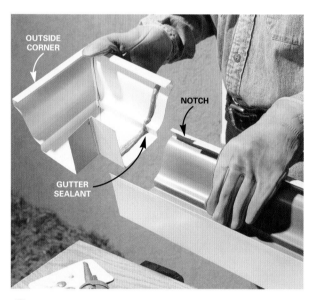

3 Lay a bead of gutter sealant along the corner 1-1/2 in. back from the edge. Hook the front lip of the corner over the notched section of gutter and snap it over the gutter.

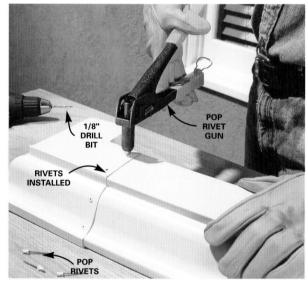

4 Join the gutter to the corner with six rivets in the locations shown. Start by drilling a 1/8-in. hole (for 1/8-in. rivets) at the front of the gutter and installing the first rivet with the rivet gun. Now drill the remaining holes and install the rivets.

Preassemble gutters

It's much easier to join sections on the ground than to work from the top of a ladder. Photos 1 – 8 show how. Instead of butting parts together and covering the joints with a seam cover as recommended by the manufacturer, lap all seams from 2 to 4 in. Then caulk and rivet them together (Photos 3 – 5). We've shown joining a gutter section to a corner. Use the same process to join two sections of gutter, except overlap the pieces at least 4 in.

When you're splicing gutter sections, plan ahead to leave the best-looking factory-cut end on the outside if possible. Also lap the gutters so the inside section is facing downhill to prevent water from being forced out the seam.

Where a gutter ends, cut it to extend about an inch past the end of the fascia board to catch water from the overhanging shingles. Then attach an end cap with rivets and seal the joint from the inside with gutter sealant.

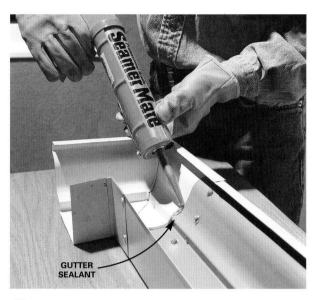

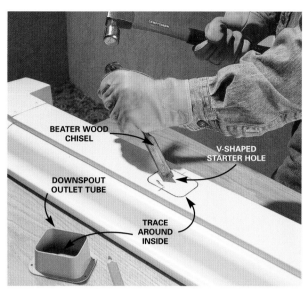

GUTTER SEALANT

BEATER WOOD CHISEL

V-SHAPED STARTER HOLE

DOWNSPOUT OUTLET TUBE

TRACE AROUND INSIDE

5 Caulk the seam on the inside of the gutter with gutter sealant. Put a dab of sealant over each rivet.

6 Mark the center of the downspout outlet on the bottom of the gutter. Center the outlet, flange side down, over the mark and trace around the inside. Cut a V-shaped notch with an old chisel as a starting hole for the tin snips.

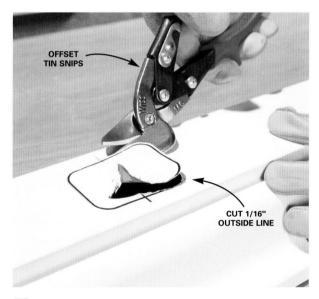

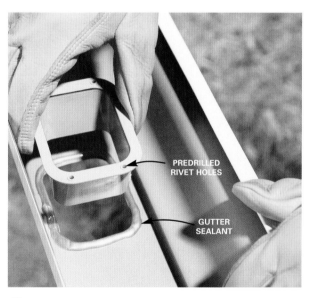

OFFSET TIN SNIPS

CUT 1/16" OUTSIDE LINE

PREDRILLED RIVET HOLES

GUTTER SEALANT

7 Cut out the outlet hole with an offset tin snips. Red tin snips cut counterclockwise. Green snips cut clockwise. Either one will work. Cut 1/16 in. outside the line.

8 Slip the outlet into the hole and predrill 1/8-in. holes for the rivets. Remove the outlet and run a bead of gutter sealant around the opening. Press the outlet into the caulked opening and install the rivets.

Cut in downspout tubes at each downspout location

First measure from the corner of the house to the center of your chosen downspout location. Double-check for obstructions. Transfer this dimension to the gutter and cut in a downspout outlet (Photos 6 – 8). This method takes

tip* Place two short scraps of 2x4 side by side under the gutter to support it while you chisel the notch (Photo 6).

a few minutes longer than using one of the short gutter sections with a preinstalled outlet, but it eliminates two seams and looks much neater. You can make this cutout with a duckbill tin snips, but a special offset snips like we're using ($15 at hardware stores and home centers) is much easier for beginners.

9 Set a slope by driving a nail 1/2 in. below the shingles on the high side of the gutter run. Measure and record the distance from the bottom of the fascia board to this nail. Subtract 1/4 in. for every 10 ft. of gutter from this measurement and mark this distance at the low end of the gutter run. Drive a nail at this mark and stretch a chalk line between the two nails. Align a level with the string to check the slope. The bubble should be off-center toward the high side. If it's not, adjust the string. Finally, snap the string to mark a line on the fascia.

10 Drive 1-1/4 in. stainless steel hex head sheet metal screws through the back of the gutter into the fascia. Install one screw every 2 ft.

A little slope is all you need

The number and size of downspouts determines how fast your gutters will empty. Sloping the gutters helps eliminate standing water that can cause corrosion and leak through the seams. Slope each gutter run down toward the downspout about 1/4 in. for every 10 ft. of gutter. If your fascia boards are level, you can use them as a reference for sloping the gutters. Check this by holding a level against the bottom edge. If they aren't level, adjust the string line until a level aligned with the fascia boards shows a slight slope (Photo 9). Snap a chalk line to indicate the top of the gutter. Then straighten gutter sections as you screw them to the fascia by aligning the top edge with the chalk line (Photo 10).

Flashing protects your fascia and soffit from water damage

Prevent water from running behind your gutters by installing a metal gutter apron flashing under the shin-gles and over the back edge of the gutter (Photo 11). If your home center or hardware store doesn't sell pre-bent flashing, ask an aluminum siding contractor or local sheet metal fabricator to bend some for you.

Ideally the flashing should be slid under both the shingles and the roofing paper or ice and water barrier. If this isn't possible because the ice and water barrier is stuck to the sheathing, or there are too many nails and staples along the edge of the roofing paper, then just slip the flashing under the shingles (Photo 11). If the flashing you're using is too short to reach down over the back edge of the gutter, slip an additional strip of sheet metal flashing under the bent flashing and over the gutters.

Install hidden hangers

With the gutters screwed to the fascia, it's a simple job to install the hidden gutter hangers (Photo 12). Install hangers every 2 ft. to support the gutters and strengthen the front edge. The hangers are designed to

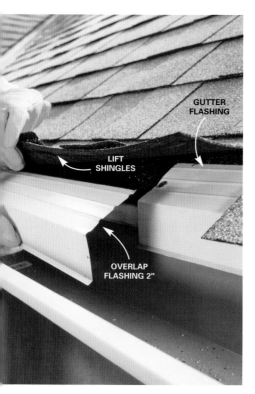

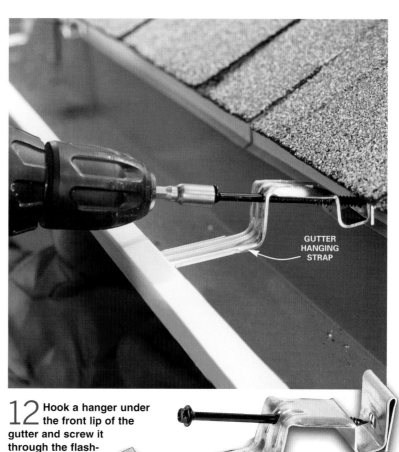

11 Slide gutter flashing under the shingles and secure with 1-in. roofing nails every 2 ft. Lap sections about 2 in.

12 Hook a hanger under the front lip of the gutter and screw it through the flashing into the fascia. (The gutter apron will prevent you from slipping the hangers over the back edge of the gutter as intended.) Install hangers every 2 ft.

slip over the back edge of the gutter, but since we've covered this edge with flashing, just hold them level and drive the screws through the flashing and gutter back into the fascia. The large screws included with the hangers we used are a little tricky to get started, especially through steel gutters and flashing. Spin them at high speed without applying much pressure until the screw tip bites into the metal. Then lean on the drill and drive them into the fascia.

A special crimper tool eliminates downspout frustration

Photos 13 – 16 show how to install the downspouts. We're using standard 2 x 3-in. downspouts, but the procedure for oversized 3 x 4-in. ones is the same. Assemble the elbows and downspout tube with the crimped ends facing down to prevent water from leaking out of the joints. Use sheet metal screws rather than rivets so you can disassemble the downspouts to clean them if neces-

sary. Pros prefer prepainted 1/4-in. hex head screws with very sharp points, called "zippers" because they're easy to install. We found these screws in the aluminum siding section of a home center, but a gutter supplier would be another good source.

You can cut downspout tubing with a 32-tooth hacksaw blade, but the pro we talked to uses a circular saw with a standard 24-tooth carbide blade. A power miter box also works great for cutting both gutters and downspouts. Use an old blade, though. Protect yourself from flying bits of metal with goggles, leather gloves, jeans and a long-sleeve shirt.

Each length of gutter and every elbow is squeezed, or crimped, on one end to allow the pieces to fit together, one inside the other. Since 10-ft. lengths of downspout are only crimped on one end, you'll have to crimp one end of any cutoff piece to make it fit inside the next elbow or downspout section. If you only have one or two downspouts to install, you can use a needle-nose pliers

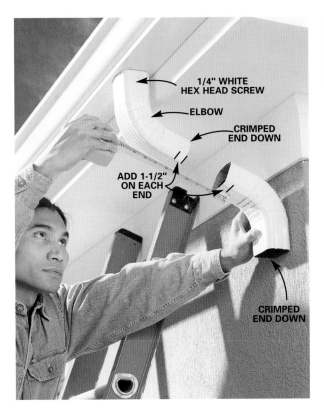

1/4" WHITE HEX HEAD SCREW

ELBOW

CRIMPED END DOWN

ADD 1-1/2" ON EACH END

CRIMPED END DOWN

DUCT OR DOWNSPOUT CRIMPER

CRIMP

13 Screw an elbow to the downspout outlet. Hold another elbow against the wall and measure between them. Allow for a 1-1/2 in. overlap at each end. Use a hacksaw to cut this length from the uncrimped end of a downspout tube.

14 Crimp one end of the short length of downspout with a special sheet metal crimper. With the three blades on the inside of the tube, hold the crimper against the inside corner of the tube and squeeze. Crimp three times across both long edges and twice on the narrow sides. Attach this short section of downspout to the two elbows with two 1/4-in. hex head sheet metal screws into each joint.

to twist crimps into the end. But a $15 crimping tool will save you tons of time and frustration (Photo 14).

Finish the gutter job by attaching the downspouts to the wall. If you can't find U-shaped brackets, make them from sections of downspout (Photo 15). They look better than the bands that wrap around the outside and make it easier to hang the downspouts.

tip* Clean leaves from your gutters twice a year, or hire a company that specializes in gutter cleaning and maintenance. You'll extend the life of your gutters and eliminate problems like backed-up gutters and plugged downspouts.

Buying gutters

Ten-foot lengths of metal gutters, downspouts and accessories are available at home centers, lumberyards and full-service hardware stores. Standard colors are brown and white. Matching inside and outside corners, downspout elbows and accessories are also available. Buy special gutter sealant to seal the seams. It's available in small toothpaste-type tubes or 12-oz. caulk gun tubes. Complete gutter systems cost about $2 per linear foot.

Using many of the same basic techniques we show in this story, you can install your own "seamless" gutters. Listed under "Gutters" in the Yellow Pages, many seamless gutter companies will come to your house, measure and form continuous lengths of aluminum gutter to fit, and sell you all the installation accessories you'll need. At about $3.50 per linear foot, it costs a little more, but you'll be able to choose from dozens of colors and eliminate seams in the gutter runs. You'll also save the hassle of measuring, shopping and hauling the parts home.

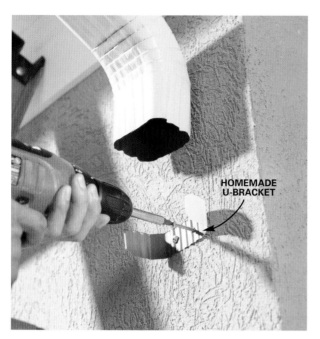

HOMEMADE U-BRACKET

CLIP CORNERS

1/4" WHITE HEX HEAD SCREW

HEX HEAD DRIVER

15 Cut strips about 1-1/4 in. wide from the end of a downspout with a tin snips. Cut out a U-shaped bracket and snip off the corners. Measure from the corner of the building and mark the locations of each bracket, spacing them about 6 ft. apart. Attach the brackets to the house with stainless steel screws. (Drill a clearance hole through stucco siding with a masonry bit. Use plastic anchors for brick. Use 1/4-in. long hex head screws for vinyl siding.) Cut and screw downspout sections to an elbow at the bottom. The bottom of the elbow should be about 6 in. above the ground. Slip this assembled downspout section over the crimped end of the top elbow and secure it with two screws.

16 Drive screws through the brackets into the assembled downspout. Complete the assembly by adding a length of downspout tube to the bottom elbow to direct water away from the foundation.

Handy Hints®

Gutter straightener

Ice coming off your roof can bend the spikes that secure your gutters to the fascia board. One simple way to straighten them without removing them is to use a 2-ft. length of angle iron and a link of heavy metal chain. The angle iron and chain link provide sufficient leverage to straighten the spike and pull the gutter back into alignment.

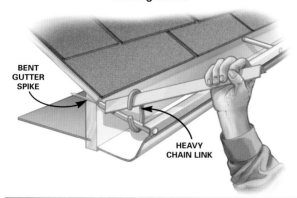

BENT GUTTER SPIKE

HEAVY CHAIN LINK

Gutter bucket

Snip the wire handle of a 5-gallon bucket in half and bend the free ends into small hooks. Hang the bucket on the edge of your gutter, then slide it along and fill it as you clean out the gutter.

Renew your wood fence

Shabby to handsome in three easy steps.

When did your cedar fence lose its rich, warm glow? Who invited that discolored, shabby-looking impostor into the neighborhood? Don't worry—underneath that thin gray skin, the glow still remains. All you have to do is remove the surface layer of aged wood cells to expose a fresh layer of wood. With a power washer, it's as easy as washing your car. Then apply an exterior wood oil stain to preserve this new layer of wood. It'll prolong the life of your fence to boot.

project at a glance

skill level
beginner

special tools
power washer
staining supplies

approximate cost
varies

Wash

Repair

Stain

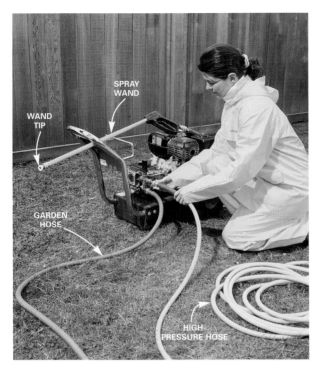

1 Connect a garden hose and the power washer hose to the machine. Snap a 25-degree tip onto the end of the wand. Turn on the water to the garden hose and pull the trigger on the spray wand until water squirts out. Now start up the power washer's engine.

2 Hold the tip of the wand about 18 in. from the fence and move it the length of the boards. Pull the trigger and keep the sprayer tip moving to avoid gouging the wood. Use a variety of attack angles to strip inside corners.

Power washing makes the huge cleaning task easy

Power washers are aggressive. They'll strip the wood as well as clean off the dirt and grime, but you can also erode the wood too deeply and ruin it. The key is to use the right sprayer tip and technique. In any case, the power washer's spray will slightly raise and roughen the grain on smooth wood. That's actually good—it allows more sealer to soak in and improves the finish.

SPRAYER TIP

Power washers cost about $40 to rent for four hours. Rent one that operates at 1,500 or 2,000 psi and avoid more powerful 3,000 or 3,500 psi units. Be sure to get both 15- and 25-degree spray tips. Have the rental people demonstrate the washer's use. It's an easy machine to run.

To avoid damaging the pump, don't run the power washer without first filling the pump and hoses with water. To do this, attach both hoses (Photo 1), snap in a 25-degree tip, turn on the garden hose spigot and hold down the trigger on the wand until water squirts out. Release the wand trigger and start the engine. If it's hard to pull the start cord, pull the wand trigger to release the water pressure.

Start spraying with the wand tip 18 in. from the wood surface. Move in closer as you swing the tip slowly along the length of the board (Photo 2). Keep the width of the fan spray aligned across the boards. The wood's color will brighten as the surface is stripped away. Watch closely and stop stripping when no more color change occurs. You don't have to remove too much surface to expose fresh wood, and continuing to spray won't improve the color.

It takes a little practice to arrive at the proper tip distance and speed of movement, but you'll catch on fast. It's better to make two or three passes than to risk gouging the surface trying to accomplish this job in one pass. As you gain experience, you can switch to a 15-degree tip. This tip cuts more aggressively and works faster than the 25-degree tip.

tip* Clear the area along the fence by tying back plants that are growing alongside it. Wear water-repellent clothing—you will get wet from the spray.

3 Glue split and broken pieces when the wood has dried for at least 24 hours. Apply waterproof glue and clamp or tape the pieces firmly together.

4 Drive weather-resistant or stainless steel screws to tighten loose boards. Recess the head 1/4 in. and fill with a light-colored caulk.

5 Realign sagging gates with a turnbuckle. We spray-painted the shiny turnbuckle black to make it less conspicuous.

6 Brush a wood preservative into the posts around the base to help prevent rot at this vulnerable area.

Simple repairs add years to the life of your fence

With the fence clean, it's time to fix or replace damaged boards, refasten loose boards and countersink any protruding nails. Use waterproof glue (Photo 3) to repair any split and broken boards. Drive corrosion-resistant screws (Photo 4) instead of nails to pull loose pieces tightly together. If a gate is sagging, straighten it with a turnbuckle support (Photo 5). Also coat the posts (Photo 6) where they emerge from the ground or concrete with a wood preservative. This is the area that rots first.

7 Roll into the dry wood a soaking coat of semitransparent stain. Coat about 3 ft. of fence, then proceed to the step shown in Photo 8.

8 Brush the stain (backbrush) into the wood grain and all corners and gaps. Brush out any runs or drips.

Stain makes the fence look brand new

To preserve the natural color of the wood, use an exterior semitransparent oil stain. It seals the wood while allowing the grain and color variations to show through. And its pigments add an overall color tone. Make sure the stain contains ultraviolet inhibitors, which will slow down bleaching by sunlight, and a mildewcide to slow fungal growth. Look for samples applied to cedar at the paint store, or bring in your own piece of wood to test. A test sample is the best way to ensure a satisfactory result.

9 Work the stain into small and tight areas with a trim roller and a 2-in. brush. One generous coat should be enough.

Before applying the stain, be sure the fence is dry. Allow at least 24 hours. If it's cool and humid, allow another 24 hours.

Use a paint roller with a "medium nap" cover (Photo 7) to apply a soaking coat to the wood. Let the wood absorb as much sealer as it can. Roll about a 3-ft. section of fence and then brush (Photo 8) the sealer into the wood. If the wood still appears dry, roll on additional sealer. Work the sealer into all recesses and corners. The roller applies the stain, but you need the brush to work it well into the wood's surface. Coat detailed areas with a trim roller and smaller brush (Photo 9). Keep wet edges to prevent lap marks.

Most semitransparent oil stains are guaranteed to last two to five years. (Solid-color stains last longer but are more difficult to renew.) Fences usually face severe weathering, so expect the finish to last no more than three years. Plan on recoating the fence within this time frame to keep your fence looking fresh. Before recoating, wash the fence with a garden hose sprayer and use a bristle brush on stubborn dirt deposits and stains. Let the fence dry and stain it using the same method.

Energy-saving tips

Low-cost ways to save fuel, electricity and cold hard cash.

ENERGY-SAVING COMPACT FLUORESCENT BULB

● Change furnace filters every month, or more often if needed.

● Have a furnace tuneup to clean and adjust burners and improve fuel-burning efficiency.

PIPE INSULATION

● Insulate pipes, especially if they pass through an area you don't want heated or cooled. Have your air conditioner serviced to clean hard-to-reach evaporator coils and adjust coolant pressure to achieve maximum efficiency.

● Replace light bulbs used more than two hours per day with compact fluorescent bulbs. Fluorescent bulbs last longer and use only one-third as much energy as standard bulbs.

● Wrap the tank of your gas-burning water heater in a special fiberglass blanket to decrease heat loss. Check your owner's manual to make sure a blanket is recommended for your model.

MOTION SENSOR

● Install light controls like motion sensors, photocell switches and timers to shut off lights automatically when they're not needed.

● Install and use an automatic set-back thermostat. You can reduce your heating and cooling costs by 5 to 15 percent.

● Replace worn-out thresholds and weatherstripping around windows and doors.

Stop faucet drips

You can fix almost any drippy single-lever kitchen faucet in about an hour.

Doing your own faucet repair may seem daunting, but once you learn the basics, modern faucets are pretty easy to fix. In fact, the hardest step is usually finding the right replacement parts. In this article, we'll tell you how to find replacement parts and show you how to stop spout drips on the three main types of single-lever faucets: rotary ball, cartridge and ceramic disc. We're showing kitchen faucets, but you can fix most single-lever bath faucets using the same procedures. We'll also show you how to stop leaks around the base of the spout.

The tools you'll need vary a little depending on the faucet you're repairing. You'll probably need an Allen wrench to remove the handle. Buy a set of small Allen wrenches ($6 to $12), and you'll be prepared for any faucet. Most repairs also require screwdrivers and a large slip-joint pliers.

project at a glance

skill level
beginner to intermediate

special tools
Allen wrenches
slip joint pliers
screwdrivers

approximate cost
$15–$50 per replacement parts kit

Rotary ball faucets

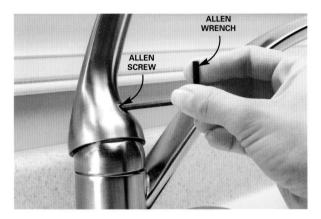

1 Lift the handle and pry off the decorative cover to expose the Allen screw. Turn the screw counterclockwise until it's loose enough to lift the handle up from the stem.

2 Unscrew the cap by turning it counterclockwise with a slip-joint pliers.

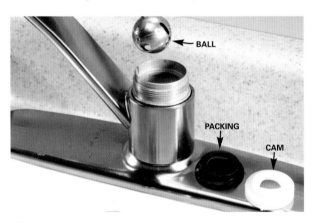

3 Lift off the plastic cam and packing. Lift out the ball and inspect it. Replace the ball if it's scratched, cracked or visibly worn.

4 Lift out the two rubber seats and springs with a screwdriver. Make note of the orientation of the tapered spring and install the new springs and seats the same way. Reassemble the faucet.

Water flow and temperature in a rotary ball faucet are controlled by a hollow ball that rotates in a socket (Figure A). Delta and Peerless are two of the major brands. Your faucet may have a brass or plastic ball. Both work well, although the long-lasting stainless steel ball comes with most repair kits. We recommend that you buy a repair kit that includes the ball, springs, seats and O-rings for the spout, as well as a small repair tool, for about $15. With this kit, you'll be prepared for almost any repair.

If water is leaking out around the base of the handle, you may be able to fix the leak by removing the handle (Photo 1) and simply tightening the adjusting ring slightly (Figure A). Turn it clockwise with the spanner tool included in the repair kit. If the faucet drips from the end of the spout, replace the seats and springs (Photo 4). To stop leaks from the base of the spout, see "Spout Leaks," p. 191.

Reassembly is straightforward. Drop the springs in the recesses and press the rubber seats over the top with your fingertip. Then align the groove in the ball with the pin in the socket and drop the ball in. Align the lug on the plastic cam with the notch in the valve body and set it over the ball. Thread on the cap with the adjusting ring and tighten it with the slip-joint pliers. Now you can turn on the water to check for leaks. If water leaks from around the ball stem, use the spanner tool to tighten the adjusting ring until the leak stops. Replace the handle and you're done.

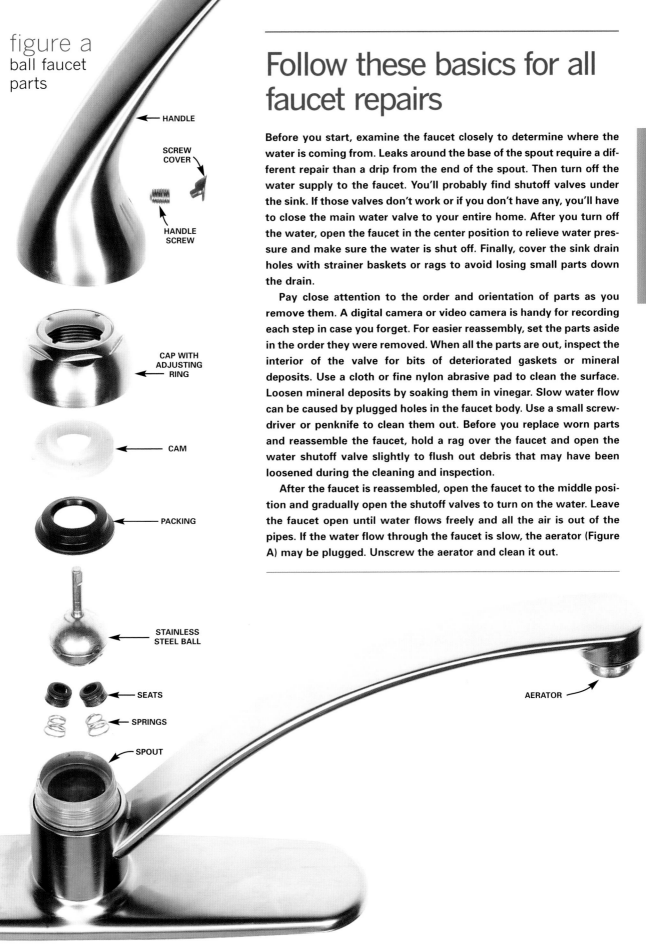

figure a
ball faucet parts

HANDLE

SCREW COVER

HANDLE SCREW

CAP WITH ADJUSTING RING

CAM

PACKING

STAINLESS STEEL BALL

SEATS

SPRINGS

SPOUT

AERATOR

Follow these basics for all faucet repairs

Before you start, examine the faucet closely to determine where the water is coming from. Leaks around the base of the spout require a different repair than a drip from the end of the spout. Then turn off the water supply to the faucet. You'll probably find shutoff valves under the sink. If those valves don't work or if you don't have any, you'll have to close the main water valve to your entire home. After you turn off the water, open the faucet in the center position to relieve water pressure and make sure the water is shut off. Finally, cover the sink drain holes with strainer baskets or rags to avoid losing small parts down the drain.

Pay close attention to the order and orientation of parts as you remove them. A digital camera or video camera is handy for recording each step in case you forget. For easier reassembly, set the parts aside in the order they were removed. When all the parts are out, inspect the interior of the valve for bits of deteriorated gaskets or mineral deposits. Use a cloth or fine nylon abrasive pad to clean the surface. Loosen mineral deposits by soaking them in vinegar. Slow water flow can be caused by plugged holes in the faucet body. Use a small screwdriver or penknife to clean them out. Before you replace worn parts and reassemble the faucet, hold a rag over the faucet and open the water shutoff valve slightly to flush out debris that may have been loosened during the cleaning and inspection.

After the faucet is reassembled, open the faucet to the middle position and gradually open the shutoff valves to turn on the water. Leave the faucet open until water flows freely and all the air is out of the pipes. If the water flow through the faucet is slow, the aerator (Figure A) may be plugged. Unscrew the aerator and clean it out.

Cartridge-style faucets

Many faucet brands use a cartridge of some type (Figure B). We show how to replace a Moen cartridge, but the process is similar for other brands. To stop drips at the spout or correct problems with hot and cold mixing, remove the cartridge and either replace the O-rings on the cartridge if they're worn or replace the entire cartridge. Take the cartridge to the home center or hardware store to find a replacement ($10 to $15).

Photos 1–6 show how to remove the cartridge. Replacement cartridges for Moen faucets include a plas-

1 Pry off the handle cap (gently) with a knife. Turn the Allen screw counterclockwise to remove it and lift off the handle.

2 Unscrew the dome assembly under the handle. Then unscrew the metal handle adapter and lift it off. Lift off the plastic pivot stop.

3 Remove the retainer nut by turning it counterclockwise with a large slip-joint pliers.

4 Pry out the brass retainer clip with the tip of a screwdriver. Grab the clip with a pliers and pull it the rest of the way out to avoid losing it.

5 Loosen the cartridge by slipping the plastic spanner cap (included with the new cartridge) over the cartridge and twisting it back and forth.

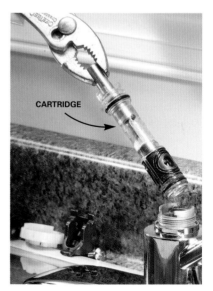

6 Grab the cartridge stem with a pliers and pull it straight up and out. Replace worn parts and reassemble the faucet in the reverse order.

tic spanner cap that allows you to twist and loosen the cartridge to make it easier to pull out (Photo 5). It may take considerable force to pull out the cartridge. Really stubborn cartridges may require a special cartridge-pulling tool. Moen's version costs about $15 and is available at most home centers.

Reassemble the faucet in the reverse order. Pull the stem up before inserting the cartridge. You may have to twist the cartridge slightly to line it up for the brass retainer clip. Use the plastic spanner cap or the tips of a needle-nose pliers to rotate the cartridge. Slide the brass clip into the slots in the valve body to hold the cartridge in place. Look for the small notch on top of the stem and rotate the stem until the notch faces you (Photo 4). Install the remaining parts and reattach the handle. The directions that come with the stem will help orient you here. Then test the faucet. If the hot and cold water are reversed, simply remove the handle, dome assembly and handle adapter and rotate the stem 180 degrees.

Take the old parts to the store to find replacements

You'll often find the brand name stamped on the faucet. And this information will help when it comes time to find repair parts. But in most cases, the safest bet is to take the worn parts to the store with you.

If you have a Delta or other rotary ball faucet (Figure A), you're in luck because you'll find repair kits in most hardware stores and home centers. Cartridges and repair kits for Moen "cartridge-type" (Figure B) faucets are also readily available. But if you have another brand or a disc-type faucet, you may have to order parts, since there are too many variations for most stores to keep in stock. It helps to know the faucet's model name or number when searching for a replacement cartridge. Otherwise, take the cartridge with you to the store so you can match it to a photo in the parts catalog. Plumbing supply specialists are also a good source of repair parts. If you're having trouble finding parts, call the manufacturer of your faucet for help.

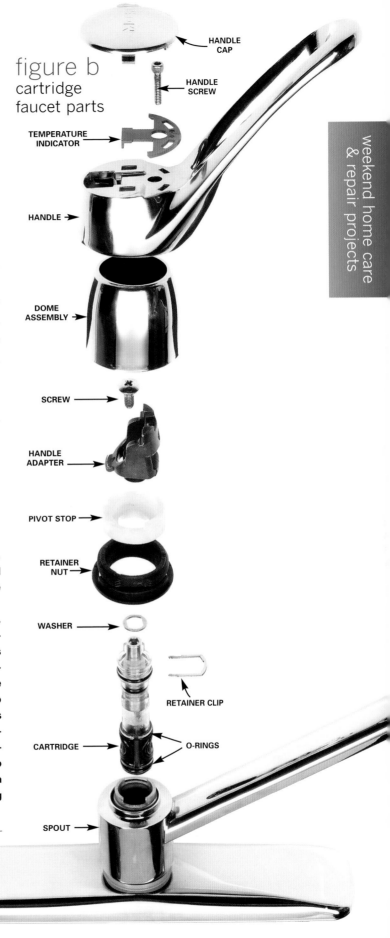

figure b
cartridge faucet parts

HANDLE CAP

HANDLE SCREW

TEMPERATURE INDICATOR

HANDLE

DOME ASSEMBLY

SCREW

HANDLE ADAPTER

PIVOT STOP

RETAINER NUT

WASHER

RETAINER CLIP

CARTRIDGE

O-RINGS

SPOUT

Ceramic disc faucets

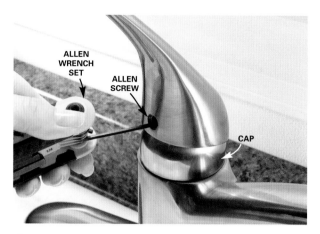

1 Pry off the decorative screw cover with your fingernail or the tip of a knife. Unscrew the handle screw by turning it counterclockwise with an Allen wrench. Lift off the handle. Unscrew or unclip the cap.

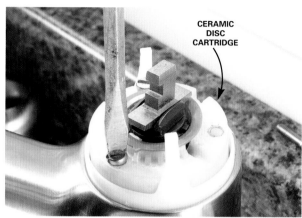

2 Remove the screws that hold the disc cartridge to the faucet body and lift out the cartridge.

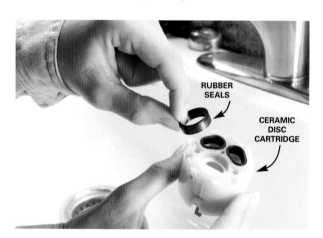

3 Inspect the cartridge for mineral buildup and carefully clean it out. Then replace the rubber seals on the underside.

4 Lift out the plastic disc (on some faucets) and replace the O-rings under it. Inspect the holes in the faucet body and clean them out if they're clogged.

Ceramic disc valves are simply another type of cartridge. Discs inside the cartridge control the water flow. This type of valve is sturdy and reliable and rarely needs fixing. In fact, many manufacturers offer a lifetime guarantee on the cartridge. If yours is damaged, check with the manufacturer to see if it's covered by a warranty. Leaks can result from faulty rubber seals or a cracked disc inside the cartridge. Since it's difficult to spot a cracked disc, and disc cartridge replacements are very expensive ($20 to $50), it's best to start by replacing the seals and reassembling the faucet. Then if the faucet still leaks, remove the disc cartridge and take it to the store to order a replacement.

Early versions of ceramic disc faucets may be more fragile and can crack if subjected to a blast of pressurized air. That's why it's important to leave the faucet open as you turn the water back on. This allows air trapped in the lines to escape. When the water runs smoothly, it's safe to turn the faucet off. Manufacturers have improved the strength of ceramic discs on newer faucets to withstand air blasts, as well as abrasive debris that may get dislodged from the inside of pipes.

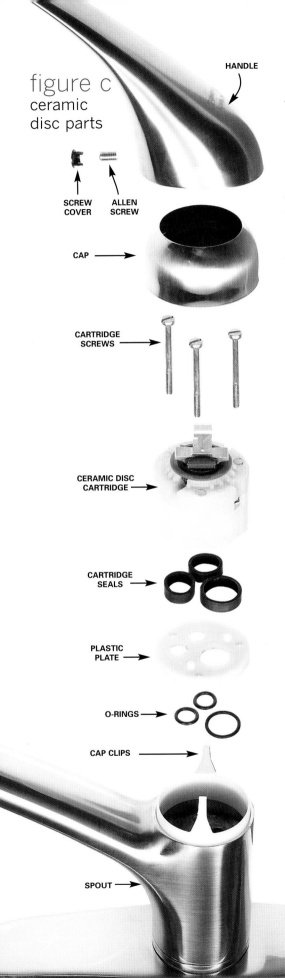

figure c
ceramic disc parts

HANDLE

SCREW COVER

ALLEN SCREW

CAP

CARTRIDGE SCREWS

CERAMIC DISC CARTRIDGE

CARTRIDGE SEALS

PLASTIC PLATE

O-RINGS

CAP CLIPS

SPOUT

Spout leaks

Leaks around the base of the spout are caused by worn O-rings located under the spout. All that's usually required to access these O-rings for replacement is to wiggle and pull up on the spout to remove it (Photo 1). Depending on the faucet, you'll also have to remove the handle and other parts to access the spout. Be persistent. The spout may be a little stubborn. Spout O-ring kits are available for many faucets, or you can take the old O-rings to the hardware store or plumbing supply store and match them up with new ones. Remember to pick up a small toothpaste-type tube of plumber's grease while you're there.

In Photo 1, you can see the diverter valve, which controls water to the sprayer. Their appearance varies considerably among brands, but you'll usually find them under the spout. If your sprayer isn't working properly, first clean it in vinegar or simply replace it ($5 - $22). If this doesn't work, the diverter valve may be clogged. If it doesn't simply pull out, contact the manufacturer or ask a knowledgeable salesperson for help with cleaning it.

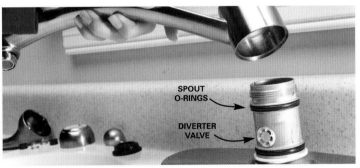

SPOUT O-RINGS

DIVERTER VALVE

1 Remove the handle and cartridge. Twist and pull up on the spout to remove it and expose the O-ring seals.

NEW O-RINGS

2 Slip the tip of a screwdriver under the O-rings to slide them out of the groove. Install the new O-rings, lubricate them with plumber's grease and reinstall the spout.

22 money- and energy-saving ideas that don't cost a dime

1. Lower the indoor temperature a few degrees in winter (you'll save about 2 percent per degree). Set it even lower at night and a full 10 degrees lower when you're on vacation.

2. Close the fireplace damper when the fireplace isn't in use. If it's never used, seal the flue with a plastic bag stuffed with insulation.

3. Open shades and blinds to let in sunlight during the day and close them to reduce heat loss at night. For cooling, close them during the day.

4. Close off unused rooms and lower the temperatures by adjusting the registers and dampers. You'll save up to $50 per year.

5. Clean your furnace's blower fan with a soft brush and vacuum cleaner.

6. Turn off lights not in use. Reduce bulb wattage and use dimmers when you can.

7. Ventilate and cool your home with window or whole-house fans during the cooler hours of the day.

8. Clean the air conditioner condenser coils and fins when you see grass and airborne debris collected on them.

9. Skip the dishwasher's drying cycle (and cut the energy use by about half).

10. Wash clothes in cool rather than hot water.

11. Fill clothes washers and dishwashers for more efficient energy use, rather than cleaning partial loads.

12. Clean clothes washer and dryer lint screens after every use.

13. Run major appliances late in the evening or early in the morning when electric loads are less (off peak).

14. Recycle. Reuse. Take your bike instead of your car.

15. Cook more efficiently using microwaves, Crock-Pots and pressure cookers.

16. Turn off room air conditioners when you leave for an hour or more. You can quickly cool the room later.

17. Flush your garbage disposer with cold water rather than hot. Grease solidifies in cold water and will wash away.

18. In warm weather, set the thermostat higher (75 to 78 degrees F) and rely more on ceiling and table fans for cooling, even when the air conditioner is running.

19. Reduce humidity in bathrooms and kitchens with exhaust fans. When dehumidifying a basement, keep basement doors and windows closed.

20. Consider higher-efficiency appliances when purchasing new refrigerators, freezers and dishwashers. The energy savings usually pays back the extra costs within a few years. The same goes for furnaces and water heaters.

21. Lower your water heater setting to 120 degrees F for both energy savings and safety. (Measure hot water temperature at a faucet with a cooking thermometer if the water heater setting isn't calibrated in degrees.)

22. Clean refrigerator coils with a soft brush annually, or more often if you have pets that shed.